D0590417

# STEVEN**TYLER**
### THE BIOGRAPHY

# STEVEN**TYLER**
## THE BIOGRAPHY

**LAURA JACKSON**

PIATKUS

PIATKUS

First published in Great Britain in 2008 by Piatkus Books

A CIP catalogue record for this book
is available from the British Library

ISBN 978-0-7499-5180-1

Edited by Jinny Johnson
Typeset in Great Britain by
Action Publishing Technology Ltd, Gloucester
Printed in the UK by CPI William Clowes
Beccles NR34 7TL

Papers used by Piatkus Books are natural, renewable and recyclable
products made from wood grown in sustainable forests and certified
in accordance with the rules of the Forest Stewardship Council

Mixed Sources
Product group from well-managed
forests and other controlled sources
www.fsc.org Cert no. SGS-COC-004081
© 1996 Forest Stewardship Council
FSC

Piatkus Books
An imprint of
Little, Brown Book Group
100 Victoria Embankment
London EC4Y 0DY

An Hachette Livre UK Company
www.hachettelivre.co.uk

www.piatkus.co.uk

This book is dedicated to
David, my remarkable husband.

# PICTURE CREDITS

# Contents

# Acknowledgements

The following helped with this book: Michael Lindsay-Hogg; Dr Stephen Perrin; Vicki Wickham; Clive Whichelow; Elgin Library staff; *Kerrang*; *Rock Power*; *Vox; Classic Rock*; *NME; Billboard*; *Q Rock Stars; Details; Rolling Stone; Mojo; Gibson; MTV; Globe & Mail; Times; Washington Post; Boston Globe; Wikipedia; Face; VH1; IMDB; Vintage Guitar; Circus; Newsday; Toronto Star; Daily Mirror; Seventeen; Raw; Musicians; Record Mirror; Melody Maker; USA Weekend; Associated Press; Daily Telegraph; Independent; Sunday Times; Metal Hammer.*

Special thanks to David for his invaluable help and support, and to Denise Dwyer, Alice Davis and everyone at Piatkus Books.

# CHAPTER 1

# Survival Of The Fittest

**S**TEVEN TYLER is the quintessential sex, drugs and rock 'n' roll superstar. Widely recognised for almost four decades as one of the most charismatic and distinctive figures in popular music, he has lived a rollercoaster life of excess – and survived. Inspired by the cream of British sixties bands, the Rolling Stones, The Kinks and The Pretty Things, with a passion for performing, Tyler propelled himself into rock as a lean and hungry teenager, and as the ear-blasting, raucous, high-energy lead singer fronting Aerosmith he quickly acquired the nickname, 'The Demon of Screamin'.

His lust for life has led to a tangled and turbulent love life and to a near deadly attraction to narcotics. In a drug-soaked meltdown during the late 1970s and early 1980s, he would, on occasion, snort pure heroin just prior to going on stage then black out mid-performance in front of the shocked audience. Tyler's heady highs always preceded desperate depths. By his own admission, he recklessly blew over a million dollars on dope. Broke, physically and mentally ravaged and staring bleakly into an unimaginable emotional abyss, he sank so low he may not have come out of it alive. Denial that he had a problem at all delayed him seeking help for his addictions, but entering rehab in the mid-eighties ultimately saved his life.

With his wiry, snake-hipped build, his trademark thick lips and his suggestive, supple movements on stage, Tyler was dogged early in his career by unfavourable comparisons to Mick Jagger, but unique, irrepressible and with an infectiously roguish twinkle in his eyes, Steven Tyler is no clone. He has proved all his detractors wrong. Aerosmith have long since earned their place in the pantheon of legendary rock bands, racking up album sales of around one hundred and fifty million; today they remain stadium fillers around the globe. In addition to his singer/songwriter abilities, Tyler is also an accomplished musician on eight instruments.

Once the epitome of the mercurial wasted rocker, he is proud to have remained sober, although his health did take another serious body blow in 2006, when he had to undergo extensive chemotherapy treatment for the potentially fatal disease hepatitis C. They say that the apple does not fall far from the tree, and that is true in Steven Tyler's case. A natural born survivor, talent and tenacity are in his genes.

Born Steven Victor Tallarico on 26 March 1948 in Yonkers, New York, to Susan and Victor Tallarico, the dark-haired, bright-eyed boy came from exotic stock – Polish, Russian and Swedish on his mother's side, Italian and German on his father's. Steven's paternal grandfather, Giovanni Tallarico, and three of his brothers were all musicians; forming a chamber music quartet, they played to the well-heeled clientele frequenting the swish hotels dotted along America's north-east seaboard in the early 1920s. Giovanni's wife, Constance, was also an accomplished pianist. So it was small wonder that their son Victor proved to be naturally gifted, too. Victor became a classically trained pianist, helmed the Vic Tallarico Orchestra and for many years taught music at the Cardinal Spellman High School in the Bronx, where the Tallarico family lived.

The northernmost of New York City's five boroughs, the Bronx is separated from the island of Manhattan by the Harlem

River and is home to the Yankee baseball stadium. Famous Bronxites include Al Pacino, James Caan, Anne Bancroft and Woody Allen, but the borough is a tough environment, definitely not for the faint-hearted. Along with his parents and an older sister, Lynda, Steven lived in a small sixth-floor tenement apartment, and one of his earliest recollections is of his handsome father diligently practising Beethoven, Bach and Brahms on the gleaming Steinway grand piano squeezed into the cramped quarters. Not born with a silver spoon in his mouth, Steven fought his way through life, yet in later years when psychiatrists tried to pin his problems on these early hardships Tyler was quick to mark their card. He revealed: 'A lot of therapists would like to believe that the reason I joined a rock band was to rebel because my parents were terrible. That simply wasn't true. I had a wonderful warm childhood and my parents were amazing.'

Naturally inquisitive, Steven had a vivid imagination from the start. Attending church on Sundays, when he was about six years old he became fascinated during worship by the table laden with burning candles; he was mesmerised by their blaze against the pristine white altar cloth. 'I thought God lived under that table,' he later revealed. More significantly, while bawling out the hymns he was stimulated by a sense of the energy inherent in singing and the evocative meaning in songs. Perhaps predictably, music became his ruling passion. 'I grew up under a piano,' said Tyler. 'When you take life's emotions and you lay them over a Bach or a Brahms sonata, they take on different meanings.'

Something of a dreamer, the skinny, up-for-anything kid pushed everything to the limit. As soon as he was old enough to be let outdoors alone, he rigged up a rope swing in the yard behind the old apartment building and practically gave himself vertigo by constantly attempting to swing dangerously faster and higher. In this way, he was reaching for the moon. With music the dominant influence at home, Steven proved to be naturally gifted, and quickly became adept on the flute, harmonica, violin, drums, bass guitar, mandolin, recorder and piano. His skilled father's attempts to teach him the piano had often been an exasperating business, however. Tyler confessed: 'I yawned so much, it blew his head!' He added: 'Ever since I was a small dude, I guess I always had this urge to show off.'

Outside the secure environ of the family home, Steven encountered a variety of pressures – some of them very personal. From an early age he was made the target of relentless teasing over his unusual looks. Steven Tyler grew up to be a striking man with very distinctive features, which sits fine with the cushion of fame. As a youngster growing up in the Bronx, however, having pointy ears and oversized thick lips brought him ridicule from seemingly every kid around the block. He spiritedly fended this off in public, but it got to Steven and made him even more determined to make something of himself.

This inner fire strengthened when, already music-oriented, in summer 1957 he turned on his radio and first heard the Everly Brothers sing 'Bye, Bye Love'. Their close Appalachian harmonies soaring over acoustic guitar work got Steven's juices going, and by the time the duo's 'All I Have To Do Is Dream' became a million-selling chart topper the following spring, the ten-year-old Tyler was hooked on this new brand of music. He fixed up a makeshift aerial outside his bedroom window so that, despite static interference, he could pick up the AM radio station WOWO Fort Wayne Indiana, which belted out all the latest hits. Immersing himself in these exciting sounds, Steven adored the freedoms expressed by a flourishing flood of new artists, including the hugely provocative Elvis Presley. For a rapidly developing restless spirit, it was intoxicating stuff. Of rock music Tyler recently declared: 'Before I had sex, it *was* sex!'

Come 1960, the twelve-year-old, self-taught drummer was pounding the skins behind his first drum kit and would soon go out with his father playing at dances on the local scene. He loved the chance to perform in front of an audience, and from Victor he embraced the ethic of practising his art every day – a discipline which would stand Steven in good stead later in life. The counterbalance to these happy weekend evenings remained school and street life in the Bronx.

Steven's parents tried hard to impress on their son the wisdom of knuckling down at school, to have something to fall back on if a career in music – already clearly his first love – did not pan out but, while bright, Steven had no interest in academic study. At school he enjoyed the chance to sing with a choir and found physical education exhilarating, although when it came to field games he often frustrated his teammates by getting distracted; instead of waiting to catch high balls whizzing his way he would be frantically stomping about the grass, crushing ants underfoot.

With a distinct lack of imagination, some of his peers continued to disparage his looks, particularly making fun of his wide mouth and big lips. His fightback by now was not always successful, however. Tyler explained: 'My mother tried to bail me out, saying: "Just tell them, they're all the better to kiss girls with." But then I got decked out for being a wise guy!' Being decked out too often was not an option in the Bronx where, as the years went by, the streets only got meaner. Steven rapidly learned how to stand his ground, and became embroiled in bruising bare-knuckled mass brawls in the neighbourhood. 'Street fights went on for an hour and a half and I'd come home bloody as hell,' he later recalled. Confronting at times a cesspool of bigotry, Tyler grew up grasping the putrid nature of prejudice. 'Jewish white kids were constantly picked on. It was terrible.' Despite the tribal atmosphere around him, Steven never had an aggressive gang member mentality. Knowing what it felt like to be hassled, indeed, he tended to be very protective of the underdog and of kids with learning difficulties.

Already a poor area, suffering from a chronic lack of investment and raging crime, the Bronx sank to new depths when a wave of arson attacks began amid the borough's many overcrowded apartment buildings. Rundown and like dry bracken anyway, homes were going up like touchpaper, which was an added nightmare for the 1.4 million residents. The Tallaricos decided that it was time to move house and so the family relocated to Steven's birthplace. The largest city in Westchester

County, Yonkers borders the Bronx and has an undulating landscape rising dramatically from sea level to hills high enough to
be seen as landmarks from as far away as New Jersey. Steven's
family moved into a house just off Central Avenue in the north-
east quarter, which had a large Italian-American community.

One constant source of delight throughout Tyler's life was the
time spent at the summer town of Lake Sunapee in New
Hampshire. In the 1920s, the Tallarico family had bought property and a few hundred acres of land there for about $5000, and
over the ensuing years they had developed it into Trow-Rico, a
small holiday resort. To Tyler it was a magical place. The state has
over eighty mountain peaks, of which the White Mountains are
its most famous range. With picturesque villages and lakeside
resorts it was extremely popular as a holiday destination; Trow-
Rico proved to be a good investment.

From a young age, Steven quit the city every summer and
headed with his family to Lake Sunapee to visit his grandparents
for the vacation season, where he became very much a barefoot
mountain boy. Hunting and trapping all day long, he grew familiar with guns and was particularly deadly with a slingshot. He
hunted for raccoons, skunks and possum until he acquired a
baby raccoon as a pet, which altered his entire outlook. 'It got to
be my buddy and I could never kill anything after that,' he
recalled. He named the raccoon Bandit, and the pair went fishing
together along the riverbanks. 'Deer were my friends,' said
Steven. 'I would spend time walking through woods, looking at
the most beautiful things.' He was extremely happy whenever he
was at Lake Sunapee – a teenager's place of dreams.

Already used to live performance from playing drums with
his father's band at New York dances, he was always up for it
when amateur stage shows were mounted at a makeshift
theatre at Lake Sunapee. The small audiences comprised holi-
daying families, who were indulgent to a fault with the many
gaffes, but it still gave Tyler such a frisson of excitement; he
knew in his bones that a stage was his natural habitat. He
began to live the dream vividly in his head. 'I'd close my eyes,

picture crowds, and shivers would start at the base of my spine,' he remembered.

As for many future rock stars, February 1964 was a pivotal point in Steven Tyler's life when America got its first taste of Beatlemania. With 'I Want To Hold Your Hand' topping the US singles chart, the Beatles arrived at New York's John F. Kennedy International Airport amid chaotic scenes, with hundreds of screaming hysterical teenagers forming the welcoming committee. When the Liverpool lads made their live US debut on CBS TV's *Ed Sullivan Show*, they drew over seventy-three million viewers. The British invasion had begun.

For Steven Tyler, British bands were the best, and over the coming years his focus fell not on the lovable mop-top Scousers but rather on grittier bands. He explained: 'I was listening to The Who, The Pretty Things, The Kinks, and when the Rolling Stones came along I thought Mick Jagger was the baddest boy on the block!' Steven avidly collected all the British rock publications he could lay his hands on, soon adding the Yardbirds to his roll of heroes. Playing in a band became his main aim in life. 'I was crazed,' he confirmed. 'I wanted to play rock 'n' roll.'

In 1964, along with other teenagers from Yonkers, Tyler formed his first band. The line-up would change, as would the band name. It started off as the Strangers until it transpired that another band had that name. Initially, they played around with the spelling but in time switched to calling themselves Chain Reaction. Irrespective of the band's line-up or billing, Steven threw himself wholeheartedly into performing as drummer and lead vocalist, scraping up bookings wherever he could. He also moonlighted occasionally as a vocalist with Yonkers' other best-known band, the Dantes, in which his neighbourhood friend Raymond Tabano played.

By the age of seventeen, Steven was already dabbling in drugs, smoking pot. At 5'10", he had an incredibly lean, near skeletal, physique. His dark brown hair was luxuriously thick and, in keeping with the times, grew down on to his shoulders. He may have been relentlessly teased when he was younger about his unusual looks but the vibrancy he now radiated, the glint in his eyes and the stimulatingly unpredictable aura he oozed attracted the girls, all the same. In 1965, Rolling Stones' music topped the soundtrack of Tyler's teens. 'I grew up with 'em!' he declared. 'I smoked so many joints, listening to their albums, fucked so many girls in high school. That was my whole youth, man! I spent it with the Stones.'

That autumn, with *Out of Our Heads* having recently topped the US album chart, the Rolling Stones launched an extensive North American tour, during which they courted controversy every step of the way. Their gig at the Memorial Auditorium in Rochester, New York, in early November had to be stopped by police after only seven minutes when three thousand delirious fans tried to storm the stage; all of this fuelled their raucous, rebellious reputations. Tyler lapped up all this bad press and tried to see his idols in the flesh. In New York one day, he got his chance to rush up alongside Mick Jagger stepping out on to a pavement and had his photo taken with him. It was a different story when Steven stumbled across the Stones' founder and musical genius, Brian Jones. The most striking Stone, the blond-haired Jones was actually extremely approachable but he had an indefinable presence. Brian was sitting enjoying a quiet drink in a club in Central Square when Steven walked in and did a sharp double take. The usually irrepressible Tyler froze. 'I was so taken aback, I couldn't talk,' he recalled. Someone who can well relate to that reaction is Vicki Wickham, one of the producers of Britain's best sixties pop show, *Ready, Steady, Go!* She reveals: 'Brian Jones was absolutely stunning! The band were all eclipsed by Jones. You had to be around him in person to truly grasp what I mean.'

Steven clamoured to see all his favourite bands when they hit town. He managed to see the Kinks in summer 1965, when they made their US live debut at the Academy of Music in New York. Completely carried away that night, he yelled his head off until he was hoarse. Fired up, he put even more into his own personal performances. He was insatiable when it came to music. 'I love the buzz,' he explained. 'The only other thing that gives you a buzz like that is drugs, but music is stronger.'

In the mid-1960s, Steven experienced adrenalin rushes from landing the chance to play support to several top acts. His band opened for the Yardbirds at New York and Connecticut gigs, when Tyler was so keen to connect with the British band he eagerly helped the roadies handling the equipment. He was in seventh heaven supporting the incomparable Byrds at a concert at Westchester County Center in White Plains, New York, enjoyed supporting the Lovin' Spoonful, and was blown away when his band opened for the Beach Boys before thousands of screaming fans at Iona College in New Rochelle. At home in Yonkers, Steven had for years absorbed the Beach Boys' immaculate vocal harmonies and the brilliant production values in songs ranging from the jaunty 'I Get Around' and 'California Girls', to the more introspective 'In My Room', which Dennis Wilson dubbed a classic make-out song. Asked what it had meant to him backing the Californian band, Tyler succinctly said: 'Fucking everything!'

The year 1966 saw some significant changes in his life. With Chain Reaction he recorded two singles, 'The Sun'/'When I Needed You' and 'You Should Have Been Here Yesterday'/'Ever Lovin' Man'. All four songs were recorded between August and September at New York's CBS studios, and S. Tallarico appears on the songwriting credits for both 'When I Needed You' and 'The Sun', along with fellow band members of Chain Reaction, Barry Shapiro, Don Solomon, Alan Strohmayer and Peter Stahl. The first single was released late that summer on Date Records, part of CBS Records. Tyler reflected: 'I can't ever forget how excited I was about being in an actual recording band. It was a total dream come true.'

That Tyler's destiny lay in music and not academia was just as well, for 1966 was also the year he was expelled from Roosevelt High School, having been busted along with others by an undercover narcotics cop for taking marijuana. Tyler explained: 'They put this narc right there in the school. Right up until he popped us, he was selling us nickel bags of good shit.' Several students were nabbed in the bust and dragooned to the police station. Their worried girlfriends were all crying, and many a dismayed parent was forced to face up to their offspring's drug taking. Tyler went on: 'They took me from my front door in handcuffs as my father was arriving home from work.' Steven's mother, Susan, stood on the doorstep in tears and with the neighbours rubbernecking to get a better view of what was going on, Tyler felt for his parents. The drug bust made front-page news next day in a Yonkers daily newspaper.

Steven faced felony charges, and when he appeared in court he promised the judge that he would walk the straight and narrow from then on. In that split second as he said it, he probably meant it, for he was numb with fear at the idea of being sent to prison. He was given one year's probation and was now classed as a YO – a youthful offender.

Not surprisingly, Steven quickly learned that he was not welcome back at Roosevelt High when term started in September, so his parents sent him to Quintano's Professional School in New York, which catered for kids with aspirations in the arts – music, acting, dance. Steven mainly gave this school a miss, teaming up instead with the other 'black sheep' to spend most days hanging around the parks, smoking dope.

His other high continued to come from gigging, and he especially enjoyed playing at The Barn with Chain Reaction. A nightclub held literally in an old barn on a farm in the village of Georges Mills, near to Lake Sunapee, it was a bring-your-own-booze venue and was locally *the* place to perform. As a recording band, Chain Reaction appeared an enviable cut above the ordinary to the other music-mad teenagers, a distinction which delighted Steven. The Barn itself, he adored. From the tiny lip of a stage, he could look out at the crowd jostling intimately up close to him, and there was a loft area with wooden spar fencing. As Tyler belted out cover versions of Stones, Beatles, Animals and Yardbirds songs, legs would dangle and sway within touching distance above his head. When his band's second single, 'You

Should Have Been Here Yesterday'/'Ever Lovin' Man', was released on Verve Records (part of CBS Records), it only enhanced Tyler's local hero status up at Lake Sunapee. He did not know it, but future Aerosmith members Joe Perry and Tom Hamilton would hang around outside The Barn, as yet too young to get in, listening to Tyler's rafter-rattling performances.

A child of the sixties, by 1967 Steven embraced the summer of love – the make love, not war ethos, sharing joints with total strangers and opposing the Vietnam conflict. His youthful offender status kept him clear of the draft, but he has maintained that he would have refused to fight in Vietnam anyway. 'I didn't believe in it,' he stated. He once expanded: 'When they said: "Don't smoke pot," we said: "Fuck you!" When they said: "Go to Vietnam," we said: "No." And it wasn't just because we were stoned and high. It was because we were right. I got into the paraphysical. I was into the Maharishi and trying to get spiritual.'

He continued to open for big bands working the clubs around Greenwich Village and over almost the whole of New York. He also played to a lot of what he called 'strait-laced' audiences when his band hit the grand ballroom circuit. His father had long ago imbued in him the need to nurture his craft, and so Tyler chose to see these unbending audiences as good training grounds. He did still play the drums but was more and more prone to grabbing the microphone stand and singing lead.

Mick Jagger continued to be his idol. 'I can remember when I was just another teenager from Yonkers going to Madison Square Garden to see the Stones and looking down and saying to myself: "Wow, man! Is that tiny figure all the way down there *really* Mick Jagger?"' In 1968, the Rolling Stones released the hard-rocking number 'Jumpin' Jack Flash', the promotional clip for which had been shot by director Michael Lindsay-Hogg. Although crude in quality by today's sophisticated video standards, at the time it was considered innovative and dark, with the Stones wearing face paint and looming through the gloom into the camera lens.

Michael Lindsay-Hogg recalls of the shoot: 'We had started at midnight and were going to work till dawn. By halfway through the night we had filmed it straight, just a performance with some flashing lights, and it was fine. Then Brian [Jones] came up with the suggestion that they should alter their whole look by using dramatic make-up and as it was a tough number, they should give it a harder edge. I liked it, so we shot a second version. When we had finished, *that's* the version everyone liked and it was the very first pop promo that had that extra something in it which set it apart from the normal performance clips.' When Steven Tyler saw this moody promo clip for the US chart-topping single, it played directly to his own developing sense of the dramatic and stage theatrics. He had turned twenty by now, but still hoped to bump into Mick Jagger for a chat, and he often hung around outside the Scene Club in New York, which the Stones frequented, just on the off chance.

Any involvement in music excited Tyler, and he guested in a recording studio on back-up vocals with a band called the Left Banke whose bass player, Tom Finn, recalled of Tyler: 'He was hungry and a good singer, so I put him on there.' One thing that seemed to escape Steven was that not everybody was *quite* so hungry for success and focused on attaining it as himself. To his way of thinking, the members of Left Banke were pretty laid-back. He later stated: 'I'll never forget being in their apartment one day and one of them saying: "What's the date today? Are we recording tonight? What are we going to record?" I couldn't believe they were taking it so lightly!'

Steven had continued to co-write songs with keyboard player Don Solomon, and the band had made demos of another handful of songs, with a view to recording an album, but in the end it never materialised. By this time, the band personnel had changed again and the name had been switched to The Chain.

Times were changing in more ways than one. Dr Stephen Perrin, a specialist in 1960s counter-culture, explains: 'In 1967, you'd had Scott McKenzie singing about people going to San Francisco wearing flowers in their hair but then the original hippies moved out of Haight-Ashbury and the mafia moved in and controlled the drug supply. They caused an LSD famine and flooded the place with speed and heroin. So where we had the flower children before, we now had a bunch of very strung-out people.'

Over on America's east coast, Steven Tyler had placed his feet on an increasingly darker road in relation to his drug consumption; he was taking speed and dropping acid. In August 1969, Tyler went to the now-famous Woodstock festival at Yasgur's Farm, close to the village of Woodstock in Bethel, New York state, but it was all a blur to him as he was tripping his brains out. He was so far gone, he had no idea even of where he was. He revealed: 'My brain was on LSD, not just one tab because I had snorted another.'

When he came back down to earth, Steven knew that as the decade was dying things were not working out for him. He was going nowhere fast. With his huge well of optimism he had promised his mother that he would become so famous in a rock band that it would change the Tallarico family's whole way of life, but when he hitch-hiked back to Lake Sunapee that summer he felt his tail wedging dejectedly between his legs. He could not know it, but he was about to meet a guy who would soon breathe new life into his folding world.

# CHAPTER 2

# Fake It, Till You Make It

**W**HAT STEVEN inwardly craved, come the summer of 1969, was a creative partner – a soulmate. 'I wanted a brother, that Ray Davies/Dave Davies thing,' he recalled. That soulmate came in the shape of Joe Perry, a gifted young guitarist who was also heavily influenced by British bands, and whose parents owned property at Lake Sunapee in New Hampshire.

Born Anthony Joseph Perry on 10 September 1950 in Lawrence, Massachusetts, Joe was raised along with a younger sister by their parents, Mary, a high school physical education teacher, and Anthony Perry, an accountant, in the small town of Hopedale, Massachusetts. His father was ex-military and Joe grew up interested in guns, becoming handy with a .22 rifle. Drawn from an early age to music, he tinkered with the ukulele before progressing to guitar, persevering to teach himself to play right-handed, despite being naturally left-handed. When he was fourteen, he sat up and took notice as the Beatles hit America, but Joe was most influenced by much meatier musicians such as Jeff Beck, Jimi Hendrix, Fleetwood Mac's Peter Green, and John Mayall.

School held no attraction for Perry and, as a loner, he tended not to hang out with the crowd. He preferred to hole up in his bedroom, practising guitar for hours on end, but with a goal in mind. Throughout his teens he became involved in several bands – Flash, Plastic Glass, Pipe Dreams, Just Us and the Jam Band. Joe Perry perhaps did not have the openly irrepressible nature of Steven Tyler, but in his quiet, stubborn way he was also a renegade spirit. A slender, handsome young guy, Joe grew his black hair so long it brought him into conflict first with school authorities, then with employers, but he stuck to his guns and refused to cut it.

As an eighteen-year-old, Joe swapped Hopedale for summer at Lake Sunapee with his family, where he took a job in a café-cum-ice cream parlour called the Anchorage at Sunapee Harbour. His tasks there included anything from sweeping the floor and washing dishes to frying chips and hamburgers. In the bustling kitchen he kept up with the latest sounds via the radio; he also kept tabs on a local rock star – Steven Tallarico. Chain Reaction singles featured on the jukebox at the Anchorage, and he could not help but notice Steven around the resort. For one thing, the New Yorker dressed very trendily and was not shy of lapping up the local hero status his band acquired through playing gigs at The Barn. Steven would frequently barge into the Anchorage with his mates and take over a booth, where their high-spirited capers sometimes got a bit out of hand – food would end up flying through the air – and their general exuberance could annoy other patrons. Joe said years later: 'I guess that's how you were supposed to act when you had a rock band – dress like you came from Greenwich Village and be loud.' As soon as Steven and his crowd dispersed, Joe would emerge from the kitchen and watch the guys heading off as he cleared up the mess they had left behind. At this time, Joe was plugging away with the Jam Band, comprising drummer Dave Scott and another friend and future Aerosmith member, bass player Tom Hamilton.

Blond-haired, brown-eyed Thomas William Hamilton was born on 31 December 1951 in Colorado Springs, Colorado, to George and Betty Hamilton. Because his father was in the air force, Tom and his three siblings moved house quite a lot. Suffering a serious brush with scarlet fever and falling prey to the odd boyhood accident, Tom was a cautious sort who took time to develop a more outgoing attitude to life. Overawed by his father's military exploits as a World War II pilot, he very much looked up to him as a role model. A love of music then kicked in and he began to teach himself the guitar at the age of twelve, quickly switching to bass.

The following year, by now living in New London, New Hampshire, seeing the Beatles on the *Ed Sullivan Show* sent his passion for music into overdrive. 'I used to go to bed imagining myself as one of the Beatles, up on stage, singing those songs,' Tom recalled. Like Joe Perry, however, Tom's focus shifted towards a rockier sound; the hypnotic heartbeat of some of the Rolling Stones' early rhythm and blues-influenced numbers strengthened Tom's attraction to bass guitar. In his teens, Tom joined a variety of bands with weird and wonderful names before teaming up with Joe Perry – whom he had met at Lake Sunapee – in Plastic Glass, Pipe Dreams and the Jam Band. By this time Tom had acquired a rather lurid local reputation, having been busted for dropping acid. It was later claimed that this brush with the law was the first acid bust in that particular part of New Hampshire. The local notoriety this incident brought Hamilton in such a small town left him feeling uncomfortably like public enemy number one; this outlaw image was only enhanced by his avid interest in the nubile young ladies around him in class. Years later, with brutal candour, Tom confessed: 'I was just about the horniest little bastard you could possibly imagine.'

Ploughing his pent-up energies into playing gigs with the Jam Band, he especially enjoyed nights at The Barn. Just a couple of years earlier, he and Joe Perry had lurked around outside The Barn listening to Steven Tyler fronting Chain Reaction, and the passage of time had deepened Tom's respect for Steven. He felt it obvious that Tyler was destined for big things, so he was impressed when, in August 1969, Steven showed up to see the Jam Band perform.

According to Tyler, he has no clear recollection of why he went to see the Jam Band that evening. He does recall having no great first opinion of what he saw. In inimitable fashion he has frequently declared: 'They sucked!' To his trained musical ear, the Jam Band lacked precision, their timing was erratic and their tuning left much to be desired. Unimpressed, Steven was on the brink of going home when the band plunged into the Fleetwood Mac number 'Rattlesnake Shake', and Perry's suddenly slinky, sensuous lead guitar work stopped Steven in his tracks; he was mesmerised. Tyler later said: 'They had a lot of raunch.' Now watching the Jam Band closely, he grew strongly aware that were he to mesh his melodic qualities and discipline with their more raw abilities, they could create something very special together. The notion quickened Steven's senses – it was what he had been looking for – and he quit The Barn that night with a lighter step than he had had for some time.

The next day, still thinking about the gig, as he mowed the sloping lawn at his family's property, Trow-Rico, Steven had stopped to adjust the grass cuttings box when he looked up to see a sleek MG sports car pulling into the drive. Out stepped Joe Perry, his long black hair glinting in the summer sunshine as he pulled off a pair of dark glasses. He approached Steven, who had abandoned the electric mower and was walking over to meet him. This meeting has since assumed near-mythical status in Aerosmith's history, but at the time they were simply two music-mad young guys exchanging a few words – except that Steven did instantly sense a compatibility between them. His parting shot was that maybe someday they would play music together. Steven Tyler and Joe Perry went their separate ways that day, and Steven trained his sights on forming another new band. He fronted an outfit called Fox Chase, which included Don Solomon from Chain Reaction, with whom he also went on to form a band called William Proud.

Come the end of the 1960s, America's unsettled mood had grown even darker. For many this was epitomised by the ugly events which resulted in Meredith Hunter, an eighteen-year-old black youth, being savagely beaten to death by a handful of Hell's Angels at the Rolling Stones' December 1969 concert at the Altamont Speedway track in Livermore, California. The omens had been bad from the start, and the Stones had just arrived at the site when a teenage boy rushed towards Jagger screaming hatred, and punched him in the face. Drug dealers had descended on Altamont in force and a lot of bad dope had been circulating for hours, adding to the unstable mood before the tragedy unfolded in the crowd while the Stones were performing 'Sympathy for the Devil'. The Rolling Stones' album *Let It Bleed* topped the UK charts while, with the Beatles soon to implode, *Abbey Road* reigned supreme in America's Billboard chart.

For Tyler, life was pretty unsatisfactory as the new decade dawned. In terms of his drug taking, he was now snorting the highly addictive blue crystal methedrine, which stimulated in him a latent instability. William Proud was not working out and Steven was restless. A new breed of band was coming through, spearheaded by Led Zeppelin, featuring frontman Robert Plant and lead guitarist Jimmy Page. The combination of rock and blues that Zeppelin blasted like a life force straight off the stage left Tyler hugely impatient with covering much tamer Beatles songs. He yearned to be delivering a harder rocking sound at his own gigs. William Proud comprised Don Solomon on keyboards, guitarist Dwight Farren, Raymond Tabano on bass, with Steven as drummer and vocalist; in summer 1970 they played regularly at a club in Southampton, Long Island. One evening, mid-performance, the audience was startled by an altercation that blew up on stage before their eyes. The story generally goes that bar staff had to haul an enraged Steven Tyler off Dwight Farren, prising his long fingers from around the guitarist's throat. Tyler has maintained that he *wanted* to leave his drum kit and go grab the guitarist by the neck, but in his temper he actually tripped over his hi-hat cymbal and cracked a bone in his leg when he fell, some way short of his intended target. In any event, a crossroads had clearly been reached for all concerned; that night Steven quit William Proud and hitch-hiked back to Lake Sunapee with the express purpose of seeking out Joe Perry.

He was easily found. That summer, the Jam Band was the house band at The Barn and Perry was dossing in a decrepit old farmhouse near to the venue. The place was draughty, damp and missing several floorboards, which had been ripped up for firewood. Perry's youth and resilience were keeping his ambition warm. Tom Hamilton and he were immersed in listening to the likes of the Yardbirds, Cream, Ten Years After, and were talking of shortly leaving the area to try their wings in Boston. When Steven showed up, it was a meeting of minds, hopes and dreams; the symbiosis between Steven and Joe was immediately evident.

Perry has likened their incendiary friendship to the core chemicals that create gunpowder – on their own, each element is benign, it is when they are mixed that sparks fly. For his part, Steven recognised Joe as a kindred spirit. Tom Hamilton felt separate from the connection that mushroomed between these two but was not immediately threatened by it. On the contrary, there was a welcome lift to life. The lake shimmered with a fresh clarity and the sun baked down, illuminating a new fork in the road ahead. Gingered up by the prospects, Steven went back to old habits and often took off for the woods and mountains, enjoying communing with nature and recharging his batteries. He knew intrinsically that he possessed what Joe Perry and Tom Hamilton needed, and that the opposite was also true.

The Jam Band's drummer, Dave Scott, was too young to up sticks and leave home, so it was Steven, Joe and Tom who headed to Boston when summer was fading over Lake Sunapee. Raymond Tabano came too, because Steven wanted to include his Bronx-born friend in any new band line-up. In September 1970, Perry and Hamilton set off first, on a mission to find an apartment to rent.

Boston is often nicknamed The Hub, which it certainly became for the fledgling Aerosmith. An old and gracious city with its own identity, it was also culturally rich. The band found a shabby three-bedroom apartment at 1325 Commonwealth Avenue in the Back Bay area, and their next task was to find a drummer, which would free up Steven to concentrate on lead vocals. Fortuitously, they quickly met twenty-year-old Joey Kramer.

Joseph Michael Kramer was born on 21 June 1950 in the Bronx, New York, the first of four children for Doris and Mickey Kramer, an ex-Army man who became a salesman. Like the Tallarico family, the Kramers relocated from the Bronx to Yonkers when Joey was a child, and he also attended Roosevelt High, the school Steven had been kicked out of after being busted for drug taking. Shades of Tyler, Kramer also attended the Woodstock festival and was so doped up that he missed all the action, though he would later state that he remembered seeing Steven at this hippie gathering. Playing drums in a few different cover bands including the Medallions, King Bees, Unique 4 and Turn Pikes, Kramer had caught a couple of Steven's earliest gigs with Chain Reaction. He rated the band highly, in particular Steven's vocal skills. His own musical taste centred on The Who, Led Zeppelin and Jethro Tull, and with music absorbing most of his waking hours, he had often toyed with the whole paraphernalia of being in a rock band, scribbling possible band names on jotters – including the name Aerosmith. Come late summer 1970, Joey was in Boston to attend the Berklee College of Music and, on the lookout to join a band, he fell in with Raymond Tabano. Soon he was the latest recruit to swell the ranks of this as yet unnamed new outfit. Joey Kramer has never claimed to be a technically sophisticated drummer – he plays by instinct and has honed his talent well. The personalities in this new group were all different, and life at 1325 Commonwealth Avenue proved eventful for the five of them.

Like the others, Steven was permanently broke and eternally hungry. Tom Hamilton recalled: 'We lived in this basement dump and we ate peanut butter and jelly sandwiches for breakfast, lunch and supper.' Steven later reminisced about how they had all existed on a great deal of brown rice and nourishing soup. 'In those days,' he wistfully remembered, 'a quart of beer was heaven!' As he pointed out, they did not have enough money to get fat and so these were literally lean times, during which Steven resorted to shoplifting to survive. Despite these dire financial straits, Steven still managed to scrape up the cash to buy speed. He was not the only one in the band taking drugs, but this chemical consumption did not stop them from knuckling down to serious rehearsals, which they held in a basement room they managed to get the free use of at the West Campus dormitory at Boston University.

His bandmates have credited Steven with metaphorically whipping them into shape, instilling in them a discipline towards practising and an intolerance for anything less than the very best they could deliver. Without a scrap of false modesty, Tyler has laid claim to having taught these guys how to be a proper, professional band, even though his methods sometimes caused upset and a deal of strain.

It could come down to personalities on both sides of the fence. Steven is a forceful and forthright guy, who does not shrink from letting someone have blunt criticism square in the face. Not everyone is equipped to like or to deal with that kind of direct approach. In Aerosmith, therefore, tensions frequently ran high during this period and Tyler has confirmed that his tough taskmaster attitude towards relentlessly honing the band made him, for spells, extremely unpopular. Battles often broke out, too, over the high volume at which the musicians liked to play, making it difficult for Steven to hear himself sing. Compromises on this front were sometimes only achieved after pieces of furniture had been hurled angrily around the room. Steven said that therapy was later used by all the guys in the band to enable them to let go of lingering resentments and anger dating from way back to this time. In a lighter vein, but no less meaningfully, Tom Hamilton described life under Tyler's rehearsal room tutelage during this period as 'rock and roll boot camp!'

With their collective musical influences, they not unnaturally strove for a powerful, hard rock sound with a raunchy swagger to it. As to the name, Aerosmith? Joey Kramer proffered it for consideration and the others liked it. While frequent attempts have been made over the years to attach some special significance to the choice of band name, Steven has recalled: 'It's just a name. We sat around for months coming up with different ideas – the Hookers, Spike Jones – and Aerosmith was great because it doesn't mean a thing.' The tighter Aerosmith's sound became, the more they were champing at the bit for exposure, and so the band began to perform on the Boston University campus. Said Steven: 'During lunch we would set up all our equipment outside of the university, in the main square, and just start wailing. That's basically how we got ourselves billed.'

Aerosmith played cover songs to rehearse, but from the outset Tyler wanted to write original material, and the symbiosis between himself and Joe Perry made for a natural collaboration. Perry began producing riffs, which inspired Tyler to put pen to paper. The first song Steven and Joe came up with was 'Movin' Out', which drew on their mutual influences. Joe vividly remembers sitting on a bed at the apartment developing this song, imbued with a strong sense that he and Steven had begun something exciting. Tyler exclaimed: 'It was like hitting pay dirt!' That said, sometimes it was hard for Steven to see any tangible sign that he and his band were not just living on pipe dreams.

Life at 1325 Commonwealth Avenue could scarcely be described as idyllic, and there were some downright hair-raising moments. One day, when Steven and Tom Hamilton were at home, a group of angry men burst in. They were on the trail of a suitcase stuffed with thousands of dollars, which they insisted had been left at the apartment. They were not prepared to believe an understandably alarmed bass player that he had never seen this suitcase about the crummy apartment and had no idea what these intimidating men were on about.

Steven had been in another room, and the intruders did not know that Tom was not alone. Realising from the different voices that he and Tom were outnumbered and out of their depth, thinking quickly, Steven managed to slip out unnoticed and rush off to beg help from an ex-marine who lived nearby. To Tyler's surprise the obliging former soldier came to Tom's rescue wielding a sharp, four-foot-long sword. As Steven gaped, the cavalry he had summoned kicked his way into the apartment, brandishing the weapon. Tom's would-be assailants immediately trained their drawn guns on the armed newcomer, who showed no signs of backing down. An intense battle of wills prevailed for what seemed like an eternity, but in the end it was the intruders who lost their bottle and fled, leaving Steven and Tom startled out of their wits but eternally grateful to their colourful neighbour.

When Aerosmith hit the Boston band circuit, life on the road was just as crazy. At the end of a bar room stint one night, with applause ringing in their ears, when they went to pick up their fee for the gig, the owner pulled a loaded gun on them – the grim message being: thanks very much, now beat it and be thankful that you are still alive. Aerosmith paid their dues as, hungry for work, exposure and cash, they played anywhere from high school auditoriums to the dingiest, dodgiest dive. Steven admitted: 'It was hard in the beginning to play and play and play, five sets a night – forty-five minutes a set – even when there was no one there and it was like for beer sometimes when we had no food!'

Some atmospheres were so fraught that it just took Steven's fatal forthrightness to light the touchpaper. Once they were on stage at what Tyler described as a 'bucket of blood Boston biker bar' when a woman swaggered across the dance floor and rudely gave Steven the finger. Without thinking, he snapped something crude at her over the mike, then thought nothing of it until the band was getting ready to go home, when an ashen-faced man tapped on their dressing room door. Joe Perry recalled: 'The guy said: "There are guys lined up outside and they're gonna kill you!" Steven had insulted the girlfriend of the leader of the bikers. We had to have the police come down because this was a place where periodically people got shot.'

Developing nerves of steel, the band plugged on, building a strong local reputation for turning in high-energy, adrenalin-driven performances, and they liked people to get up and enjoy themselves. Tom Hamilton reflected: 'When we played the Naval Officers' Club in Boston they would flip out. Then, we would play a frat house and they would get smashed and dance their balls off.'

Energised that Aerosmith was starting to create a smidgen of the sensation he planned to become, Steven was firing on all cylinders. He was also a red-blooded, unattached young guy very much on the loose, and virtually insatiable when it came to bedding women. Indelicately he once maintained: 'I like to ball everything I see – well, not *everything*, but at least one a day.'

Rampant skirt-chasing aside, Steven's serious eye was firmly fixed on what he could see amid the ever-growing crowds they attracted to gigs. He was also carefully weighing up how his individual style was going down. Tyler has become synonymous with his frenetic stage act, with dressing in lurid, revealing clothes and with grabbing the mike stand, itself festooned with flowing colourful scarves, as he suggestively grinds his body to raunchy lyrics. In 1970, he had not yet perfected that act but his bold behaviour at the mike already provoked a reaction. He recalled: 'I vividly remember the first time in Boston when I came out on stage and it really clicked. I *knew* the kids were digging what I was doing.'

Steven diligently rehearsed for the bigger venues he envisaged Aerosmith playing, and would privately practise addressing vast audiences. Without diluting the ambition in each of his bandmates, Steven believed that he wanted success more than anybody – it was impossible for him to imagine anyone wanting it more than he did. He once said: 'Rock and roll is just entertainment. If people pay their money and walk out happy, then you have done what you're supposed to do.' But he also revealed: 'I walked around in a fantasy land for years. I thought of it [attaining success] every second of the day.' He was convinced deep inside that it was only a matter of time before his band would achieve the breakthrough it needed. Aerosmith's following in and around Boston now ensured that more and more clubs were packed wall to wall with a growing number of grassroots fans. As Aerosmith thrashed out the raucous hard rock songs, probably many punters were inwardly comparing Steven

Tyler to Mick Jagger, but Steven was doing his own thing and his mindset was clear: 'Pretend to be somebody, until that somebody turns into you!'

# CHAPTER 3

# The Nature Of The Beast

**WHILE IT** cannot be said that Steven Tyler's ambition or determination waned, by late 1970 times were tough on a day-to-day level. Money was in desperately short supply. Steven was given a start at a bakery but was soon out the door. A spell waiting at tables did not last long either, and it was clear that he was not cut out to hold down a regular job. Joe Perry worked as a janitor at a Boston synagogue. Meantime, Tom Hamilton and Joey Kramer battled with health problems that winter; all of which also weighed things down.

Continuing to pick up bookings playing ballrooms, high school dances and at clubs and bars around Massachusetts, Tyler perfected his delivery of Yardbirds and Rolling Stones hits, but at 1325 Commonwealth Avenue he bent his mind even harder to writing original compositions. Stimulated by what he saw emerging, by spring 1971 Steven had produced sheet music for particularly promising songs but his rising optimism was tempered by an awareness that there was unrest in Aerosmith. It was not working out with Raymond Tabano as rhythm guitarist.

Years later, Tabano candidly confessed that, in terms of musicianship, he did not match the others in the band, a fact that became increasingly apparent that summer. He also had a life separate from the band – personal relationships, other calls on his time and attention. He would sometimes be late for rehearsals or unavoidably have to miss some practice sessions altogether, which irked the others. 'When Raymond did show up,' recalled Joe, 'he would try to take over.' Arguably, a personality clash was the biggest problem. Raymond has suggested that the others believed him to be a tougher guy than he really was, and Tom Hamilton did later state that he had felt intimidated by Tabano. Perry felt that there was someone out there who would make a more complementary match for the band, but not everyone was at ease with ousting Raymond.

Drummer Joey Kramer was saddened to see the man who had helped secure him his place in Aerosmith becoming isolated, and Steven had the toughest time of all reconciling matters. He and Raymond went way back to when they were children, and because of these shared roots he did not take kindly to wielding the axe. One sunny summer's afternoon, Joe Perry tried to let Raymond know over a pint of beer that he was being dropped from the band, but Tabano was not prepared to go without a fight. He perhaps believed that, if push came to shove, his longtime friend would not eject him. With tensions running high, after Steven and Raymond got into a shouting match at a gig Aerosmith officially dropped Raymond Tabano as its rhythm guitarist. Although they eventually made up and remained good friends, Raymond did not return to the band; his vacancy was filled by Brad Whitford.

Bradley Ernest Whitford was born on 23 February 1952 in Reading, Massachusetts, to Joyce and E. Russell Whitford, the middle child in a family of three sons. The brown-eyed, brown-haired boy began playing the trumpet at junior school before turning his sights on an electric guitar, an instrument about which he was sufficiently serious to seek tuition at a local music shop. In time-honoured tradition, however, he taught himself to play more by listening to records on the radio. Like Steven Tyler, the young Brad was an early aficionado of the British music scene. Newly a teenager, in summer 1965 Brad caught the Dave

Clark Five live during their US tour. Synonymous with foot-stomping melodic pop songs such as 'Bits and Pieces' and 'Glad All Over', this five-piece outfit ignited in Whitford the spark to join a band. Starting younger than most, he played rhythm guitar in a succession of local groups including the Cymbals of Resistance, Teapot Dome, Earth Incorporated and Justin Tyme, cutting his teeth in often less than salubrious joints. As a long-haired, music-mad eighteen-year-old, Brad left high school in 1970 and enrolled to study at Boston's Berklee College of Music when the clean-cut, suited Dave Clark Five was soon replaced in his affections by Britain's hottest hard rock export, Led Zeppelin. On tour, smashing attendance records in a blaze of publicity, Led Zeppelin was everywhere, and like so many others Whitford was bowled over by the stage wizardry of lead guitarist Jimmy Page. Energised, Brad threw everything into developing his guitar skills, and it was the following summer that he played at Lake Sunapee in New Hampshire, coming into casual contact with Joe Perry and Tom Hamilton. Brad went to see an Aerosmith gig there and something clicked. Everything about Tyler, Perry and co seemed right to him. The blues rock music Aerosmith belted out dovetailed with his tastes. Days later, to his surprise, Brad received an offer to join the band. He said: 'They were incredible, so there was not much to think about.'

Brad Whitford's first appearance with Aerosmith was at the Savage Beast, a club in Brownsville, Vermont, in late summer 1971, and soon after that he entered the belly of the beast by moving in to 1325 Commonwealth Avenue in Boston, where he encountered a far harder drug scene than he had been used to. Several people came and went at this apartment, many of them drug dealers. Taking a rather romanticised view of things, Joe Perry saw these people as being like rock bands – pariahs in conventional society. Columbian pot and cocaine got smoked or snorted in this dingy den, which was such a potential target for America's drug enforcement agency that even when a fire broke out there it had to be dealt with by the spaced-out occupants themselves; they dared not call in the fire service because of all the illegal drugs littering the place. Steven had stepped up from taking crystal meth to a higher class of drug, acquiring an appetite for cocaine, which in turn fuelled his rampant desire for sex – to Tyler, the combination of both was best. 'Once you've tasted coke and got blown at the same time, it's fuckin' bliss!' he declared. 'When you've gone to a party and made love to three girls it really does not suck.'

The band, however, remained Tyler's top priority. He now knew that the line-up was right and he was keen to progress. Not shy of putting in the roadwork, Aerosmith picked up a few hundred dollars per gig wherever they could over that perishing winter, travelling to venues courtesy of a converted, clapped-out red school bus that they had scraped up the money to buy. Staunch self-belief aside, the reality was that life continued to be a hard slog, and Steven still resorted to stealing food from shops to keep the wolf from the door. Maybe it was meant with tongue in cheek, but one Boston shopkeeper wanted to offer Tyler a job – it being cheaper to pay Steven a wage for working there than to stand him stealing from the premises! Despite Steven's resilience, it was not difficult to imagine packing it all in. Even if only fleetingly, he must have questioned the sheer viability of the band being able to stay together, living on little more than burning ambition.

Just when they needed it, they landed a break. By now John O'Toole, the manager of Boston's Fenway Theatre, was allowing the band to rehearse there free of charge when the theatre was dark. It was draughty and the heating was switched off, which meant practising muffled up to the eyeballs. Undaunted as the band played, Steven sang with his breath clouding the freezing air before him. He had recently moved lodgings to a place in Kent Street and the remaining occupants of 1325 Commonwealth Avenue had been served with an eviction notice, just as a white knight came to the rescue in the shape of a well-known Boston promoter, Frank Connelly, whom John O'Toole had tipped off about this diligent and ambitious band.

Connelly came to the Fenway Theatre and watched and

listened unobtrusively from the gloomy shadows. Liking what he found, he offered the five a management contract. Given the dire straits Aerosmith were in, it was a no-brainer anyway but, like the others, Steven was thrilled to sign the deal. Back at 1325 Commonwealth Avenue, with the threat of eviction hanging over their heads, it was brought home to them all just how close the band had come to falling apart.

Frank Connelly gave Aerosmith something more valuable than just money and terms. He breathed new impetus into the band at a desperately low point. He saw them as the rock world's new sensation in the making, and his faith was invigorating. Said Brad Whitford: 'Frank was the first guy who said we were on to something.' Initially, Tyler was not keen on Connelly's master plan to set Aerosmith to work playing the pub and club circuit, since he himself was well seasoned in that sphere but he was persuaded to see the need, now that the line-up was right, to knit the unit into its best ever shape. While sharpening its act, the band played some memorable nights – particularly when they opened for Johnny Winter and Humble Pie in December 1971 at the Academy of Music in New York City.

Missouri-born blues guitarist Jonny Winter was a top live attraction in the US. In the early 1970s, he succumbed to drug addiction, for which he received treatment before successfully returning to recording and touring. Hard-rocking headliners Humble Pie from Britain boasted ex-Small Faces frontman Steve Marriott, but amid a great deal of rancour the band had recently lost guitarist/vocalist Peter Frampton, who had decided to go solo. Steven recalled rushing to borrow some extra equipment for this support slot – by far Aerosmith's biggest gig to date – and getting to New York in their beat-up old bus. 'That night, Johnny had just come back from a rehabilitation centre,' said Steven. 'We did all original numbers and it went down quite good – well, no boos and just a couple of shouts.'

Away from the stage, rehearsals took place wherever Aerosmith could get a foot in the door. Although no one in the band hailed from Boston, they had already played so much in the region that they were viewed as a local band in many quarters, and Steven's vibrant personality was making an indelible mark. Doors opened to them. Theatre bosses were content to let the hard-working band play their hearts out overnight to empty auditoriums, so long as they were gone in the morning before the cleaners arrived. During these practice sessions, as Tyler heard his strengthening voice echoing out, he had to imagine all the bums on seats that Aerosmith would eventually pull in.

Come early 1972, the raw winter had taken a worse grip, but even though getting to remote venues in a ramshackle bus was an arduous experience, they stuck it out tenaciously and did not let blizzard conditions thwart them. Very much the main motivator in the band, Tyler made certain that everyone stayed focused, while manager Frank Connelly ceaselessly attempted to interest the music industry's movers and shakers in Aerosmith. Sometimes he persuaded record producers to come and listen to the band, but as yet the professional consensus was that Aerosmith was not quite up to scratch. This changed in summer when, realising that they needed more help than he alone could provide, Frank Connelly unselfishly brought the New York management team of Steve Leber and David Krebs into the picture.

Connelly invited Leber and Krebs to check out Aerosmith's live performance at Max's Kansas City, the Manhattan club that was then *the* watering hole for rock stars and the arty set. For hyped-up, over-eager hopefuls, showcase gigs are notorious for going pear-shaped, but within one explosive set that night Aerosmith won over the two managers. Steve Leber later maintained that they were the closest band he had seen for some time to rival the Rolling Stones, whereas David Krebs absorbed from the jumping ecstatic audience around him just how potent Aerosmith was in live performance and he, too, was sold. In July 1972, Steve Leber and David Krebs officially became the band's managers.

That month, Aerosmith was given the use of a back room at the Boston Garden to rehearse and it seemed inspiring that right then the Rolling Stones should come to perform at this venue.

The Stones' *Exile on Main Street* was nearing the end of a four-week run topping the US album charts when the controversial rockers courted yet more headlines en route from Rhode Island to Boston to play at the Garden. Mick Jagger, Keith Richards and one or two others were arrested after an altercation with a photographer, and it took the intervention of Boston's then mayor, Kevin White, to have the stars released on bail to enable the Rolling Stones to play the scheduled gig.

The Boston Garden held a resonance. In addition to staging rock concerts and sporting events, the fifteen-thousand-seater arena had also been used for political rallies, including one in November 1960 when John F. Kennedy had given a famously stirring speech. At the Boston Garden, Steven left Aerosmith's back room rehearsal and wandered out on to the stage, which was set up for the Stones' show. There, he stared out at the deserted venue. Playing to crowds of a few hundred was not what he yearned for – *this* was his dream and he soaked in the moment. Tyler would have to get by on his imagination for a bit longer yet, although events were moving fast.

Within weeks of signing to Leber and Krebs, Aerosmith played another showcase gig at Max's Kansas City, this time to impress all the influential record label executives who could be enticed to attend. The upshot of the night was that, in early August, Aerosmith was signed by Clive Davis to Columbia Records for $125,000. Again, it took just one set to spark Davis. Blown away by their talent and enthusiasm, he also absorbed Steven Tyler's personal force as a front man, his infectious impudence and marketable charisma that connected with every person in the place. Tyler will always remember Clive Davis delivering the hackneyed old line to him that night: 'I'm gonna make you a star.'

The $125,000 advance sounded a lot of money, especially in 1972, but by the time it was carved up in all directions and when it became obvious exactly what this sum would be offset against, the truth was that Steven and the others were left far from flush in the pocket. Tom Hamilton has maintained that it was the mid-

1970s before the band members received any more money from record royalties. Obtaining gigs remained a top priority for visibility and cash. Nonetheless, being signed to a major label and having a strong management team in place gave Steven a massive lift. Creativity was bursting to get out of him as a songwriter and as a magnetic performer. He was quickly cast in the role of a rock and roll gypsy because of his penchant for dressing in bright colours and containing his long hair with flowing headbands. His use of dramatic make-up to accentuate his striking features, and in time his propensity to dangle a bottle of Jack Daniel's from one hand on stage also ensured that he made an impact. But above all it was his full throttle delivery of punchy hard rock numbers which made people take heed of him and would earn him the nickname the Demon of Screamin'. It was hard for anyone to tear their eyes away from this explosive entity attacking the scarf-festooned microphone stand. That said, Tyler never forgot that he was part of a unit and as team leader he relentlessly geed up the troops. 'I used to tell the guys all the time: "Next year, at this time, *we're* gonna be on that radio!"' Their work schedule over the entire state of Massachusetts was exhausting though, turning Tyler into a nocturnal being. He quipped: 'Since this band started, I ain't seen daylight!'

In summer 1972, most members of Aerosmith were pushing the boundaries in one sense or another. It was then that Joe Perry first tried heroin, and at 1325 Commonwealth Avenue a visit from the narcotics detectives was always just a door knock away. The apartment was still a hub for nefarious types to come and go. The cops did mount a surveillance operation outside and at one point charges were laid, but then dropped. It was a volatile time when Steven and Joe, both strong personalities, constantly clashed. It is not something that either man has ever denied or tried to dilute. They would have rip-roaring bawling matches backstage after gigs. There were times when tensions ran so high that they found it easier not to speak to each other for spells. A good old barney over something quickly came to be par for the course. Although both Steven and Joe have been frank about the incendiary nature of their creative partnership and friendship, the degree of volatility did create an extremely fraught environment that was further complicated when the lead guitarist became involved with a young woman named Elyssa Jerret.

Elyssa Jerret's family owned a house at Lake Sunapee and initially she knew Steven only by seeing him around the resort. Frequenting the Anchorage, she had encountered Joe Perry when he worked in the kitchen there. She began spending time with the budding guitarist, but on a purely platonic basis. She grew to know Steven better by attending his gigs at The Barn, before leaving America in the late 1960s for London, where she became involved with a guitarist. Steven and Joe separately corresponded with Elyssa while she was living across the pond, mainly sharing news of their burgeoning band. Elyssa was beautiful and lively, and when she returned to America in summer 1972, just after Aerosmith had signed to Columbia Records, she had parted company from the musician in London and was a free agent. When she met up with the band soon after her return, she and Joe became romantically involved. The dynamics of the already spiky friendship between Tyler and Perry instantly became skewed.

Elyssa was an independent spirit who fearlessly spoke her mind; sometimes, she has confessed, her mouth pre-empted her brain getting in gear; her unwillingness to be a delicate presence waiting patiently in the background until Joe was free to pay her attention suited Perry's nature, too. The couple quickly became closer than two coats of paint, and the more Joe vanished with his new girlfriend, the more rejected Steven felt, breeding mounting jealousy. For all the fireworks in their friendship, Steven had waited all his life to have a buddy like Joe Perry. Suddenly, it felt as if Joe did not value that friendship any more. For a man who had taken such an interest in British bands, Steven must have noted that all too frequently women, or sometimes one particular woman, coming on the scene is a recipe for monumental disruption.

It was not only Tyler who was affected by this change in the wind. Tom Hamilton, who had been mates with Perry before Joe and Steven had met, now felt excluded. A bust-up one day, when Joe was leaving 1325 Commonwealth Avenue to move into the Kent Street apartment building where Steven lived, did some damage to their particular bond. Outside Aerosmith activity, Joe's total absorption was with Elyssa, and this imbalance would not be a temporary blip. Tyler recalled: 'I clearly saw that Joe was pulling away and it really bugged me!'

Although the Commonwealth Avenue apartment was shabby, it had been home for two years for most of Aerosmith, but with the lease expired each guy now went his own way into different lodgings. Steven headed for Lake Sunapee, where his mind turned to which songs they ought to put on the band's debut album. Seven of the eight songs ultimately selected were Tyler compositions; songs he had been squirrelling away for some time. A particular favourite of Steven's was 'Mama Kin', so much so that he had 'Ma' Kin' (the song's original title) tattooed on one arm. Perry's initial reaction was that musically 'Mama Kin' was a little too simple. 'Steven obviously loved that song,' Joe recalled, 'and inevitably the best ones are the easy ones.' 'Movin' Out', which Steven and Joe had co-written sitting on a bed at 1325 Commonwealth Avenue, was a cast-iron certainty for inclusion. Tyler felt this first songwriting collaboration between the friends had cemented their bond. Although Steven created 'One Way Street' alone at the piano in that crummy apartment, drummer Joey Kramer remembered working on it with Tom Hamilton. He confessed: 'We drove the old lady downstairs crazy – Tom on his bass and me on a kitchen chair using a pedal on a cardboard box.'

'Write Me a Letter' was the product of six months' development, and Brad Whitford recalled how the musical arrangement had been thrashed out during rehearsals in the back room at the Boston Garden. As a lyricist, Steven reacts spontaneously to something he sees or hears; he has the knack of picking out the gems in the mud and creating songs around them, and he puts pen to paper anywhere. 'Make It' was written in a car on his way back from Lake Sunapee to Boston. For a long time, Aerosmith would use 'Make It' to open their shows. 'It's a great way to get things going,' revealed Tom. Besides 'Movin' Out', the only other co-composition was a song called 'Somebody', on which Steven had collaborated with Steve Emsback, a guy he had known in the pre-Aerosmith days. It was 'Dream On', however, that became the album's standout track.

'Dream On' began life one late, dark night at Lake Sunapee when Steven, aged seventeen, was feeling very lonely and a little emotional now that summer was over. Drifting indoors at Trow-Rico Lodge in a preoccupied mood, he sat down at the upright piano and tried to translate his feelings into music. From nowhere a melody gradually emerged which he could not get out of his head. At the time he left it at that, with no specific notion of developing it into a song. At the Commonwealth Avenue flat he returned to the piano ballad in the key of F minor, as Tom Hamilton can vouch for. 'When we were all living together, mine was the only room with a piano in it and I remember waking up hearing Steven playing this song over and over again,' he said. 'It pissed me off at the time but I'm sure glad he kept playing.' Its heartfelt lyrics were about holding on to the hope of fulfilling aspirations and the grit needed to take life's knocks. Tyler has been blunt: 'This song sums up the shit you put up with when you're in a new band.' With its haunting quality and the way it builds to a crescendo, 'Dream On' made a lasting impression on Aerosmith fans and is classed as the prototype for today's hard rock power ballad. '"Dream On" is one of my favourite songs to play live,' stated Joe Perry.

To put the finishing touches to this batch of songs, Aerosmith spent time that autumn holed up at the Sheraton Hotel in Manchester, Massachusetts, before moving into a rented house. This concentrated time helped the five men to focus purely on their debut album, free of all other distractions. It was when they headed back to Boston that Steven decided to change his surname to Tyler. Though it is commonplace for singers to adopt a stage name, some stars become irritated when reminded of their real name. In the case of Queen's Freddie Mercury, Farookh Bulsara had yearned to reinvent himself as someone synonymous with glamour and strength – hence Mercury, the messenger of the gods. But Steven did not want to shut a door on his past. He did not want to deny his heritage. He simply saw changing Tallarico to Tyler as giving him a snappier name in preparation, he hoped, for when he hit the big time; he has little patience with those who attempt to apply cod psychology to his name-changing. He recently blasted: 'I got that shit in rehab – "I want you to keep Tyler out of here." Fuck! I *am* that guy. Steven Tyler and Steven Tallarico are the same guy!'

Over two weeks in October 1972, Tyler joined the other four at Boston's Intermedia Sound Studios to record their debut album with producer Adrian Barber. In addition to the seven songs Aerosmith had prepared, they recorded a cover version of the Rufus Thomas rhythm and blues number, 'Walkin' the Dog'. Though recording their debut album was what they had all dreamed of, they were too uptight and scared of making a mistake to be able to relax and enjoy the experience. Strain tautened every aspect of the recording process and this tension made relations fraught. Joey Kramer later recalled Tyler's growing frustration when nerves made his timekeeping while drumming less than perfect. For some, it was also claustrophobic and a rushed affair.

In 1976, Steven recalled: 'Bob Ezrin [a producer] heard our first album and thought we needed a lot of work, which we did, but we're honest. We're not a band that puts track over track.' Tom Hamilton has since reflected: 'When we recorded our first album, it was done with very little studio experience. Unfortunately, we made a sort of crude album.' Brad Whitford confirmed this when he revealed: 'It was recorded on a recording console that was literally homemade. Part of it was cardboard with knobs the size of headlights!'

Steven was dismayed when reaction appeared to be decidedly cool at Columbia Records during the first playback of Aerosmith's debut album, and a comment from one label executive that there was no immediately recognisable single among the tracks leadened Tyler's heart even more. Along with the others, Steven went through the process of shooting the album cover but even this was a downer when they realised that there was a dearth of material to chose from to help hype the band in the album's liner notes. The Boston media had yet to notice Aerosmith. Feeling the way he did, it did not help Steven when he picked up at the record company that there was, by contrast, enormous excitement about another artist who was about to launch his recording career with the label.

The previous summer, the New Jersey singer/songwriter Bruce Springsteen had signed a worldwide ten-year, ten-album deal with Columbia Records. His debut offering, *Greetings from Asbury Park*, had been recorded in just three weeks and was due for release the same month as Aerosmith's album, but Springsteen was already being touted to critics and the music media as the new Bob Dylan.

A hot-off-the-press copy of Aerosmith's first album was sent to the band, and they all sat around Joey Kramer's Boston apartment and listened to it in complete silence. Low though their expectations already were, the general feeling at the end of the final track was one of dense dismay.

*Aerosmith* was released in America in mid-January 1973 and went into instant oblivion. Despite their best efforts the record company could not drum up any promotion for the album, so it had absolutely no chance of impinging on the music-buying consciousness. Depressingly for the whole band, when scouring the record shops it was hard even to stumble across a copy on the packed record racks. What made it worse was that, rightly or wrongly, they did not feel they had a support network beneath them, at least not the kind and strength of network they had always imagined there would be when launching a new band on the highly competitive music scene.

Expressing his personal belief, Tom Hamilton once declared: 'When the album was released, Columbia Records hated it, all of their reps hated it and the disc jockeys also hated it!' Steven remembered that those rock critics who did give *Aerosmith* a fleeting mention did so only in order to pan it thoroughly. Said

Joe Perry: 'By this time, we had fans in Boston who loved us and packed out the clubs wherever we played. So it was only ever the critics who did not give us the credit we deserved.' In the midst of a bleak mid-winter January, that was very cold comfort.

# CHAPTER 4

# Spliffs, Tiffs And Stiffs

**A**EROSMITH ARRIVING on the music map with the merest whimper did not suit Steven Tyler and the situation was exacerbated when critics weighed in deriding the band as the poor man's Rolling Stones. Rock journalists came away from gigs and wrote of how, from a distance, the blond Tom Hamilton to Tyler's right could be Brian Jones, the brooding guitarist to the left resembled Keith Richards, while a skinny, prancing front man bawled out lead vocals. Understandably irked by this, in a *Rolling Stone* interview Steven revealed: 'Anybody who says I'm a Jagger rip-off because I look like him a little has no intelligence. And what am I supposed to do – get plastic surgery?' He had more pressing concerns than that, however. With the debut album's poor chart performance, Tyler knew that Aerosmith had to break on the live circuit beyond the confines of New England. So, while they continued to play five nights a week at clubs and colleges, he was on the lookout for work supporting established bands that would take the group all around America.

Like most major bands, Aerosmith suffered the growing pains associated with going out on grossly mismatched bills. Their first proper tour was playing support to the Mahavishnu Orchestra – an outfit that fused music and mysticism. The instrumental group's Top 20 album, *Birds of Fire,* released in March 1973, set them up to hit higher heights a few months later with *Love Devotion Surrender.* The only adoration Aerosmith saw was reserved for the headliners. As for surrender? That is what Steven and the others had to do with their pride. It was a true baptism of fire for the five. Tom Hamilton recalled of Mahavishnu Orchestra: 'The band would meditate before they started playing and we were not into that! We'd already found our own way to meditate, chemically.' Often dispirited before even stepping on stage, they came off stage thoroughly dejected after performing to stoically unimpressed audiences who were never going to get into Aerosmith's gutsy act. Slow handclaps and calls for Mahavishnu demoralised and angered Tyler by turn, though he knew well that they were flogging a dead horse. He said: 'It was weird, like Jimi Hendrix opening for the Monkees, but it was to get us out on the road.' Stubbornly ignoring the boos and catcalls, Aerosmith tried to rise to the occasion every night, telling themselves to put it all down to experience. They had to be resilient, for the music press switched its attack and now dubbed Aerosmith a punk band. Tyler did not appreciate this – to a New Yorker, a punk meant a slob. Manager David Krebs recalled: 'Aerosmith was not a press favourite. The press thought they sucked.' Happy to relegate this first support slot to history, in spring 1973 Tyler was excited to be opening for one of his all-time favourite bands – the Kinks.

Although afforded legendary status – and to this day often cited as hugely inspirational to a new generation of music stars – the Kinks had found it impossible to mirror the chart success attained in America by their sixties' peers, the Rolling Stones and the Beatles. In March 1973, *The Great Lost Kinks Album* peaked at number 145 on Billboard, but the ultra-English band had begun to gain ground at concert level in the States. When Aerosmith opened for them, though, it was not exactly the joy Steven and the others had been so eagerly anticipating.

It is perhaps too strong to say that Aerosmith discovered that their heroes had feet of clay, but they were certainly deeply disappointed, on a practical level, not to be given a sound check before playing. Also, it was maybe the case that a very London sense of humour missed the mark with the Americans and caused unintentional irritation, but Steven did not find much to laugh about. In performance, however, he thrust out his chest, plunged his fingers into his hair and raised the roof with high-octane renditions of hard-rocking numbers. Road-testing their own original material gave him a buzz. His flat-out enthusiasm could not help but elicit a response, and like any self-respecting support act Aerosmith was out to steal fans from the headliners. With relentless drive, Steven was bent on building Aerosmith a hardcore following, throwing everything into his act. This paid off, and led to them securing a slot at Boston's Orpheum Theatre, albeit stapled last on to the bill of a charity gig. Needless to say, they were delighted, and when they reverted to club and college gigs their fee per night had quadrupled.

The bugbear continued to be the reaction of the music media. After gigs, Steven would eagerly rifle through national music magazines in the hope of finding a mention, only to come up blank or else find Aerosmith still being dismissed as copycats. Keeping his spirits up was not easy, but his rascally personality was ever ready to burst out – as was evidenced when a Rhode Island newspaper featured Aerosmith on its front cover. Inside, the paper printed a shot of a clowning Tyler cheekily mooning. Signs of a breakthrough came, however, when *Creem* magazine provided Aerosmith with its first nationwide review, picking up on the sheer sexuality of the band's lyrics and performance style, and affectionately dubbing them 'delinquents'. While Tyler appreciated this he was inwardly concerned that because *Aerosmith* had under-performed, Columbia Records may already be considering cutting the band loose.

Welcome green shoots burst through when 'Dream On' was released in June 1973 as the first single off the debut album. Nationally, it reached a modest number fifty-nine on the US chart, while regionally it became a hit across the north-west, upstate New York and in New England. The rock ballad was also voted the number one song of the year by listeners of two Boston radio stations, WVBF and WBCN; all of this helped *Aerosmith* to creak its way, months after its release, to number 166 on Billboard. Drawing what encouragement he could from 'Dream On', Tyler and the others concentrated on performing at summer festivals across New Hampshire and at high school proms, fraternity parties and occasional week-long club residencies. This gigging entertained thousands and drew the eye of *Variety* magazine, which commented on Steven's grinding groin action at the mike and his eye-popping stagewear. It tailed off by dubbing Tyler the undoubted focus on stage. Other publications followed suit and began to single out Aerosmith's raw raunchiness.

Steven set out to turn his audiences on every night, but sometimes the smouldering flame ignited in unexpected ways. At one show at the Suffolk Downs horse-racing track near Boston, the audience became so worked up that they began throwing beer bottles at the band. Once two or three did it, others got in on the act until Steven was faced with the daunting sight of all these missiles raining down on the stage. Despite these reactions, they persevered and completed their tour. When Aerosmith came off the road late that summer they decided once again to share an apartment; they found a place on Boston's Beacon Street, where they had to devote their energies to creating songs for their second album.

Invigorated by their experiences over the year and spurred on to prove themselves, the band's creative juices were flowing; from this songwriting blitz emerged a mixed bag, with hard rock numbers such as 'S.O.S. (Too Bad)' and 'Lord of the Thighs' perhaps coming easiest to Steven. Of the Joe Perry/Steven Tyler collaboration, 'Same Old Song and Dance', in 1992 Steven recounted to *Rock Power*: 'That was a real classic Joe Perry riff. I just filled in the blanks. I hate to spell things out too much but that was about one girl who was pulling on my guitar player's balls.' Tyler also collaborated for the first time with drummer Joey Kramer on the slower-paced 'Pandora's Box'. Said

Kramer: 'We were up in New Hampshire and I had this old guitar I'd found in a dumpster and I came up with the riff. I played it for Steven and he went to work on it.' The most atmospheric number was a ballad called 'Season of Wither'. Perry preferred to steer clear of ballads – he only made slow blues an exception – but he was impressed by this Tyler composition.

Steven tended to leave writing lyrics to the last possible moment, believing that he worked best when under pressure. Naturally, strong emotion motivates him best, but whereas loneliness had inspired 'Dream On', 'Season of Wither' stemmed from a fusion of melancholy and anger over his financial status. In threadbare basement surroundings, having doped himself up with pills, he strummed on a guitar and produced this song. Drugs, of course, played a prominent role in life at Beacon Street, where the chemical buffet included Tuinals, Seconals, blue crystal meth and quaaludes, while a surfeit of hash ensured spliffs rolled the size of fat cigars.

All the same, for several weeks the band diligently rehearsed this clutch of new numbers to the best of their budding ability. In the main, Tyler managed to maintain his dream of success, but in autumn 1973 he suffered a fleeting crisis of confidence. The differing personalities in Aerosmith made for some heavy-duty clashes, and arguments tended to break out all the time. Steven was as guilty as anyone of sparking a row, and while a set-to could sometimes alleviate the tension, at this moment in time when Steven felt little support from any section of the music business, the fact that he and his bandmates were so quarrelsome made him fear that Aerosmith was just *too* volatile to make it. With his quirky sense of humour he once declared that fine stood for: 'Fucked up, insecure, neurotic, emotional'. Banishing doubt, Tyler overcame this wobble and looked forward to returning to live performance, again on support duty; this time they were backing the British band, Mott the Hoople.

Fronted by Ian Hunter, and with singles 'All the Young Dudes' and 'All the Way from Memphis' to their credit, Mott the Hoople was making an impact that autumn on US audiences.

Aerosmith hitched their trailer to this wagon in October, garnering much-needed experience in playing large coliseums and auditoriums. At first, Hoople was happy that the warm-up act was so effective in building the atmosphere, but before long awareness dawned of just *how* avidly the crowds were reacting to the scantily clad, snake-hipped singer with outrageously overt sex appeal. For Steven, however, this tour established the point at which he could put even fleeting doubts aside. Near nightly, to his immense satisfaction, he watched overwrought teenagers leaping barriers and scrambling to climb on stage, making a grab at his legs. In December, when Aerosmith played at the renowned Whisky A Go-Go club on Sunset Boulevard in Los Angeles, Tyler's on-stage charisma reaped rave reviews, helping to elevate the band to a new level.

It was with a spring in their step, then, that towards the end of the year Aersomith headed to New York to record their second album at Record Plant Studios, where they would work with Jack Douglas. The influential New York-born record producer already had impressive credentials, having worked as an engineer on The Who's album *Who's Next?* as well as on John Lennon's *Imagine*. At Record Plant he had brought his studio skills to bear on offerings from the New York Dolls and Patti Smith, among others. Earlier in 1973, Jack Douglas had caught Aerosmith in performance around Boston and was attracted to their raw, hard-rocking ethos. He had met them briefly in person and liked their defensive edginess – something, as a native New Yorker, that he well understood. He developed such a strong bond with the band that for a while he was nicknamed the sixth member of Aerosmith. No one was under any illusions as to how vital it was to make inroads with this follow-up album. Tom Hamilton has bluntly revealed: 'The record label said: "If your next record doesn't do a lot better, that is the end."' Initially a little intimidated to be recording in such a famous facility, they soon overcame their nerves and knuckled down with their experienced producer at the helm. Although drug-fuelled squabbles broke out, recording was completed in January 1974 and *Get Your*

*Wings* was released on Columbia Records two months later. Though the album spent eighty-six weeks on the charts and eventually went gold on the back of future success, its highest Billboard ranking was number seventy-four. Three singles from the album were released throughout the year: 'Same Old Song and Dance'; 'S.O.S. (Too Bad)'; 'Train Kept A-Rollin'. All failed to register on the US singles chart, hardly helping Steven to feel secure. Holding their nerve, in March, Aerosmith launched themselves on a gruelling touring schedule playing mainly support to virtually the A–Z of pop and rock bands. Said Tom Hamilton: 'We got on the best tours we possibly could and projected as much fun as we pos-sibly could and gradually we became popular. We did that everywhere so eventually people started buying our albums. I'd say the secret to making it big in rock, and keeping it that way, is to play your balls off touring.'

Starved of radio airplay, Aerosmith had no chance of breaking that way but their grassroots following was strengthening with every live performance. This growing fan base soon came to be known as the Blue Army, largely because the band attracted strong support from America's blue-collar community, but partly in recognition of the fact that the majority of the fans showing up for gigs were denim-clad teenage boys. In demographic terms, certainly in these early days, Aerosmith's testosterone-driven music appealed predominantly to guys with attitude. *Rolling Stone* once described fans rolling up for a particular Aerosmith gig as akin to 'a boozy army of hard hats coming to dismantle the place'.

That year Aerosmith headlined in their strongholds around New England, playing sold out shows at Boston's Orpheum Theatre, shining too as emerging stars in pockets across the US. Though Steven was gaining a reputation as a flamboyant frontman, a role that came completely naturally to him, he has revealed that he often regrets not playing on tour. 'I miss playing instruments very much. I play on the albums, a little guitar, drums here and there, but I definitely miss that when I'm touring. It's something to do. There are a lot of dead spots up there on stage so I just hide behind my scarves.'

The fractiousness inherent in Aerosmith was not the only source of tension. Elyssa Jerret accompanied Joe Perry wherever he went and her constant presence was later said to have aggravated matters, while Tyler and Perry's ever escalating drug use further fuelled feelings of resentment which could only add to the cauldron of unrest. By Tyler's own admission he was stoned much of the time – it had become essential to him constantly to chase the elation he craved, for without that feeling he became nervy and irritable. He could not do without a fix even for the couple of hours each night he was on stage, which was why he had pockets stitched into some of the long flowing scarves dangling from the mike stand to hold his back-up stash of drugs. During performances, he could feed what was becoming a serious habit.

Steven's stage style was now very much the ragamuffin gypsy look – torn clothes made of floaty material that swirled around him as he gyrated manically about the stage. Joe Perry, the black-clad epitome of Mr Cool, once groaned: 'Oh man, he definitely gets dressed in the closet, with the light off!' But visually, it was extremely effective. Steven's lurid stagewear had started off being provided by friends who would run him up outfits as favours, but he had progressed beyond that and soon he rasped to journalists: 'You have no idea how much it costs to look this cheap!' Despite his cheek, Steven was still not at all secure, a fact that showed when the rock media began knocking on Aerosmith's door for interviews. Looking back, he wished that he had been a little less nervous when sitting down with journalists but, having received bad reviews and criticisms from the press in the past, his distrust of the music press was understandable.

When Aerosmith returned to Boston in late 1974 after such a hectic year the rewards were plain to see. The reception at gigs was now so wild, state after state, that cops were becoming nervous about controlling hyper fans on the verge of spiralling out of control, and the money the band coined in was at last steadily rising. With a real feeling that Aerosmith was taking wings Steven focused on writing songs for their next album. The ceaseless roadwork had sharpened the band, helping to infuse Steven with a positive attitude, but it is also true that their troubles behind the scenes provided grist for the mill. Brad Whitford believed that in the song 'No More No More', Tyler cleverly held up a mirror to life inside the band at that time. Joe Perry agreed, describing this number as representing 'a page from our diary'. The pacy tempo of 'Toys in the Attic' appealed greatly to the lead guitarist, while Tyler was later not too certain where his head had been when writing 'Adam's Apple'. Tyler collaborated on numbers with Whitford, Perry and Tom Hamilton, and he fell back on a pre-Aerosmith song, 'You See Me Crying', which he had penned with Don Solomon. He also opted for a cover version of 'Big Ten Inch Record', but two particular songs written for this third album would stand apart from the others.

At the start of 1975 recording work had begun, once again at Record Plant Studios in New York with producer Jack Douglas. Joe Perry had stumbled upon a stimulating riff while messing around during a sound check, but coming up with lyrics proved annoyingly elusive. With nerves fraught and fatigue setting in, Douglas suggested the band took a break, so they quit Record Plant late one night to get some fresh air. Passing the prostitutes plying their trade alongside the drug dealers in shady Times Square, the band wandered into a cinema showing the Mel Brooks-directed comedy *Young Frankenstein* starring Gene Wilder, Gene Hackman and Marty Feldman, famous for his startlingly bulging eyes. Feldman's character in the movie would croak 'Walk this way' at people, and that clicked with the band.

Although Steven Tyler's confidence could drop when he had to come up with lyrics, he was more than capable of stepping up to the task when the pressure was on. Back at the studio, with the song title to stimulate him, he clamped on a pair of headphones and let fly. 'That was me just throwing my hands in the air and going with a retching sound. I loved that,' he said. Ideas were coming thick and fast, and as he had lost his notepad he ended up rushing out to pen the lyrics to what became one of Aerosmith's most famous hits on a wall by the staircase.

Unashamedly, the song is saturated with sexual innuendo suggesting masturbation, three-in-a-bed sex and romps with older sirens. Said Steven of 'Walk This Way': 'It's about what I went through in high school, the relationships with girls. It reeks of teenage sex.'

The other notable number was 'Sweet Emotion' which, despite what the title suggests, stemmed in part from a bitterness that had taken root inside Steven. He has stated that he cannot pinpoint when he physically sat down and expressed himself so poignantly in this song, but he does not dispute that some of the lyrics were inspired by his complex feelings for Elyssa Jerret. He has candidly admitted to blaming her for being a barrier between himself and Joe Perry. Considering that Joe and his girlfriend were growing even closer, this release of Steven's frustration and naked hurt was unlikely to be well received, and did not help the suffocating pressure under which they were all living. More money purchased a better grade of dope and now what Perry termed 'unstepped-on cocaine' became the drug of choice. As cocaine often induces paranoia, this was the last thing anyone needed.

In late March 1975, with recording over at Record Plant Studios, when Steven led the band out on tour around America just prior to the release of *Toys in the Attic*, their faith in the new material proved to be well founded. The album reached number eleven on the US chart, but more than creating Aerosmith's commercial and artistic breakthrough, *Toys in the Attic* became a hard rock classic. Billboard said: 'The band's sound has developed into a sleek, hard-driving, hard rock powered by almost brutal blues-based riffs. Aerosmith strip heavy metal to its basic core, spitting out spare riffs that not only rock but roll. Steven's lyrics are filled with double entendres and clever jokes and the entire band has a streetwise charisma.' The single 'Sweet Emotion' was released in May and made number thirty-six.

With this welcome impetus, the band worked hard that summer, turning in electrifying performances, such as at the Schaefer Music Festival held in New York City's Central Park. At gigs, the mercury was teetering on the verge of exploding back-stage where the aggravation between Steven and Joe Perry was now noticeable to total strangers; in a different way fans out front were becoming crazed. At one Central Park gig in the 1970s, a female fan scrambled on stage and launched herself on to Steven, clawing at him in such a frenzy that he was left with a large bleeding hole in his left earlobe. New safety measures had to be implemented both to protect the band in performance and to dissuade the teenagers from harming themselves in their fever to get on stage.

At the same time, after a period in rock when androgyny had left audiences not sure what to make of sexually ambiguous stars, Steven Tyler oozed full-on heterosexual lust. He has declared: 'The stage is my mistress and I fuck her to death every night. I do feel sexy up there.' Sex permeated Steven's whole life. He wrote about it, adored to sing about it and continued to be insatiable when it came to slaking his desire for women. He saw no reason to limit his horizons. As he plainly put it: 'It's a trip seeing girls with big tits and tiny asses just dripping with sex, throwing themselves at you – especially if they've brought a girl-friend with them! Man, that's orgasmic! I haven't had it [three-in-a-bed sex] as much as I would like but when I have had the pleasure, it has *truly* been a pleasure!' One of Tyler's later regrets was that there had been times when his drug consumption left him flaked out on his back alone in bed, too stoned to get it up.

But if sex was Steven's mistress, drugs were rapidly becoming his master. He flatly denounced those who decried drug users as being empty-headed fools, arguing that drug abuse was rooted in the search of feeling great. Comparing the similarities between the molecular structure of cocaine and heroin and that of adrenalin and endorphins, he reasoned: 'Taking drugs is very akin to feelings that humans get when they are elated.'

Building a relentless head of steam increasingly resulted in trouble erupting at gigs, bringing with it reports of riots at some venues – just the juicy kind of notoriety that was guaranteed to bolster a band's reputation. Aerosmith was widely credited as being the hardest-working band on the road in America throughout 1975 – in terms of pulling crowds they stood shoulder to shoulder with Led Zeppelin, Jethro Tull and Queen. The previous year, rivalry had reared between Aerosmith and Queen when both bands had been booked to back Mott the Hoople at a gig at the Harrisburg Farm Arena in Pennsylvania. A row broke out between the two groups as to which should be first on stage. Joe Perry and Brian May wandered off with a bottle of Jack Daniel's, leaving Steven Tyler and Freddie Mercury to go heatedly head to head over the issue.

In 1975, Tyler had his own take on Aerosmith garnering recognition. He said: 'This band is like cold butter on hot bread – it sinks in after a while.' 'Walk This Way' and 'Toys in the Attic' were released from the new album towards the end of the year and did not initially make much of a splash. Rock critics at the time did not give Aerosmith much of a break. Steven let these attacks get under his skin and although a new kid on the block, in the mid-1970s he was not shy of airing *his* forthright views on reviewers, highlighting examples of what he termed their ignorance. In *Melody Maker* he blasted: 'I go through a lot to write lyrics to songs like "Walk This Way" – I'm very fond of those lyrics – and the critics never stopped to listen to the words. They don't give a shit. So why do I have to respect their opinions?' With the fans, where it counted, Tyler continued to see proof of Aerosmith's burgeoning status; by December, *Toys in the Attic* went platinum and his band was a bone fide major concert draw in the States. For Steven personally, however, the picture was not quite so rosy.

# CHAPTER 5

# When The Fur Starts Flying

**I**N SUMMER 1975 the tense dynamic between Steven, and Joe and Elyssa worsened. Tyler now felt to an intolerable degree that Elyssa was depriving him of Joe's friendship and companionship. Her presence in Perry's life seemed to be all-consuming. The lead guitarist disputed this, in the sense that whenever he was needed for Aerosmith he was there, but the singer clearly hankered for his brother-in-arms. It was not only Tyler who felt this way – other Aerosmith members were concerned at the influence Elyssa's presence had on the band – but, in a display of raw emotion, Steven left himself vulnerable to further rejection when he attempted to explain his feelings to the besotted couple. On reflection, Steven has acknowledged that it was not one of his wisest moves; indeed, at the time he believed that his frank soul-baring had only led to him making a fool of himself. It was a very painful time and maybe Steven's substance abuse heightened his sensitivity.

Elyssa Jerret became a firmer fixture in Aerosmith's world when she and Joe married on 5 August, with the reception being held at the Ritz in Boston. It highlighted the stark contrast in the band's fortunes. Guys who had not so long ago huddled in a hovel of an apartment across town on Commonwealth Avenue, with an eviction notice hanging over their heads, were now being waited upon at the city's plushest hotel. Family members from both the bride and groom's side afforded the nuptials traditional values and respectability, while the groom became so stoned his insides were spinning and Steven discreetly disappeared around speech time to inhale heroin.

That month, Aerosmith again hit the road. Said Tyler: 'I've been going to a lot of concerts lately, watching groups who are so fuckin' outrageous on record that you'd think they'd get out there on stage and shake ass but they just stand there. The songs we write aren't the kind that you come out and fucking genuflect. We play kick-ass music!' Following an exhausting schedule as headliners and as a support act, Aerosmith played gigs in over a dozen states coast to coast across America. Racking up the air miles, hotel rooms all started to look the same, and weeks passed by in a drug-induced off-duty haze; fuelled by cocaine and vodka, every night felt like it was New Year's Eve. For the unattached Steven the on-road debauchery became crazy, elevating Aerosmith's raunchy reputation to Rolling Stones and Led Zeppelin realms. Along the way, Aerosmith played on bills with the likes of ZZ Top, Reo Speedwagon and Rod Stewart.

Aerosmith set out to thrill their audiences to the core, and Tyler's stage act had become breathtakingly physical. As lithe as an acrobat, he could leap to astonishing heights and perform slick somersaults, and he whirled dizzily back and forth across the full length of the stage. His endless energy was incredibly exciting to watch; he wielded the heavy microphone stand like a weapon, at times coming within an inch of unwittingly braining his guitarists. He shook his bony body as hard as he did the maracas and his deft harmonica playing was very Dylanesque. Tyler was Tyler, not emulating anyone on stage, although *Rolling Stone* recorded around this time that when Steven sang the ballad 'Dream On', his voice sounded like Robert Plant's.

Yet, for all that Tyler was beginning to live the dream, with his latent anger he could erupt like a volcano for a variety of reasons. After a performance, exhausted and loaded with drink and drugs, something as simple as taking against one dish among the generous buffet laid out backstage could make him lose his temper and tip over the whole trestle table, sending food and drink flying. It would be years before he admitted to taking a long hard look at this behaviour, which had felt so good to him at the time. By his own admission, throughout the 1970s he smashed up expensive wristwatches by hurling them against walls whenever something pissed him off. 'I was so far out on the edge that I felt I *had* to trash something quickly,' he revealed.

The fact that Steven is not a man to always mind his ps and qs, meant that he nearly had his collar felt in Memphis for flouting local laws by swearing on stage, and in Lincoln, Nebraska, some high jinks with fireworks resulted in the cops calling at the band's hotel. He could explode with fury about some of the media coverage his band attracted. In particular, he found it profoundly irritating to see Aerosmith dubbed an overnight success. In one frank exchange with journalists he talked of his intense dislike for those people who had not believed in Aerosmith at the outset, mourning the fact that there was no way he could get back at them. Not vindictive by nature, it was an interesting indicator as to how deep previous cuts had gone with him.

Aerosmith started the new year as one of America's hottest rock properties; by securing the hitherto elusive AM radio airplay their debut album finally peaked at number twenty-one. Also in spring, 'Dream On' lodged at number six on Billboard's singles chart, providing the band with their first Top 10 hit record. Soon the tangible signs of their increasing wealth came in the shape of luxury cars. As the era of merchandising was taking off, Aerosmith acquired a logo featuring wings, the initial A and the band name. The business side of affairs flourished, establishing their identity even more firmly in the public's consciousness.

The year before, bassist Tom Hamilton had married his girlfriend, Terry Cohen. Now, in February 1976, rhythm guitarist Brad Whitford wed Lori Phillips. By this time, work had already begun on the band's fourth album at the Wherehouse, a rented converted warehouse in Pond Street, Waltham, Massachusetts. This hard rock song collection included 'Lick and a Promise', which Steven said dealt with setting out to win over an audience, and 'Rats in the Cellar', a counterpoint in one sense to 'Toys in the Attic'. Of 'Rats in the Cellar', Tom Hamilton declared that Tyler and Perry were: 'taking the thing the Yardbirds created and making it balls to the wall'. 'Rhythm and sex go together,' maintained Joe Perry, who co-created with Steven the ambiguous 'Back in the Saddle'. Another hard rock song was 'Nobody's Fault' – a Tyler/Whitford number about the San Andreas geological fault that runs through California. Steven and Tom came up with 'Sick as a Dog', and one of Tyler's favourite songs was 'Last Child', on which he and Brad again worked. Said Brad: 'Steven likes some oddball things, kind of out of the way riffs.' Steven's only solo composition was a ballad titled 'Home Tonight', while Joe Perry's first solo song, 'Combination', proved to be a cautionary tale about the dangers of giving drugs free rein – advice that was being completely ignored by everyone in the band.

With substance abuse in Aerosmith plumbing new depths, Steven was sinking further into the mire. Once asked what his favourite drug combination had been, he replied: 'I guess that would have been Brumpton's Cocktail. That's a mixture of cocaine, alcoholic spirits, morphine and syrup – delicious!' Joe was later brutally honest about the seductive allure of heroin before it turned on him. He confessed to writing the music to songs for this new album while lying on the floor, totally stoned on heroin.

At the Wherehouse in Waltham, rehearsals got under way. The fan mail in Steven's office in-tray was mushrooming by the day, and they were surrounded by a circus of people, including drug dealers who came and went. Years later it emerged that Aerosmith's growing riches were not being handled with the tightest possible rein. One decided downside of being as high as kites or dope-sick was not knowing precisely what was going on around them.

On the other hand, Tyler credited drugs with helping him to

become more creative. He was working mainly in a spontaneous way, responding to a sound and finding inspiration flowing forth. When recording got under way at Record Plant Studios in New York, with producer Jack Douglas, Tyler would again vanish to the cold stairwell and furiously scribble lyrics, sometimes by the ream. Writing while stoned was one thing, but being high also made recording an arduous process; often dozens of takes were required to get a single song down properly. Yet when Aerosmith did pull it together, their development, honed by constant touring, shone through. The burden was made even greater because while they recorded this new album, they also gigged, so subjecting themselves to tiring shuttle flights back and forth between cities and the studio. It could be argued that without chemical assistance they would never have managed to sustain such a gruelling schedule. That and the resilience of youth kept them going. Tyler found sufficient reserves to main-tain his live wire presence in rehearsals and could not resist leaping behind the drums, picking up the sticks and letting rip. His exuberant energy on the skins jolted Joe and Brad to ginger up their guitar action. Likewise, Steven happily slipped into backing vocals when Perry sang lead when recording his song, 'Combination'.

With recording completed, Aerosmith had begun prepara-tions for a summer tour when they quit Boston for a special trip to New York. The British hard rock band Black Sabbath, fronted by Ozzy Osbourne, was touring America to promote its new album, *We Sold Our Souls for Rock 'n' Roll;* on 10 May 1976 they were to headline at Madison Square Garden, supported by Aerosmith – their first appearance at this hallowed venue. A bundle of excitement and nerves, on the day Steven became alarmed when with early evening approaching Joe Perry had not shown up. He made it at the last moment, but only after he had been roused back home from a drug-induced stupor and rushed to New York to take the stage. For Steven, that night still proved to be special. Apart from performing on this famous stage where so many of his music idols had appeared, his parents, Victor and

Susan Tallarico, were sitting in the front row, lapping up this first-hand proof of just how far their go-getter son had come.

That month, Columbia Records released *Rocks*, a classic hard rock album that uncompromisingly defined Aerosmith's identity. It shipped platinum, meaning that it had a million copies on order before it hit the record shops. Dubbed Aerosmith's most sophisticated effort yet, *Rocks* was voted the number one favourite album by *Creem* magazine readers, ultimately reaching number three on the US album chart, and remaining on this chart for a year. To back the new album, the band launched a 58-gig tour of the US, kicking off in St Louis in May.

Sheathed in sleek black satin, with his long, dark hair hanging about his face and his tongue lolling out lasciviously, Steven made his most pronounced effect yet on audiences across the country. Experience and confidence combined to elevate his vocal delivery and stage presence to new levels. Tyler's natural charisma extended well beyond the first few rows, commanding the attention of every kid crammed into the increasingly bigger arenas. Steven had no truck with the by now popular stage effects such as smoke bombs, or with staging spectacular stunts. Apart from believing that such flashy capers detracted from the music, he recognised that with each new tour it would become absurd trying to outdo previous antics.

Of the three singles released from *Rocks* over the coming months, 'Last Child' fared best, reaching number twenty-one in America in summer. 'Home Tonight' dropped anchor later at number seventy-one, with 'Back in the Saddle' ultimately making it into the US Top 40. The band that had initially struggled to get noticed by the media, now had journalists hard on the trail of exclusive interviews. The combination of dope, drink, adrenalin, lust and fatigue could make Tyler wildly indiscreet during such sessions. At the mercy of his own irreverent sense of humour, he would shoot his mouth off, only to cringe when he opened the rock magazine to discover just how unguarded he had been.

Backstage at gigs, Tyler was snorting lines of cocaine from

mirrors that must have reflected the visible ravages of what he was doing to himself. Whether Aerosmith was headlining at the LA Forum or the RFK Stadium in Washington, it was becoming patently obvious that Tyler was in trouble, but he took years to confess that he was in a mess. Before stepping on stage his stomach would be churning with nausea, and his heart hammering with adrenalin and drugs. On stage, mid-flight, his head would be so all over the place that there were moments in the middle of the whirlwind when he would grind to an unsteady halt and find himself spooked and bemused. Coming off stage, usually with helping hands ready to drape a towel around his sweat-soaked shoulders, he would be so drained that it was a struggle to walk. Dehydration must have been a major concern, too; all of this was taking a relentless toll on his system. He was exhausted much of the time and felt a great deal older than his twenty-eight years.

Aerosmith headlined their first stadium gig in June 1976 when they performed before eighty thousand fans at the Detroit Lions' stadium in Pontiac, Michigan. Boston newspapers now hailed Aerosmith as 'Boston's Biggest Export' and the event had a decisive impact on the band. Joe Perry later stressed: 'We were America's band. We were the garage band that made it really big – the ultimate party band.' Playing in a venue of this size was an odd experience, however. Tyler had become accustomed to avoiding getting too close to overwrought fans, when a split second's mistiming could see him hauled into the seething, hysterical mass. In this massive arena the fans seemed so distant and there was a wall of helmeted security guards in between.

Acclimatising to Aerosmith's rising status was not exactly a chore to Steven, but the road was becoming bumpier in other ways. When *Rolling Stone* wanted to feature Aerosmith with a six-page spread, the news came through that for the magazine cover they preferred to picture just Steven. From the Rolling Stones to Bon Jovi, this kind of situation was guaranteed to create strain within a band. Although Tyler was the lightning rod in Aerosmith, Steven did not class himself as the boss – all major decisions were made jointly by the five members. The issue of this cover photo caused problems. Influential publications inevitably win out, and *Rolling Stone* ran its cover story featuring Tyler with the title 'Aerosmith's Wrench Rock: Music for the New Stone Age'.

Aerosmith induced pandemonium at gigs, and the key to their success, according to Steven, was that the band did not try to be clever, did not attempt to philosophise. They went all out to rock the fans clean out of their seats. It was a mutual admiration society, because just as Aerosmith's guts and passion bled straight off the stage into the crowd, the fans' wild enthusiasm energised the band as strongly as any stimulant. Steven definitely took time to accept the need for security guards forming a ring around the massively high stages at stadium gigs – sometimes he felt he was singing to the helmets. The pace of life had so quickened that whole chunks of the year just seemed to have evaporated. The strain that the Demon of Screamin' put on his vocal cords also threatened to be a problem, but Tyler's periodic need to rest his voice was a luxury the band could not afford; there was no longer time even to fit rehearsals into their hectic schedule.

Come September 1976, after four months on the road, Steven was ready to run to Lake Sunapee, where he rented accommodation while a property he had recently purchased was renovated to his specific design. It was the old yacht club, and he spared no expense in getting it just as he wanted. He had special stone transported to New Hampshire from Belgium, and his plans included having a rope bridge erected to join his property to an islet on the lake, while a solarium was to be built on the roof. At his rented house he kept his collection of guns; they ranged from hunting guns to guns used in Vietnam and, closer to home, guns that had been used (not by Steven) on the dodgy streets of New York. Used to the lake, Steven enjoyed taking a powerful speed-boat out for a spin on the shimmering water. Though lapping up Lake Sunapee's tranquillity, Tyler continued to indulge in coke-fuelled evenings.

The sex, drugs and rock and roll trip was hardly wearing thin, but Tom Hamilton confessed: 'It's getting to the point where it is not cool to go running around getting laid because you wind up with your shlong falling off. The whole novelty of the pull is kinda fading away.' Certainly, in his personal life, Steven lately had had much to think about.

A woman Steven had been involved with had become pregnant but it was not the right time for either of them to contemplate bringing a baby into the world – both of them were young and Tyler's drug addiction had to be a consideration. They had, therefore, mutually decided to abort the pregnancy. It was not a decision taken lightly and, for Tyler's part, not one that proved particularly easy to live with afterwards. By late summer 1976, Tyler had become involved with another woman who would subsequently have his child – she was fashion model Bebe Buell.

Born Beverle Lorence Buell on 14 July 1953 in Portsmouth, Virginia, 5'9" Bebe began modelling, encouraged by her mother Dorothea, when she was seventeen. Two years later, she moved to New York, and while living in a women's hostel run by the Catholic church, the beautiful blonde was signed to the Ford Modelling Agency. Soon, Bebe also met and became involved with the Philadelphia-born rock star and producer Todd Rundgren. They moved in together but it was, in the spirit of the times, very much an open relationship – both Bebe and Todd dated other people.

In 1974, photographed by Richard Fegley, Bebe posed nude for *Playboy* and was that November's centrefold Playmate of the Month. She was one of the first top fashion models to do this, and it is said to have cost her her association with the renowned Ford Modelling Agency. Although she soon signed to other modelling agencies in America and Britain and continued to carry out assignments for top glossy fashion magazines, as a *Playboy* Playmate Bebe Buell became more known as the 1970s progressed for her rock star lovers – including David Bowie, Jimmy Page, Iggy Pop and Mick Jagger.

By 1976, Bebe had cast her eye in Steven Tyler's direction. In

August, she had accompanied Todd Rundgren to England, where he was one of the support acts at Knebworth where the Rolling Stones were headlining. At Knebworth, Jagger is said to have teased Buell: 'Why go for Steven Tyler, when you can have the real thing?'

Bebe had briefly encountered Steven years earlier, but their paths crossed again in 1976 at a record convention in Los Angeles. Tyler had not missed her *Playboy* centrefold spread and was immediately taken with the busty blonde, who seemed to have taken a shine to him. Exchanging phone calls first while Aerosmith was on the road, the pair finally got together in New York and she subsequently accompanied Tyler to Lake Sunapee in September. Their time together may not have proved to be that long, but it was extremely passionate from the outset.

The arrival of another foxy lady in the Aerosmith camp cranked up the existing tension; according to Buell, she and Elyssa Perry did not get along from day one. Interestingly, Steven had battled with deep hurt at the thought that Joe did not care about being his buddy because he had Elyssa. Yet Bebe has maintained that Joe had quickly made it plain to her in private that he was concerned that she not hurt Steven emotionally. At any rate, it was a stifling environment for the young and free-spirited Bebe, but she still opted to accompany Steven when Aerosmith now left America to embark on their first European tour.

Aerosmith's confidence was entitled to be high since, by mid-October, *Rocks* had gone double platinum. In advance of the band hitting British shores, Steven had been asking around, and his information was that not many rock bands were holding sway in the UK right then. On the back of the success of 'Bohemian Rhapsody', Queen had been catapulted to new heights but otherwise the UK charts read: number one single, 'Mississippi' by a Dutch outfit called Pussycat, and the top UK album was currently *Abba's Greatest Hits*. Tyler could have been forgiven for thinking that when Aerosmith came to kick off their first European tour at the Empire Theatre in Liverpool, Merseyside, they would be welcomed with open arms by hard rock lovers and the music media. In truth, Aerosmith came in for a rough ride.

The UK rock press annihilated Aerosmith. Tom Hamilton recalled how tough it was performing live: 'Playing England was a lot like when we first started in New York, because both places had been hearing the best for years and they were not easily impressed. A lot of our style is patterned after English bands but we felt resistance from the audiences and the press.' Tyler called the entire tour hell, and later declared of these first UK dates: 'All we were worried about was finding the best bottle of wine and the best cocaine. I did no sightseeing, no shopping and it was fuck the music – let's get high!'

Despite that remark, it still gave Steven a massive rush to go on stage. He adored the whole ritual of when, pumped up and poised, he and the band were escorted by bodyguards from the dressing room along corridors, up a ramp and let loose on a stage before tens of thousands of people. No matter how often it happened, for the first few minutes he always felt in a state of shock. The other side of the coin was his heightened awareness of how vulnerable any rock star was to the unhinged mind in the audience. It would be another four years before the world was stunned by John Lennon's callous murder, and while Lennon was not gunned down in concert, Tyler knew of performers who had been faced with some wild-eyed teenager at a gig brandishing a loaded weapon. His reasoning was that in a world full of people with problems, people high on dope and in a country with a gun culture like America, there was a worryingly high possibility that a rock star would one day be shot dead on stage. In late 1976, he made no bones that since a moving target is harder to hit, this inner fear contributed to his manic darting about in concert.

He was conscious, too, that the band's crazed fans were becoming increasingly difficult to corral safely. At Aerosmith gigs now a special barrier was erected six feet away from the stage and designed so that teenagers could not scale it. To reduce the risk of restiveness and because Tyler preferred to keep shows running like a racehorse there was not much in the way of conversation either between band and audience.

Off stage, between drink and drugs, Tyler's temper still erupted at times, when he continued to cause localised carnage. In England in 1976, he later revealed, he trashed the band's tour bus because of another drug-fuelled fit of rage. He and Bebe also rowed, sometimes publicly. When asked about the ructions among Aerosmith, Tyler confessed that these invariably stemmed from Joe Perry playing guitar so loud that it threw his singing clean off. He balanced this criticism by praising his bandmates as 'beautiful people'.

The true extent of Tyler's drug taking really only came to light many years later, and Tyler has laid a portion of the blame for this serious substance abuse at the record industry's door. Speaking in broad terms, he explained that industry figures knew well what rock stars were shoving up their noses or injecting into their veins, but that it did not matter so long as the tour-album cycle remained in force. Tyler does not deny that taking drugs is the individual's own responsibility, but perhaps it exposed a hint of bitterness when he maintained that if he had had a heart attack induced by dope there were those who would have falsely claimed that they had no idea he was an addict.

Bebe Buell was an uncomfortably close witness to how scary this side of Tyler's life had become. He also had no peace of mind, and was continually pushed to keep to a debilitating schedule. At times he felt like climbing the walls. None of this made it the best time for Buell to break some sensitive news to Steven.

By early October, she knew that she was pregnant, and had started to suffer from morning sickness on Aerosmith's European tour. About a year before, on the subject of possible domesticity, Tyler had stated that he had no wish to get married and start a family because he knew that his lifestyle was too wild and it would not be fair on any children, but he did add the rider that before he completely screwed up his life he would like to father a child. Come autumn 1976, however, what Bebe saw made her take a hike.

The European tour was over and Steven and Bebe were back at Lake Sunapee when one day he had a drug-induced seizure. She tried her best to help him through it but it was the catalyst to her deciding to pack her belongings and leave. Bebe went to Todd Rundgren in New York and told him that she was carrying Steven Tyler's child. They agreed to resume their relationship, nonetheless.

For Steven it was extremely confusing. He and Bebe had not been together for very long. When it became known that Buell was pregnant, poison was dripped in his ears from here and there suggesting very clearly that he was not the father of Bebe's child, and when she and Todd Rundgren resumed their life together, Steven did not know what to believe. In any case, he knew that his drug taking and drinking meant that he was in no shape even to consider fatherhood, and so it was left at that – for now.

Aerosmith business carried on regardless. 'Walk This Way' reached number ten in the US singles chart a year and a half after its original release. Then, when Aerosmith headlined a sold-out show at Madison Square Garden that December, they were the toast of New York. *Rocks* was acclaimed as capturing Aerosmith at their most raw and rocking, and the band's star was at its highest point to date. Privately, however, Steven was about to drop to one of his darkest, most dangerous levels yet.

# CHAPTER 6

# The Toxic Time Bomb Ticks

**I**T IS fair to say that the last place on earth you would think to stumble across Steven Tyler is a convent, but after Aerosmith completed their first tour of the Far East in early 1977, he joined his bandmates at the Cenacle in Armonk, upstate New York. The impressive former nunnery nestles isolated in one hundred leafy acres; it was built on a huge scale, with endlessly long corridors connecting all its three hundred rooms. Its serenity and solitude offered Aerosmith an ideal situation in which to work on material for their next album, but this would be squandered, for by now their drug consumption was unleashing new demons. When Tyler arrived in the massive hall with its grand staircase he could have been forgiven for thinking that he had entered a lunatic asylum – the sound of gunfire reverberated in his ears. Along with a mountain of luggage, a fleet of flash cars and motorcycles, an arsenal of more than two dozen weapons had been brought to the retreat, including handguns, rifles, even a semi-automatic sub-machine gun and live rounds. Joe Perry had already rigged up a makeshift firing range in the long attic and was busy blasting away, intent on turning suspended targets into sieves.

It was a destructive time in many ways, and as Tyler's mental meltdown continued, his slide towards becoming a fully fledged junkie was inevitable. In addition to consuming Tuinals and other strong pharmaceutical drugs, his increasing use of cocaine and heroin meant that if he did not black out, much of the time he had trouble even seeing straight. It was a sordid scene, as every member of Aerosmith was getting into harder narcotics. Said Steven: 'We became professional drug addicts who dabbled in music, instead of professional musicians getting high once in a while.' His grasp of reality slackened further as one day simply ran into another in this secluded environment. He could not sleep because of the level of stimulants in his system, so he lived in a blur in which anything could happen. Once, he passed out in the driveway with a loaded rifle in his hands. On another occasion, he had a drug-induced seizure while driving. He lost control of the Jeep, crashed it into a tree trunk and blacked out. Miraculously he was not injured, but he was found slumped over the steering wheel with a loaded shotgun in his lap. By their own admission, the band went wild, spending most days cruising crazily all over The Cenacle's grounds, the surrounding country-side and around Armonk itself on two or four wheels, high as kites and therefore oblivious of the danger to themselves or to anyone else. Ostensibly, the nights were set aside for recording, but Steven had not written a single song before arriving at the retreat and nothing was likely to materialise there considering his condition and the state the others were in. Various recording facilities had been built inside the convent, which meant that the guys did not record on the same floor as each other, let alone in the same room, and that was only *if* they all turned up for recording duty after midnight.

In recent years, Joe Perry has maintained that he always made sure that ultimately he did not go too far, but at The Cenacle he was in pretty bad shape. Doped to the eyeballs and often sick, he would turn up to play guitar scarcely able to walk in a straight line. Once he was discovered flaked out in an upstairs doorway, having failed to make it into the room, with a hypodermic needle sticking out of his arm. If anyone did show up for work there was no guarantee he would be able to remain awake long enough to complete a session of work with producer Jack Douglas, who was also staying at the former nunnery. Everything was unravelling. It was noticeable that Perry was becoming less inclusive about his music. Tyler needed the music to stimulate him lyrically – no music meant no modelling clay – but by now Steven had stopped caring. At this place of former spiritual reflection and worship, individually every member of Aerosmith was reaching into darker, more unnerving realms.

After weeks of indulgent drug abuse and delirium, the band left The Cenacle at the end of May. Even then, drama unfolded. On the highway, on his way home, drummer Joey Kramer fell asleep at the wheel of his Ferrari and crashed at 135 miles per hour, cutting himself badly on his shattered windscreen. Days later, Joe Perry had a car accident, writing off his Corvette. 'I can't even count all the smashed-up cars among us,' admitted Perry.

Work on the new album now got under way at Record Plant Studios in New York; in the circumstances it was hardly surprising that there was a complete lack of cohesion to the material. Gone was their clarity, and confidence was clearly absent, which showed most in the negativity of the lyrics. Only three numbers were Tyler/Perry collaborations – 'Get It Up', 'Draw the Line', which featured one of Joe Perry's all time favourite riffs, and the reflective 'I Wanna Know Why', of which Tom Hamilton later said: 'I always thought that song was a reaction to all the shit Steven was getting into at the time.' The bass player, along with Tyler and producer Jack Douglas, came up with a number called 'Critical Mass', while 'Bright Light Fright' was every step of the way a pure Joe Perry project. Both 'The Hand That Feeds' and the dynamic 'Kings and Queens' seemed to involve everyone except the lead guitarist. 'Sight for Sore Eyes' included input from David Johansen, lead singer of the New York Dolls. Only one cover version would be added to the album – 'Milk Cow Blues' by Kokomo Arnold. Although working at Record Plant Studios brought some structure to the material, it would take several more months to actually complete. The album title became *Draw the Line* which, bearing their drug abuse in mind, had other connotations, but they opted to reflect the title literally on the cover illustration. At The Cenacle they had been visited by Al Hirschfeld, an artist whose line drawing of the five produced the caricature ultimately featured on the album sleeve.

The album was still a work in progress when Aerosmith went out on the road in June. Opening acts included AC/DC and Ted Nugent, and audience reaction varied from gig to gig. To diehard Aerosmith fans Tyler and co could do no wrong. Other times, the shows clearly went down in spectacular flames. Steven confessed that one Cleveland concert was later denounced in regional radio polls as the worst show of 1977.

Steven did not know that while he was gigging around America, at Mount Sinai Hospital in New York City Bebe Buell had gone into labour. On 1 July 1977, she gave birth to a daughter she named Liv. One of Bebe's earliest visitors in the maternity ward was Mick Jagger, who found that he had to share the model's attention with the newborn. Buell later said of Jagger: 'He said: "All right, put her away now. I can see you're a mother."' Jagger's appearance in the maternity wing sparked talk that Bebe's daughter might be his illegitimate offspring, and for a while Jagger quite enjoyed the speculation. Todd Rundgren, though, was widely assumed to be the girl's father, while Liv's biological father had no idea; sunk in his own degenerating world, he continued to push himself to the limit.

The fast-moving UK and Europe tour that summer was a huge drain on Tyler. After playing to an appreciative crowd of American troops stationed in Stuttgart, West Germany, gigs followed in Hamburg, Munich and Frankfurt. Europe was experiencing unusually heavy rainfalls, and many a gig turned into a quagmire. Steven would not deny that some shows were dire. Early into one performance he passed out before thousands of bemused fans, and his voice was already a problem. One evening he spat up blood as he threw himself about the rain-drenched stage. Yet he failed to recognise that his health was breaking down.

Off stage the tour was the classic rock riot – hotel rooms were trashed and television sets sent sailing over balcony rails to splash into swimming pools, to the background growl of a chainsaw ripping apart offending furniture. Steven was hurtling out of control. Speaking of these hedonistic excesses, he later admitted that almost everything he had enjoyed in life throughout the 1970s was either immoral or illegal and it came at an escalating cost. 'I was a junkhead,' he confessed. 'I reckon, I did over a million dollars on drugs. I was paying one thousand dollars a gram for heroin and I'd do about three to five grams a week. I would have traded in my nuts for a good ounce of heroin.'

Joe Perry had become dope-sick in Germany, and the tension between a spaced-out Steven and his lead guitarist was turning nasty. As is the nature of addicts, whatever dope they could get their hands on they zealously hoarded to feed their own habit. Tyler would become furiously frustrated when he ran out of drugs and Joe refused to share his stash with him. The aggravation between the addicts began to show in public. On stage, they would bait one another, coming to blows – or, at least, hitting one another not exactly accidentally with mike stand or guitar. Their bandmates and many people in their entourage looked on anxiously from the wings as this volcano rumbled.

When the band arrived in the UK towards the end of August, bearing in mind the frosty reception they had received last time, Tyler kept his expectations low. He felt that to break the British music market Aerosmith would need to blitz the country for a good six months, putting themselves about enough to get a groundswell going, and they did not have the time to try that. Although the foundations of new wave music had been laid in America some years before, in 1977 the punk movement was taking centre stage with bands such as the Clash, the Damned and the Sex Pistols ruling the charts. Punk would die out in roughly eighteen months, although it is often claimed that its influence was long-lasting. At any rate, the music press had latched firmly on to punk rock and were predicting the demise of hard rock acts. Steven quickly came up against this mindset when he embarked on the PR circuit soon after arriving in England, and he was blunt with his opinion. 'It seems that every time something happens in Britain, it's gotta be a big ya ya!' he remarked. 'The Beatles and the Stones were big but punk rock isn't.'

Picking up on the signs of discord within Aerosmith, some music watchers queried whether Tyler would ever consider flying solo. Steven admitted that he could do a solo album and believed that it would do well, but he stated emphatically that he had no interest in breaking away from his bandmates. Aerosmith closed their European tour by taking part in the mud-bath event that was that year's Reading Rock Festival, held in Berkshire. When their flight took off from London at the end of August, Aerosmith would not perform outside the United States for another decade.

In September 1977, with barely a pause for breath, the band hurtled headlong into playing dates around America, during which their condition deteriorated further. As tempers frayed, sound monitors were occasionally kicked over the edge of the stage to crash down into the no-man's-land between the band and the audience. One night Joe Perry took everyone by surprise by doing a Pete Townshend impersonation and dramatically smashing his guitar to the floor. He later conceded that he had snapped, but insisted that his histrionic display was not the onset of manic madness, more a dose of self-destructiveness peppered with a sense of humour.

No one was laughing to see the entire band becoming submerged by their addictions. Danger came from all directions. Towards the end of a sold-out show at the Spectrum in Philadelphia, when Aerosmith returned on stage for the encore, a small explosive device was thrown at the band, burning the cornea of Steven's eye. Panicked because he could not see, he threw his hands up to cover his face. Meanwhile, blood was spurting alarmingly from one of Joe Perry's hands. The other three men felt the concussion of the device exploding. Shaken and angry, the guys were whisked to hospital for treatment and some shows had to be cancelled that October to allow Steven and

Joe's injuries time to heal. Steven headed for New Hampshire to recover. During this enforced break, the band planned to put the finishing touches to their overdue album, but it was sometimes difficult to get Steven to the Record Plant Studios in New York sober enough to work. The others were in no better shape, and all too soon the live shows resumed.

In November, the new single, 'Draw the Line', was released but it failed to crack the US Top 40. *Draw the Line* soon followed, went platinum and peaked at number eleven on Billboard's album chart, but drew sharp critical attack from the music press. Aerosmith's disintegration as a working unit clearly showed in the end product, and Steven knew it. He knew that they had lost their edge and their direction. The album had cost half a million dollars to make, but Joe Perry commented years later that what truly cost the band dear was that they had become so arrogant that they could not see what they were doing to themselves. They had even ignored any soul who was brave enough to try to warn them. As he bleakly put it: 'The Beatles made their *White Album*. We made our blackout album.'

As performance standards at gigs degenerated, frustrated fans verged on violence – hurling not just boos and catcalls but increasingly heavier missiles at the band. Clearly sensing the alienation within Aerosmith, more and more people left the auditoriums fractious and dissatisfied. Backstage, there was belligerent behaviour, too, with reports leaking out of Steven verbally abusing those around him. When the tour wrapped up, industry rumours began to circulate that Aerosmith was on the brink of breaking up.

It was around now that Steven Tyler and Joe Perry were tagged by the music press with the moniker 'The Toxic Twins', in recognition of their voracious appetite for heroin, cocaine and other narcotics. Their volatile, creative partnership and friendship has always provided an important axis in Steven's life, just as it has always held the key to Aerosmith's fortunes. Though dissimilar in nature, the two men have an indefinable chemistry that arguably seems more potent than that of the other famed rock 'twins' – Mick Jagger and Keith Richards. The more openly emotional Tyler still did not hide his feeling that Joe's wife, Elyssa, was an obstacle. By now, however, Steven had a new distraction in his life in the shape of the woman who would become the first Mrs Tyler.

Kathleen Victoria Hetzekian was born in 1952 in Santa Monica, California. Her parents divorced when she was very young. Growing up in the Midwest, in the 1960s she became an avid fan of the Kinks and the Rolling Stones. By the age of nineteen she had left home and moved to New York, reinventing herself as a bleached blonde named Cyrinda Foxe. As an aspiring actress, she threw herself into the dizzy world of New York's nightlife, hanging out at Studio 54 and Max's Kansas City. She soon became part of the Andy Warhol circle, appearing in Warhol's movie *Bad*, starring Carroll Baker. Vivacious and ambitious, Cyrinda hung out mostly with musicians, and by summer 1973 had become involved with the twenty-three-year-old Staten Island-born New York Dolls frontman, David Johansen. The New York Dolls and Aerosmith had the same managers, and Cyrinda first saw Steven Tyler at Leber and Krebs's New York office that same year. Though not yet a star, Steven exuded a magnetism and embodied a style that caught Foxe's eye.

Over the next three years, because of her involvement with David Johansen, Cyrinda's path increasingly crossed Aerosmith's; she became friends with Joe and Elyssa Perry, although her inward attraction was always for Tyler. She fitted right in that scene and by now was experimenting with cocaine and heroin. A liberal free spirit, she maintained: 'I think sex is an art form – the entire body becomes one sense.' It was not long after she first spoke with Steven that she made it clear she was not prepared to join the bevy of groupies constantly surrounding him. Despite her attraction to Tyler, Foxe married David Johansen on Staten Island in 1976.

According to Cyrinda, this marriage was doomed from the start. Instead, she spent a great deal of time with the Perrys and had a ringside view of the tense triangle that Steven, Joe and

Elyssa made up. Attraction ricocheted all over the place, mingled with rife jealousies, rampant insecurities and drug-induced paranoia. Amid these crazy head-games, however, she continued to be drawn to Steven, and in autumn 1977 she and David Johansen split up.

To Steven, Cyrinda was not only ravishingly lovely, he adored her independence and, perhaps significantly, her continued resistance to his approaches. It drove him mad, and the chase was on. Flattered by Tyler's persistence and unable to resist his roguishness, Foxe eventually succumbed and they finally became an item towards the end of 1977. One upshot of Cyrinda switching her allegiance between frontmen was that she and Elyssa Perry fell out. Rightly or wrongly, Elyssa felt that Cyrinda had struck up a friendship with her simply as a device to get close to Steven. Tyler must have felt that he had been here before. Bebe Buell had felt unwelcome among the band members' wives – now Cyrinda and Elyssa were at odds. It went rather deeper than the two women simply not talking, however, for those close to Aerosmith could see the tension between Elyssa and Cyrinda becoming absolutely unbearable. Joey Kramer once declared that it felt like they were caught up in a real life soap opera.

There is no doubt that Steven was aware of the discord his having this very beautiful lady at his side was causing. Cyrinda *was* stunning, had a vibrant personality that drew the eye of all those around and so, by extension, this made her and Tyler the 'it' couple, snatching attention away from Joe and Elyssa. Tyler also knew that this only widened the chasm between himself and Joe.

For Cyrinda, on a personal footing, things did not get off to the start she had imagined. Her vision of life with Aerosmith's famous frontman was very different from reality. When she went with Steven to Boston she had anticipated moving into a beautiful, well-staffed luxury home. In truth, his home in the Brookline suburb dismayed her, and at all hours of the day drug dealers and other unsavoury types came visiting. While Steven could be extremely tender and loving, other times their relationship was volatile. Cyrinda called herself 'high maintenance' and she was not able or willing to become a domestic goddess. There were occasions when she would come home and find Steven passed out on the floor. Unsurprisingly, there were moments quite early on when she wondered if she had made the right decision in getting involved with him. Nevertheless, in spring 1978, the couple moved to Lake Sunapee, where Steven's dream house was still under construction.

Steven could not stay long at the lake, for a mini-tour of America loomed, plus appearances at several major festivals throughout the year. The first of these was on 18 March, when Aerosmith headlined at the California Jam II Festival, held at the Ontario Motor Speedway in California in front of an estimated 350,000 people. Other acts included Ted Nugent, Santana, Heart and Jean Michel Jarre. By the time Aerosmith took to the stage, Steven was so stoned on cocaine that he had to have the lyrics to his own songs written out on pieces of paper scattered around the stage. This performance would become infamous in Aerosmith's history, but worryingly for Steven his health was so badly compromised by his drug use that he was having difficulty breathing. In a bad physical and emotional state, Steven again ruined the backstage buffet for everyone, picking up plates and bowls of food and violently smashing them against walls.

From sinking to hideous nadirs, Tyler's seesaw world bounced up again weeks later when Cyrinda discovered that she was pregnant. Steven must have known that he was in no condition to contemplate fatherhood, but this news so excited him that he proposed to his girlfriend – the whole routine, going romantically down on one knee – and this new state of affairs had a calming effect on him for a while.

In April, 'Kings and Queens' became the second single released from the new album but it quickly stalled at number seventy. As summer approached, Aerosmith was swinging between extremes – playing in massive arenas, then performing in small intimate clubs, sometimes under assumed names. There was no hiding place, however, at either size of venue.

On stage, Aerosmith had become shambolic. One of the worst examples of this was on 4 July, when the band took part in the Texxas World Music Festival, held at the Cottonbowl in Dallas. The mercury that day had hit well over one hundred degrees in the shade, and dehydrating music lovers were on the verge of hallucinating, though very few of them missed the disastrous state that Aerosmith was in.

Tyler recalled: 'It starts off, you have a great gig and you go out and buy a gram and you get fucking shit-faced that night. You go out next day and play. Then we started getting shit-faced *before* we played. Then we were shit-faced *all* the time.' That particular day at the Cottonbowl, Steven was so drugged that he had to be physically carried to the wings and propelled out on stage, where he was barely able to move a muscle of his own accord. He was in a frighteningly desperate condition. Because of the cocaine consumed by the others, the music was played far too fast, making it an even more surreal experience for a frontman who was barely holding it together enough to stay standing upright.

Twenty years later, when the band had cleaned up, viewing footage of this 1978 event proved painful. Tom Hamilton recalled: 'Our music was the battered neglected child of that behaviour, and it's pretty sickening.' Tyler was losing his grip all round and he could not see it. He had arrived at the point of believing he could not function personally or professionally without drugs. He would get high and drunk to go out to a club or the cinema and the next day he would have absolutely no recollection of what he had been up to. It left him very vulnerable and it took him to new places. Years earlier, he had shoplifted food to keep himself and his bandmates from starving to death. Now, as a drug addict, he started thieving again. He has confessed: 'After a while, I started stealing and stuff. You take drugs initially to be with the devil and to be creative and it works, for a while but then he [the devil] goes: "Now, I'm going to steal your soul." And he does!' He added: 'Drugs raped my spirituality in the early days and I didn't see that it was hurting me.' In so many ways it was extremely sad for fans to see this unique frontman reducing himself to a shuffling wreck.

At one concert on America's west coast, the show had hardly warmed up when Steven decided that he had had enough of singing and promptly hunkered down on stage and began to tell rambling, unfunny jokes, for which he forgot the punchlines. As the audience grew angry, Tyler's bandmates tried to shunt him back on track by blasting into a song intro but Tyler would not be motivated. He ordered the music to stop, as he wanted to keep on telling jokes. It became quite mad. Lines of cocaine would be laid chopped out on top of amps at the back of the stage for people to have a swift snort between numbers. The tempo of Aerosmith shows often became either too fast or too slow, and the audiences really would have had to be as seriously stoned as their heroes to have a hope in hell of enjoying these spectacles.

There were exceptions, nights when Steven and the band's performance proved inspirational to future rock stars, among them British-born teenager Saul Hudson, who later became famous as lead guitarist Slash, in Guns N' Roses. Said Slash: 'My first Aerosmith concert was in 1978. They were playing at a festival. They were incredibly loud and I barely recognised a note but it was still the most bitchin' thing I had ever seen. Anyone who sings needs to be exposed to Steven Tyler.'

Drugs rightly take the blame for almost every aspect of Steven's bizarre or excessive behaviour, but his natural impishness also played a part in a prank he pulled off that year when Aerosmith flew for the first time on a 747 jumbo passenger jet. Someone bet him that he would not have the guts to strip naked during the flight and run upstairs into the lounge deck. The money on offer was a few paltry dollars – it was a test of whether he would have the barefaced cheek to do it. And he did. The way Tyler tells it, he also did it almost without being nabbed, for after streaking along the lower deck and hiking upstairs into the lounge, he was on his way back to base before a startled stewardess had the dubious task of tackling him.

It was the sort of daft antic more associated with one of the Beatles' 1960s screwball comedies and, funnily enough, earlier that year Aerosmith had accepted the offer to play a small part in the Michael Schultz-directed film, *Sgt Pepper's Lonely Hearts Club Band*. Produced by Robert Stigwood for Universal Films and written by Henry Edwards, the movie, based on the Beatles album and set against small-town America, starred Peter Frampton, the Bee Gees, Alice Cooper and Earth, Wind and Fire, alongside actors Donald Pleasence, Frankie Howerd and Steve Martin. Aerosmith's role was as the Future Villain Band, and they shot their scenes over three days in California. The film's daily rushes showed up to an embarrassing degree that everyone in Aerosmith was drugged to the eyeballs on set, but Tyler maintained: 'We liked making the movie. I guess it was in line with our image.' When the movie was released that summer it was comprehensively slaughtered by the film critics and bombed at the box office.

The *Sgt Pepper's Lonely Hearts Club Band* film soundtrack reached number five in America's album chart and it included Aerosmith's version of 'Come Together'. Tyler was excited at recording with producer George Martin, and at the Wherehouse facility in Waltham, Massachussets, it took several takes to complete the session. In their fledgling days, Aerosmith had belted out the odd Beatles hit at gigs, so recording this song came naturally to them. Steven purposely did not dig out a copy of *Abbey Road* to study the Fab Four version of the 1969 number, preferring to perform the song for George Martin as he remembered it. According to Tyler, the man famously dubbed the fifth Beatle remarked upon the finished take: 'Fucking great!' Aerosmith released 'Come Together' which peaked in summer at number twenty-three.

Gigs continued to be haphazard affairs. In early August, Aerosmith performed at Giants Stadium in New Jersey. By now, Steven's extreme exhaustion had hollowed out features that were already accentuated by dark-ringed eyes. Tens of thousands of fans in this impressive arena gazed dismayed at revealing close-ups of the ravaged frontman shown on huge stage-mounted screens. Whether or not they were trying to tell him something, the missiles aimed at Tyler's emaciated frame this time included unravelling toilet rolls.

When Aerosmith staggered off tour, on 1 September 1978, Steven and Cyrinda got married in Sunapee, New Hampshire. For the non-denominational ceremony, held outdoors on a mountainside, Steven wore a cream suit, while his five-months pregnant bride chose patterned silk chiffon. They were surrounded by their families and friends and Steven's band-mates, and the sun shone bakingly down. Tyler once flashed that he married Cyrinda because she and Elyssa Perry hated each other, but if that had been meant tongue-in-cheek, he did admit that he went into marriage with only half a mind to make it work. He knew, with his drug and drink addictions, that he was not ideal husband material. Steven was, though, excitedly anticipating the birth of what he believed to be his first child, although Liv by Bebe Buell was at that stage a fourteen-month-old toddler. Asked about his and Cyrinda's expected child, Tyler said: 'I guess I would like it to be a boy, but most important, I want it to be a healthy baby.'

Within a month, the newly married Tyler was back out on the live circuit. Aerosmith quickly ran into controversy at a gig at a sports arena in Fort Wayne, Indiana, in early October, when dozens of fans were arrested for defying no-drinking and smoking rules. Aerosmith stepped in and paid bail money to release the teenagers from custody – a sum which ran into several thousand dollars.

Tyler's lack of sobriety continued to be a curse. More often now the singer had to be assisted not just to the wings, but right on stage. They tried to make it look like people were just messing about for a laugh, but on these occasions Tyler was literally unable to walk on his own two feet to the microphone. Nor was it unheard of for him to be discovered dead to the world in his dressing room very close to show time. It was a nerve-racking business for those charged with the task of having frantically to find ways of stirring Steven awake and getting him compos mentis enough to at least try to get through a performance.

Amazingly, if he did remain upright, some performances came off not too badly. Once Steven had rifled through the pockets stitched into the scarves tied to his mike stand for cocaine, one hit and he was off.

It could have been cocaine-induced paranoia, but there were nights on stage when Steven would launch into 'Dream On' – a special song to him – and he would catch sight of Joe seemingly exchanging a look with Elyssa standing in the wings before bursting out laughing. Sensitively, Steven took this to mean that they were laughing at him; true or not, it hurt him very much.

In late November, Aerosmith played Madison Square Garden, then returned to the stage at the Spectrum in Philadelphia, where last time an explosive device had injured Steven's eye. At first it seemed that lightning would not strike twice, but the show had hardly warmed up when someone hurled a bottle from the crowd. It hit one of the sound monitors at the front of the stage and shattered, throwing splintered glass up like shrapnel. Brad Whitford recalled: 'Pieces of glass literally went through Steven's cheeks and into his mouth.' Steven was bleeding profusely and once again the show had to be abandoned.

That month, the last single from *Draw the Line* was released, but 'Get It Up' failed to measure up and did not chart. By now a double live set, *Live! Bootleg*, had been released, comprising sixteen songs recorded at Aerosmith concerts during 1977 and 1978. Steven knew full well that some fans were surreptitiously taping their performances and that several bootleg recordings were already in circulation. The title *Live! Bootleg* was meant to be ironic. The double album charted on Billboard at number thirteen, and *Creem* magazine reviewer Billy Altman declared: 'What *Live! Bootleg* makes clear, as it highlights the best of their past work, is that Aerosmith really is one of the best hard rock bands the US has ever produced. I don't think they set out to be an important group, had no great message to get across, no big causes to champion. They just want to be one hot rock band.'

Tyler had scarcely caught his breath after surviving the latest stint on tour when Cyrinda went into labour. Charged with the task of getting his wife to the Mary Hitchcock Hospital in Hanover, New Hampshire, Steven drove there like a bat out of hell; on 22 December 1978, Cyrinda presented him with a baby girl. Steven found being at the birth an overwhelmingly moving experience. They named their newborn daughter Mia Abagale.

By the end of the year, Aerosmith released the single, 'Chip Away the Stone'. The band liked the number but it did not find favour with the fans and dropped anchor at number seventy-seven in February 1979. Two months later, they took part in yet another massively attended California music festival, this time held at the Memorial Coliseum in Los Angeles, along with acts including Van Halen, Cheap Trick and the Boomtown Rats. At this point Steven was thirty-one years old, a dollar millionaire who was in complete denial that he was risking his wealth, his health, his life even. Many in and around the music scene could see some metaphorical red flags flying. In the 1970s so far, the music world had witnessed the premature demise of Janis Joplin, Jim Morrison, Paul Kossoff, Elvis Presley and Keith Moon, among others. Young, talented and recklessly out of control, Steven Tyler right then fitted the profile and seemed ripe to become rock's next tragic casualty.

# CHAPTER 7

# Crying Over Spilt Milk

**A**FTER REHEARSING at the Wherehouse in Waltham, Massachusetts, in late spring 1979, Aerosmith headed to Media Sound Studio, New York, to start recording their next album. The pressure pot lid was already rattling when it quickly transpired that Tyler had failed to come up with any workable lyrics. They tried to motivate themselves but it felt as if a lead weight was on their shoulders, and the forced struggle to be creative caused increasing friction in the camp. On the other hand, it was easy for apathy to set in and so the slow progress practically ground to a complete halt. There were no incentives, and to top it all they were demoralised by looming financial problems and rising debts.

The ructions erupting between Steven and Joe became more heated as summer approached. Said Tyler: 'We got in each other's face but we never came to blows. I guess because I'm Italian and he's got Italian in him.' Perry confessed that there was an invisible line that neither was prepared to cross, no matter how intense the confrontations became. That said, the lead guitarist recalled: 'We certainly went head to head on a lot of occasions and stuff would fly around the room. We'd be like bull gorillas.' Their drug consumption ensured that this volcanic state worsened as the weeks went by, what with feeling stale in the studio and zoning out at hotels. Verbal abuse was strangely less hurtful than refusal to speak to one another. Against this miserable backdrop Steven battled to come up with lyrics to lay over the tracks recorded in the studio, aware that he was the brake on anything happening, conscious that frustration all around him only added to his difficulties.

Perry became so infuriated at doing next to nothing that he hightailed it off to Boston, where his thoughts turned to launching a solo career. On his way back to New York he suffered a seizure, blacked out and was rushed to hospital, where doctors were alarmed at his emaciated condition. Tyler, too, was fading virtually before everyone's eyes. If inwardly he was aware that he was weak, at the same time he knew that the band needed to get out and earn some money. Production on the album had stalled, forcing the record company to bump back its release date, and now industry rumours were muttering that the album would never see the light of day. Continuing with their schedule of stadium appearances, Steven led the band out before tens of thousands at the JFK Stadium in Philadelphia before heading to Ohio to take part, on 28 July, in the World Series of Rock concerts held at the Municipal Stadium in Cleveland. Other bands on the bill included Journey, Ted Nugent and Thin Lizzy. For Aerosmith, it marked one of the most significant nights in their lives.

The incredible tension afflicting the band members had been creating animosity among the men's wives. Often the atmosphere was so strained that some women actively avoided being in the company of others; if thrown inescapably together, one wife might not breathe a word all night to another, and the potential to take serious exception to any perceived snub was enormous. Backstage at the Municipal Stadium matters boiled over when a row erupted between Terry Hamilton and Elyssa Perry. Verbally, the two strong-minded women gave as good as they got. Then Elyssa chucked a glass of milk over Terry and all hell broke loose. Steven's wife, Cyrinda, later reduced this incident to nothing more than a playground spat, but the men could hear the noisy fracas, and when they came off stage the real fireworks began as Steven, Joe et al. got into one almighty rumpus.

Although Tom Hamilton, Joey Kramer and Brad Whitford had their own deep feelings to express, the eye of the storm swiftly centred on the harsh vitriol trading back and forth between Steven and Joe. This was not just the sort of bear-baiting they had been doing on stage, niggling and pushing each other's patience. This felt like all out war brewing. The fire had been smouldering for a long time and the set-to between the women had merely fanned the embers into flame. There had always been a chance that things would flare up one day. 'We could feel the decline in '79,' said Joe. 'We could feel what was going on but we'd been too wrapped up in our bullshit to do anything about it.'

That night, they did do something – Joe Perry quit Aerosmith. Tyler later declared: 'Drugs brought us to our knees and it made us break up. It made me say: "Fuck you, Joe," over a glass of spilt milk! Can you believe it?' From Perry's perspective he felt that he had reached the end of his tether with the way things had become in the band. Despite the ferocity of their tempers, that night the guys surprisingly agreed to keep this momentous development a secret. Certainly rumours were already circulating about their delayed album, but there was a touch of masculine pride at play here. The men, or some of them, were embarrassed at the thought of it coming out that this raucous rock band could shatter because of women squabbling and throwing a glass of milk. Within a couple of weeks, however, speculation began to surface that Aerosmith's lead guitarist – Tyler's Toxic Twin – had cut loose. In the circumstances, the band had had no option but to cancel the remainder of their live dates. This threw another log on the fire, and though music journalists were dished denials that a rift had occurred, it was said that Joe Perry was preparing to bring out a solo album. There was just too much grist not to set the millstones grinding.

Behind closed doors, Joe's departure threw up mixed emotions. Tom Hamilton admitted to harbouring relief. The terrible tension coiling around the band members and their respective wives had often produced unbearably stifling conditions, which the bass player felt had been alleviated by this bust-up. Hamilton maintained of Perry: 'He was at odds with the rest of the band generally on how we should conduct ourselves. He'd been thinking about doing his own thing – at first within the context of the band, but then things got pretty heated.' Steven battled with a kaleidoscope of feelings, none of which he could think through clearly due to the thickening fog of his drug addiction. In addition to heroin and cocaine Tyler now took opium, and was endlessly scraping up cash to be able to pay for his worsening habit.

In the recording studio, with producer Gary Lyons, Steven worked at nailing six songs for the overdue album. The five numbers credited to Tyler and Perry were a disparate lot. 'Three Mile Smile' reflected the anxiety of the nation. On 31 March that year a potentially lethal build-up of hydrogen gas inside a reactor at the Three Mile Island nuclear power station in Pennsylvania had brought the threat of a nuclear disaster into very sharp focus. The song 'Bone to Bone (Coney Island White Fish Boy)' had somewhat less lofty connotations. Explaining to the bewildered that a Coney Island White Fish was a used condom, Tyler maintained that when he had lived near the Hudson River he had often spotted such things floating by on their way to the sea. 'No Surprize' saw Tyler tell the story of Aerosmith's early beginnings, and the only solo Tyler composition was 'Mia', written for his little daughter. Three cover versions completed the nine tracks: one was an old blues number, 'Reefer Head Woman'; 'Think About It' was written by Yardbirds' Jim McCarty, Keith Relf and Jimmy Page; finally, and incongruously, 'Remember (Walkin' in the Sand)' was a 1964 number five hit penned by George Morton for the Shangri-Las all girl group.

The album was finally shaping up when, on 10 October 1979, a band press release officially announced Joe Perry's departure from Aerosmith. It spoke of the guitarist's plans to branch out into a solo career in the new year, and maintained that his leaving was an amicable arrangement, driven by his desire to seek a new musical direction. Joe soon stated: 'Considering what kind of progress I was makin' with Aerosmith, the decision [to leave] was easy to make. I'm a rock musician who likes to play and I always enjoyed playin' clubs the most. Aerosmith had become such a big cumbersome project. It was just so stifling and it wasn't movin' into the eighties.'

The notion that anyone could happily regress to playing small clubs after having hit the big time was completely alien to Tyler, and he was aggrieved when he read in the music press that Joe had complaints about some of the mixes on the forthcoming Aerosmith album, which had been such an incredibly hard slog to put together. Tyler's argument was that Perry might have been happier with the final product if he had attended the recording studio when he had repeatedly urged him to. Steven revealed: 'There were things going on that, as far as we were all concerned, had nothing to do with the band as a unit. Certain outside aggravations you don't need. When the split came, there was quite a bad taste in all of our mouths.' Steven later reflected that he had felt a fair degree of anger about the whole situation, but the underlying emotion was intense sorrow that the partnership he valued very much was broken.

Joe Perry knew that the bond between himself and Steven Tyler pivoted on their love-hate professional relationship and friendship. The wives being at war was not the issue for the guitarist. He acknowledged almost immediately that the blame lay with him and Steven for having let matters run way out of control. Even so, he had no compunction about walking away. He needed space and the freedom to try new challenges. He also felt strongly that Aerosmith had been pushing the fans' patience too much. Considering the state of some of their live performances he believed that the Blue Army's loyalty was more than the band deserved at that time. Steven could not believe that the dream was over, but in late October he welcomed in Joe Perry's replacement – lead guitarist Jimmy Crespo.

James Crespo was born on 5 July 1954 in Brooklyn, New York, into a musical family. He recalled: 'My father was a guitar player and singer. We are Puerto Rican, so we always had a Spanish guitar around. My grandfather was a violinist and I was supposed to become a violinist but I couldn't stand the way you had to hold it.' The Rolling Stones kindled the flame in the teenager to become a rock star, and his attraction to learn lead guitar was fanned by listening to Eric Clapton, Jimi Hendrix and Jeff Beck. Crespo's first guitar was a second-hand instrument with rusty strings, but his natural aptitude overcame this obstacle and throughout the 1960s he diligently honed his talent. His first band was called the Knoms and he made his debut public appearance at a school dance. By the early 1970s, Jimmy had formed Anaconda and gigged around the New York clubs, at the same time securing studio session work with artists including Meat Loaf. At that time he found the club scene tawdry, depressing and unlikely to be his springboard to recording stardom. He then auditioned for and landed a place in a band called Flame, which struck a deal with RCA Records and subsequently released two albums. Flame quickly burned down, though. 'It fell apart, as groups do when there is no money coming in,' explained Jimmy, who concentrated his energies on session work. 'I was playing music with whomever I could.'

In autumn 1979, David Krebs spotted Jimmy Crespo in performance, liked his hard rock style and sounded Crespo out about possibly playing lead guitar with Aerosmith. Unaware that Joe Perry was leaving, Jimmy considered it an academic, though tantalising, query and said that that would appeal to him very much. At this point, Aerosmith was still finishing the new album. When the call came in October, Crespo eagerly auditioned for the vacancy. Steven thought Jimmy fitted the bill both in terms of his strong musical abilities and his look – so he was in.

*Night in the Ruts* – said to be a spoonerism for 'right in the nuts' – was released in November. It peaked at number fourteen in the US album chart, went gold and drew polarised reviews. Malcolm Dome for *Record Mirror* at the time hailed: 'This is a raw hunk of macho venom that decimates the old grey matter like an overdose of neat vodka. Steven Tyler has obviously been sand-papering his larynx with great zeal.' More than twenty-five years on, *Mojo* pinpointed: '*Night in the Ruts* is the sound of the band on the brink.' The only single to be released 'Remember (Walkin' in the Sand)', stalled at number sixty-seven, by which time the album had sunk from view. Steven, meantime, was keeping an eye on Joe Perry's progress.

Since storming away from the band after that July Cleveland gig, Perry had not let the grass grow beneath his feet and by autumn he had recruited three musicians to enable him to form his solo band, the Joe Perry Project – vocalist Ralph Mormon, bass player David Hull and drummer Ronnie Stewart. After intensive rehearsals this new outfit played its first gig at an old Aerosmith stomping ground, Boston College, in mid-November 1979. Despite their fractured friendship, Steven showed up that night in the band's dressing room to say hello but he did not hang around to watch the Joe Perry Project perform. Perry described this solo band's style to *Rolling Stone* as being 'high-powered rhythm and blues, sort of funk rock'. Reinforcing his stance that he wanted to revert to playing more intimate venues than Aerosmith favoured, Perry maintained: 'I got disillusioned playing the big halls. I just don't like it and I don't need it any more.'

A strange period followed when both Perry and Aerosmith talked the talk about moving on and found new recruits to help that process along. Yet Steven and Joe kept casting a glance at, and a line to, each other. The umbilical cord between the 'twins' could not seem to snap irretrievably, and the fans clearly did not want that to happen either.

In preparation for recording his first solo album, Joe and his band rehearsed at the Wherehouse in Waltham, jointly owned by the Aerosmith members. Graffiti on the outer walls of this ware-house left Joe in no doubt that Aerosmith fans wanted him back in the fold, pronto. Indoors, knowing that his ex-bandmates would show up on other days, Joe left handwritten messages lying around for them – provocative messages at times, but still a means of keeping some dialogue going between the two camps. And Joe was not prepared to put up the slightest pretence of being pleased that just as he had moved on, so seemingly had Aerosmith by hiring his replacement. Joe secured a solo recording deal with Columbia Records and set to work with producer Jack Douglas on an album at New York's Hit Factory studio.

By the end of the year, Aerosmith with Jimmy Crespo had returned to live performance, playing dates around the east coast. Tyler was falling apart. On occasions he was too bombed to read the lyric sheets strewn around the stage, and frequently had to seek some physical support even to stay upright. During one performance he dropped like a bag of bones to the floor, was helped off stage only to return soon after, having been given oxygen backstage. The restless, disappointed fans were barely settling into the restarted show when Tyler again lost the plot mid-song. He then crowned this shambolic display by taking a spectacular header right into the crowd, having blacked out. Although he was clearly not in any condition to be performing live, the shows continued, and in January 1980, Steven collapsed in public again – this time during a gig at the Civic Center in Portland, Maine. Tyler was too drunk to perform that night, but not so pie-eyed that he did not realise that he would not get away with just staggering backstage where there were people ready to push him back out on stage. So he pretended to pass out and stayed prone on the floor despite sustained attempts to rouse him. This looked worse than anything Aerosmith fans were sadly becoming used to seeing, and when Tyler was carted off stage that night it was show over and the disappointed, short-changed horde filed quietly out.

When Aerosmith resumed their gigs, Tyler managed to stay on stage for the entire performances, only to be confronted with agitated fans yelling for Joe Perry. Jimmy Crespo, who stayed apart from the substance abuse, was playing fine lead guitar work for a band that was struggling to hold it together. He would have been fully entitled to feel aggrieved at these increasingly voluble cries from the crowds for his predecessor's return.

(*Above left*) As a teenager, Tyler played drums with his father's band, the Vic Tallarico Orchestra, at New York dances.

(*Above right*) Sex, drugs and rock 'n' roll were a way of life for Tyler throughout the 1970s.

By the mid-1970s, Aerosmith was one of America's biggest bands. Pictured here performing on NBC's *Midnight Special Show* in 1974.

(*Above left*) Steven sunk to the very depths of drug addiction in the late 1970s, often collapsing on stage or falling head first into the audience.

(*Above right*) Tyler and Joe Perry were known as the 'Toxic Twins' and their on-stage chemistry was explosive. Pictured here in concert in 1976.

(*Above left*) By the late 1980s, Tyler had regained his standing as one of rock's most iconic stars.

(*Above right*) Never an easy man to ignore, Steven is determined to capture his lead guitarist's full attention! Photographed here in the early 1990s.

(*Above left*) Sexuality saturates Tyler's stage act: he gyrates for his fans during 1993's *Get a Grip* album tour.

(*Above right*) Tyler with Jon Bon Jovi at the third annual Silver Clef Award Honours, 1990. Tyler doesn't do understated.

It was always Aerosmith's dream to make a lasting impression on rock. On 6 March 1990, Aerosmith was inducted into Hollywood's Rock Walk on Sunset Boulevard, Los Angeles.

For years Steven was tagged 'the poor man's Mick Jagger', but Tyler is no clone: photographed together in 1997.

(*Above left*) Tyler and Joe Perry photographed in the early 1990s.
(*Above right*) The Demon of Screamin' takes the stage on the *Nine Lives* tour, 1999.

That spring, Joe released his debut solo album, *Let the Music Do the Talking*, which peaked at number forty-seven on Billboard just as he launched his first tour with the Joe Perry Project. To all intents and purposes, this looked like living proof that he and Steven had each definitely taken a separate fork in the road. On the promo circuit for Aerosmith, Tyler was frequently quizzed about his feelings on this split. Steven maintained that he could appreciate Joe wanting to explore this solo path, insisting that was okay with him as he had his own thing going. It may have been convincing on radio, but during certain US television interviews Steven's expressive eyes plainly gave him away. He looked incredibly vulnerable when deflecting questions about Perry, and those close to Steven knew the truth. Jack Douglas once put it that Tyler missed Perry as one would miss a long-lost lover. In truth, all was far from rosy with Joe, too. His foursome was not gelling and personnel changes would soon take place. Plus, Perry was sliding into dire difficulties. He owed money to some serious drug dealers, who did not take kindly to waiting for payment.

Steven's lifestyle was rapidly disintegrating. He was so financially strapped that he was reduced to living in a sleazy hotel in New York, with his health deteriorating. His wife and daughter had at last moved into Steven's renovated house up at Lake Sunapee.

These conditions made it tough when the band started work on material for their next album. Brad Whitford confirmed that everyone except Jimmy Crespo was burned out, and that Steven was once more in trouble when it came to conjuring up lyrics. Steven did not have the same chemistry with Joe Perry's replacement, and his drug intake blurred too much for him, too often. It was obviously doomed to be a long, slow, hard slog and it was further hampered when in late 1980, Steven had a serious road accident in which he could have been killed.

One night, having taken drink and drugs, he climbed aboard his motorbike and took off from a bar. Taking a bend in the road at too steep an angle and too fast, he lost control and came crashing down. As parts of the motorbike flew off, the impact of hitting and being dragged along the ground almost ripped one of Steven's heels clean off – he had not been wearing protective footwear – and he slammed into a tree. It took several hours of surgery to repair the damage to Steven's foot, and he spent a long time afterwards laid up in hospital in a leg cast. As he physically recovered, the others carried on rehearsing, creating and sending him audio cassettes to listen to. This did not go down well with patients in the neighbouring beds; in Steven's words, nurses would order him to 'turn that shit off!'.

When eventually Steven left care and returned to his crummy hotel room in New York, still being in a leg cast worried him. The dive he was dossing in was not the place to be vulnerable, and as nights felt the dodgiest he would often hardly sleep. When he could make the journey, Steven visited his wife and daughter at Lake Sunapee, but relations between him and Cyrinda had soured. Cyrinda had her own problems, not least that she was battling drug addiction. She later publicly outlined how she was once so far gone on dope that she required resuscitation and that she had almost accidentally overdosed. Tyler heard tales that his wife was seeing someone, which he was unsure whether to believe. It made for a rocky relationship, and Mia was not yet three years old.

Before the end of the year, *Aerosmith's Greatest Hits* was released. The ten-song compilation album did not set the heather on fire chartwise in America, but it was destined to go multi-platinum, selling over ten million copies and earning the band a diamond award from the RIAA in 2001.

Twenty years earlier, Steven was being fed yet more stories of his wife's infidelity, and it was still difficult for him to know if he could trust his informants. Certainly, he knew that his marriage to Cyrinda was not thriving. He had moved into an apartment in New York and commuted to New Hampshire. Rows erupting between the couple, some vicious, were widening the gap. For her part, Cyrinda had no way of knowing if Steven was being unfaithful to her, and up at the lakeside property she often felt sad and lonely. When a fit, healthy, young man hoved on to her horizon in

1981, it did not take long to become physically involved with him. It was not a long-lasting relationship but it became messy and it was brought specifically to Steven's ears. Cyrinda admitted to having had, in time, more extra-marital liaisons after the dalliance with this Adonis. Being together was no longer an option for Steven and Cyrinda, each for their own reasons, and they stopped living as man and wife. Divorce became inevitable.

In the first quarter of 1981, Tyler, Perry and Aerosmith's fortunes were pretty shaky. When Joe's second solo album, *I've Got the Rock 'n' Rolls Again,* was released that summer, it failed to chart. With a new line-up, the Joe Perry Project was playing support to various bands but, still financially broke, Perry knew that he was going nowhere fast. Aerosmith fans were delighted to learn, though, that Tyler had telephoned Perry that spring, and industry rumours of a rapprochement circulated. The singer, however, was sinking deeper into drug addiction – Steven being in a stupor in the studio was not a rare occurrence. He could not climb out of the rut he had fallen into and everyone was driven up the wall with frustration at the lack of progress on this album. Tom Hamilton and Joey Kramer, too, were each abusing their bodies with unhelpful amounts of cocaine, and it was about now that Brad Whitford decided to bail out of Aerosmith.

The rhythm guitarist was numb with boredom. He needed to be performing live, and the insane lifestyle Aerosmith was leading was in danger of cracking him up. As the summer rolled on, the pressure built up to intolerable levels. He had not felt especially comfortable since Joe Perry's departure. He acknowledged Jimmy Crespo's musicianship but he did not enjoy the same rapport with Jimmy as he had had with Joe; overall he was thoroughly miserable. He would escape from the studio stalemate and head for Boston to unwind and reclaim his sanity. After one such trip, he just couldn't stand the thought of returning to the mire awaiting him in New York. The crunch came when he was at the airport; instead of boarding the plane, he called the band from the terminal building to say that he had had it, and was not coming back.

Steven was stunned. He thought Brad ought to have realised that he had it good being in Aerosmith – drugs had dulled Steven's wits in many ways by this time. The upshot was that Aerosmith lost a second original member. That same year, Brad teamed up with drummer Steve Pace, bass player Dave Hewitt and vocalist/guitarist Derek St Holmes to form the band Whitford/St Holmes, which released an eponymous album. It did not chart, nor did the spin-off single, 'Shy Away'.

Brad Whitford's departure served as a wake-up call to Tyler that he had to try harder to get his act together; in the new year he tried to create some studio magic, concentrating on working with Jimmy Crespo. Tyler stated: 'Spending such a long time in the studio really gave us a good chance to get to know each other's ways and I really like Jimmy's attitude. He is constantly putting things out. He never stops, whether or not the machines are running. The way he slotted into the band was incredible.'

Tyler and Crespo came up with four numbers: 'Bitch's Brew'; 'Bolivian Ragamuffin'; 'Jig Is Up', and 'Jailbait'. The latter particularly excited the band. Joe Perry, keeping track of Aerosmith's development without him, later admitted that he was rather jealous of the Jimmy Crespo riff on 'Jailbait'. Tyler and Crespo teamed up with Jack Douglas to create 'Joannie's Butterfly' and 'Rock in a Hard Place'. Steven's solo contributions were 'Push Comes to Shove' and 'Prelude to Joannie', and they recorded a cover version of 'Cry Me a River'; written by Arthur Hamilton, it had been a 1957 hit for the American singer, Julie London.

From winter into spring 1982, Aerosmith focused on pulling this album together. Initially, they worked with producer Tony Bongiovi (Jon Bon Jovi's second cousin) at the Power Station studio in downtown Manhattan. Work later switched to Criteria Studios in Miami, Florida, and Bongiovi relinquished the helm to Jack Douglas. Jimmy Crespo opined that Tony's approach was 'too structured for Steven's freeform style'. Tyler explained: 'It's not that we weren't happy with what Tony Bongiovi was doing but we felt it would be real good to have Jack Douglas involved again. We kind of missed the feeling we'd always got with Jack and I felt that he could capture some of those elements on this album.'

Jimmy Crespo took on the extra guitar duties until Brad Whitford's replacement was found in Rick Dufay. Born Richard Marc Dufay on 19 February 1952 in Paris, France, the rhythm guitarist had been recommended to Steven by Jack Douglas, who had produced Dufay's album, *Tender Loving Abuse*.

The abuse that was rife within Aerosmith ranks was now painfully evident to both newcomers to the fold, who had their eyes well and truly opened. Rick Dufay called the situation horrendous and was frankly appalled at Steven Tyler's rapidly deteriorating state. Jimmy Crespo confessed: 'When I joined, I was full on but after I worked with the group for a while, it just took the fire out of me.' It was not hard to understand why.

Steven had plumbed even darker depths. The once vibrant, impudent star, with his natural gift of wowing fans at gigs, was now mingling with society's bottom feeders in the relentless quest for his heroin fix. Even for a streetwise guy from the Bronx, Steven had entered a scary new stratum. One drug dealer he dealt with was found murdered one morning in his seedy den with a screwdriver embedded in his skull. Having resorted to buying dope on New York's streets, Steven would take heart-stopping risks by accompanying strangers down dark alleys to part with his cash – desperate guys who could in a split second's madness have killed him. On at least one occasion he was robbed. Speaking of a particularly precious diamond ring he had once worn, Steven revealed: 'While I was copping heroin on 79th Street, a guy put a gun to my temple and ran off with it.'

Steven had become such a junkie, however, that *any* risk was worth taking to experience the euphoria that heroin gave him, and nothing had the power to dissuade him. He knew that people from all walks of life were falling victim to heroin addiction. He would hear of addicts with collapsing veins desperately trying to find new places to inject themselves. In a few years' time Thin Lizzy's frontman, Phil Lynott, who took to injecting drugs between his toes, would die, but the addiction was stronger than any scare stories for Steven, whose hair was now falling out in places.

Worrying tales circulated on the music grapevine about Aerosmith's frontman, including untrue claims that Steven had developed throat cancer. Later that year, Tyler delivered a few broadsides at the people who had peddled these tales, calling them 'assholes'. Aerosmith's new album had been so long in the making that Tyler understood the inevitability of rumours, but that had crossed the line. Scratch the skin of Tyler the addict, however, and the incorrigible Steven was still there. He advised those critics who felt impelled to comment on his health to pick another malady – tell their readers that his dick had dropped off, he joked.

*Rock in a Hard Place* was released in October 1982; Steven was proud of its unashamedly hard rock content. He refused to agree that the three-year gap since *Night in the Ruts* had left Aerosmith out of touch with the record-buying public, and he was not shy of condemning the middle-of-the-road music that was monopolising both the charts and the airwaves. Steven was not alone. Xavier Russell for *Sounds* magazine declared of *Rock in a Hard Place*: 'As soon as the needle hit the wax, it melted and the speaker covers blew across the living room floor!' Despite this and other five-star reviews, Aerosmith's new work climbed no higher in the US chart than number thirty-seven; 'Lightning Strikes' failed to chart. It was when they went out on the road to support this new release, though, that it became inescapably obvious that the band was on the skids.

Reduced to playing in small arenas and clubs, they hit some dives along America's east coast, coming on stage in the early hours of the morning when most of the punters were too drunk to give a toss. They played one-thousand-seater clubs that, in their early days, they had been guaranteed to pack to the rafters; now they could only muster up a couple of hundred people. Tyler had maintained that he could not wait to get back into live performance, touring for the first time with Aerosmith's new line-up, and he spoke of how he had overheard fans leaving one venue saying that they had closed their eyes and had been unable to tell that it was not Joe Perry up there. The truth is, the yells from the crowds to bring Perry back were hard *not* to hear.

Jimmy Crespo and Rick Dufay tried to inject fresh verve into Aerosmith, and something like the old excitement was there at times. Steven dearly wanted to prove that the band had been missed, and he believed it best to deliver kick-ass music, but for others the writing was too clearly on the wall. Jimmy Crespo could see how passionately the diehard Aerosmith fans wanted to love the shows, painfully aware that Steven and the others were capable of delivering far better, but unable to because of the personal problems in the band. To Crespo, it was a lost opportunity. 'I was so willing to work,' he said, 'but the spirit was not there. Steven missed Joe.'

Very quickly, Steven's demons returned – forgetting the lyrics and passing out mid-performance. One November night, Steven went on stage in Massachusetts so stoned that he simply could not function. He collapsed, disappearing from the audience's sight and ending up like a limp rag on the stage floor behind one of the sound monitors. Again, it was show over.

It could very well have been game over for Steven. It seemed to some of his closest acquaintances that he had gone beyond the point of caring whether he lived or died. He was certainly in denial about how bad he had become. When worried, well-meaning friends tried to tell him that he had been behaving bizarrely the night before at a backstage party, he would flatly refuse to take them seriously. Steven was not eating properly. Ever a lean man, he was now almost literally skin and bone. When anyone warned him of others who had ended up down and out, he found any number of ways to justify his behaviour. Later he said: 'A line of blow would put you in a place you're familiar with. You experience a lot of memory loss. It's like spending all your time on the dark side of the moon – you get used to it.'

At the core of this chaos, however, Steven had faith in one safety net – a voice in his head that he believed always prevented him from accidentally overdosing. Though he was grateful for this higher power, when he was dope-sick there were times he fleetingly wished that he was dead. Some days he shook so violently that he was unable to get out of bed. In such a frightening and fragmenting condition, Steven's rein on his volatile temper could be slack, to say the least, and he threw terrible tantrums at times. It was not unknown during this period for Steven to throw things at people. He has confessed: 'I was so arrogant. I should have had the shit kicked out of me!' Intrinsically a charismatic livewire, he was pushing people who cared about him away. One of the most supple movers and electrifying frontmen in the business was being reduced to a catatonic wreck.

# CHAPTER 8

# Brothers By Choice

**S**TEVEN'S SAVIOUR was Teresa Barrick, a clothes designer almost ten years his junior, whom he met in 1983. Their paths had first crossed some time earlier when the slender blonde from America's Midwest was hanging out with a crowd of teenagers at clubs in Lahaina on the Hawaiian island of Maui. In this heaving social whirl, Teresa had been just another pretty face to Tyler, but she did not forget him over the ensuing few years as she moved in the same circles; in time a friend of her sister, Lisa, turned out to be also friends with the frontman. Teresa was at Record Plant Studios in New York with her sister and the friend when Tyler walked into the reception area. There had been a fair few foxy ladies around Aerosmith in their time but Teresa Barrick blew Tyler away. After gawping at the beauty he managed to ask her to stay a while. She did, and before long they were getting hot and heavy with each other. Separated from Cyrinda, Steven invited Teresa to his apartment.

It has to be said that no one could accuse Teresa Barrick of having an eye on the main chance. Right then, Steven Tyler was not a catch – he was loaded with drugs, not money, and though one time front cover material, he was generally feared to be heading fast for skid row. Their mutual attraction was powerful and immediate. Tyler later confessed to having read raw compassion in Teresa's eyes in that studio waiting room, and Teresa did once label herself as a good caretaker. Had Teresa been seeking a lost soul to succour, she could not have found a more worthy candidate. Tyler was broke, and Columbia Records were not going to renew Aerosmith's contract. As for his health, his condition had reached the point where there were days when he was barely able to dress himself. He was on heroin and crack. 'I must have snorted up all of Peru,' he later quipped, but people close to him, already anxious, dreaded him sinking any lower. For these friends, Teresa Barrick quickly became the one spark of hope they could see on the singer's horizon.

Steven fell head over heels in love with Teresa, although he was not an easy man to be with. Drugs distorted many aspects of life, but it did not take Teresa long to identify Tyler's Achilles heel – his lost bond with Joe Perry. It is not something that Tyler has hidden. He recognised Jimmy Crespo as a fine lead guitarist and he had successfully collaborated on creating songs with him, but said Steven: 'I used to look across the stage at Jimmy and somehow it just didn't feel right.' Joe Perry felt the same way. 'I just couldn't find a singer with whom I hit it off the way Steven and I always did,' he said. Since leaving Aerosmith in 1979, life had not been kind to Joe.

Addictions had devoured him, too. Every dollar he could scrape together went to feed his drug habit, and when he could no longer afford his usual class of drugs, he turned to copious amounts of alcohol to numb him into the required oblivion. He was such a wreck that sometimes his limbs shook, and he continued to experience frightening seizures. Clearly, he was in desperate need of professional help. His rocky marriage to Elyssa had run irretrievably aground – they were separated and heading for divorce. Broke and buried under a rising mountain of debt, Joe was reduced to living in a spartan Boston boarding house with the tax man hot on his trail.

By this time, Perry had acquired a manager named Tim Collins, whom he has credited with being of invaluable help when he was at one of his lowest ever ebbs. After his recording contract with Columbia Records expired he had secured a deal to produce an album for MCA. The Joe Perry Project's third offering, *Once a Rocker, Always a Rocker*, was released in late 1983 and failed to chart, spelling the death knell for this solo venture. The truth is, Joe had gained very little from breaking away from Aerosmith. There was nothing like the pleasure in it that he had envisaged, and personnel were hard to hold on to in an outfit that was scarcely commercially viable. It had meant a lot to him when his ex-Aerosmith friend, rhythm guitarist Brad Whitford, had joined him on stage to play at some live shows, but it was not enough.

After his split from Elyssa, in the early 1980s, for a time Joe played the role of the classic reckless rock star, partying with a succession of girls. Briefly it gave him a hitherto unknown sense of exhilarating freedom, but meaningless liaisons were not Perry's style. Interestingly, just like Steven, Joe met the woman who, to him, is responsible for saving his life – Billie Paulette Montgomery. The blonde model had auditioned for a part in the video shoot for 'Black Velvet Pants', a track from Perry's upcoming third solo album, and at the shoot Joe had been mesmerised by her. They instantly clicked, moved in together and soon became devoted to one another. Learning all about Joe's colourful life, it seemed obvious to Billie that he should reconnect with Steven Tyler and reform Aerosmith. Having no history with the band, Billie's view was not obscured by old simmering rivalries, jealousy or any mixed emotions. Initially resistant, Joe gradually began to respond to his new girlfriend's nudging to reach out to his former partner and friend.

At the same time, the new woman in Tyler's life, Teresa Barrick, was gently encouraging Steven to let go of past resentments – maybe set aside a dose of male pride – and think about extending an olive branch to Joe. Who contacted whom first is a matter of debate but, in any event, in summer 1983 the two men began talking to one another on the telephone. They then met face to face to chew over the tentative possibility of Aerosmith reforming. Tyler came away from that meeting on cloud nine. The Joe Perry Project still gigged, and Steven and Joe began turning up at each other's shows, but that itself could throw up bumps in the road to reconciliation.

At one Aerosmith gig, having come on stage very stoned, Steven stopped the show by collapsing, a familiar occurrence by now, but this time it looked so serious that some onlookers feared that he had actually died before their very eyes. Steven came round, but some were quick to blame that particular debacle on the backstage reunion earlier that night of the Toxic Twins. That resentment caused a wrinkle or two, which added to the difficulty of finding a workable way towards a reunited Aerosmith.

By the end of the year, the situation was desperate. Steven was dossing in the Gorham Hotel in New York, in a state of permanent penury. Money was also virtually non-existent for drummer Joey Kramer and bassist Tom Hamilton. Jimmy Crespo had reluctantly resorted to selling some guitars from his prized collection of vintage instruments in order to keep the wolf from the door. He dulled the pain of having to do this by persuading himself that he could always buy them back when the band's plight improved. Rhythm guitarist Rick Dufay was as skint as the others and the guy he replaced, ex-Aerosmith member Brad Whitford, had also been forced to liquidise his assets to keep his head above water for a little longer. Brad's solo venture had not worked out and he had been keeping tabs on these attempts at reconciliation between Steven and Joe. Unquestionably, for all the original members, a great deal hinged on this coming to fruition.

Rock history records that it was at a St Valentine's Day gig in 1984, when Joe and Brad went to see Aerosmith backstage at the Orpheum Theatre in Boston, that they finally decided to put the original quintet back together. Naturally, panic set in as to whether this would succeed. Would the old volatility and schisms tear them apart again? But, really, there was no question about it – they had to bite the bullet and try.

The adrenalin-driven anticipation around rekindling this

flame was tempered by the fact that this decision meant the departure of Perry and Whitford's replacements. Jimmy Crespo knew how much Tyler had missed Joe, and the way Aerosmith was placed at this point it was not hard to see that he was destined to jump ship. Having no money made life very difficult, and lacking the best showcase for his skills had left him feeling unfulfilled. Overall, Crespo saw it as a sad situation. On leaving Aerosmith, he linked up with a few musicians to form a band called Adam Bomb; later he reverted to session work, among other things. Rick Dufay knew that it was only natural that Brad would return to the fold too, and so this turn of events came as no surprise. He went on to pursue a range of other options.

Aerosmith has always been a brotherhood, and if some members took longer than others to see it that way, it probably came down to their very individual natures. The polarised characters of Steven and Joe can conceal that they each feel matters with the same underlying sensitivity – they just have wildly differing ways of expressing it. Tyler's passionate character means that he openly throws everything he has into a friendship and hopes to receive overtly the same in return. Recently reflecting on his bond with Joe, he frankly revealed that he carries a grain of sadness that he never feels entirely certain that in Perry he gets what he termed 'the full-time friend.'

In March 1984, with Joe and Brad Whitford back in the ranks, Steven felt it was a case of déjà vu as he left New York and rented an apartment in Boston to concentrate on getting Aerosmith airborne. The band began to rehearse at clubs and hotels in and around the city. Tyler later fondly recalled: 'You should have felt the buzz the moment all five of us got together in the same room for the first time again. We all started laughin'. It was like the five years had never passed and we knew we had made the right move.' There was possibly faint hysteria in the air as everyone was on tenterhooks, but at this first rehearsal they played well together. Back at their separate abodes that night, however, they all harboured anxieties that their old problems would eventually resurface.

With rehearsals under way, Tyler's temper threatened to snap one day when he heard on the grapevine that Alice Cooper was said to be interested in recruiting Joe Perry to his band, but nothing prevented the official announcement in April that the original Aerosmith had reunited and intended to tour. Prosaically, Perry agreed with journalists that money had been a factor when they had set aside their past problems to attempt the relaunch. No one in the business could deny, however, that it was an enticing prospect to put these explosive elements together again and wait to see the outcome. Before the rot had set in, Aerosmith had a special chemistry, at the core of which was the osmosis between Tyler and Perry; their loyal fans desperately hoped that that would happen once more.

Columbia Records were unmoved by the news of Aerosmith reforming and chose to stay out of the picture. The following year, referring to this label, Tyler confessed: 'They were obviously a bit fed up with seeing royalty cheques going direct to drug dealers.' Another tie to be cut at this time was with the management team of Leber and Krebs; it would prove to be an acrimonious affair. Tyler felt very aggrieved that although Aerosmith had sold millions of albums, each member had precious little to show for it. Steven acknowledged that he had squandered an absolute fortune feeding his addictions but he was certain that, even so, he ought not to be completely broke. The other band members felt exactly the same way. Steve Leber and David Krebs were, and have remained, adamant that the deal they had drawn up with Aerosmith was entirely legal and in line with deals made with other recording stars at that time. Krebs admitted that it had been a good deal for himself and Leber, but has been emphatic that nothing illegal was done in any area of their business arrangements with Aerosmith. Severing from Leber and Krebs was a painful process. Lawsuits were instigated and it was two years before a resolution was found. Tyler's emotions can still run pretty high when asked to express his personal opinion on this aspect of Aerosmith business.

By early summer, Steven preferred to focus on a major US

reunion tour that had been designed to catapult the band back into the public eye. Aptly called Back in the Saddle, this tour saw them flying without a net. They had no record deal and were not taking to the road to back a new album release. Aerosmith was in too fragile a state to be subjected to the intense pressure of trying to come up with new material good enough to withstand the close scrutiny that would inevitably fall on the reformed band, particularly as they entered the changing musical landscape of the mid-1980s. It had been tough enough attempting to put their fraught past behind them when rehearsing their old numbers. Regurgitating those same songs in the spotlight on stage before live and expectant, if not critical, audiences was going to be a stiff acid test in itself.

It is probably no more than could have been expected, but as this reunion tour rolled out, starting in New Hampshire, the picture proved patchy. On occasions, it all knitted well and the old magic was in evidence. At the other end of the spectrum, after some shows Steven quit the stage thoroughly dejected, knowing that things had gone all wrong. He was running on the same nervous adrenalin as his bandmates, and it did not help that with his track record many music critics were watching and waiting for Tyler to black out and take an ignominious header into the audience. Eyes were sharpened on the others, too, to see if the ravages of substance and alcohol abuse were going to take their toll on them. There was a willingness in some quarters to write Aerosmith off as a spent force, a tired relic of the sleazy seventies that was no longer relevant to the music-buying, concert-going public.

Steven was under a lot of pressure and as he was still heavily addicted to heroin and cocaine he inevitably did come crashing down. Quite early into the tour, he collapsed during a gig in Springfield, Illinois. The show had to be cancelled, giving Aerosmith the kind of publicity they did not want. Steven managed to get his act together and the tour continued. Tension was unavoidable and arguments broke out in the band, but each man was determined to take a less emotive attitude to disagreements this time around. None of the five had lost their fire but they were more fearful of extinguishing the flame than once they had been. Under these trying circumstances they held it together to gig throughout the summer.

Away from the stage, it was always at the front of Steven's mind to nail a new record deal; the key player in that happening in 1984 was A & R man John Kalodner. By the mid-1980s, Kalodner enjoyed a strong reputation in rock circles. Hailing from east coast America and weaned as a teenager on the best of British sixties' bands, John had immersed himself in popular music from a young age. He first worked with US bands at street level, managing local nightclubs, and for a time he drifted into music journalism. Switching to promotion, he found work with reputable record labels, graduating in time to the realms of artists and repertoire, where he quickly began to make his name. Transferring to west coast America, in 1980 he had pitched up as A & R man at Geffen Records in Los Angeles.

Kalodner had an eye for recognising untapped resources. He went to a couple of Aerosmith gigs during the Back in the Saddle tour and each night came away intrigued. All too aware of their very publicly played out troubles and their lurid reputations for debilitating addictions, he also respected them as having been one of America's greatest rock bands. Steven Tyler was just thirty-six years old – they were all still young, talented musicians. Provided that they could kick their individual habits, Kalodner believed that the band could potentially be huge again. From a record label's point of view, at that moment in time, there was great risk attached to investing in Aerosmith, but when Kalodner put his faith in an artist, it usually panned out.

Steven was thrilled when John Kalodner approached them. A good rapport quickly formed and before the end of 1984, Aerosmith was signed to Geffen Records for a reported $7 million advance. Around the same time Tim Collins, who had managed the Joe Perry Project, became Aerosmith's manager. The band's reunion tour had come to an end and Steven had to face up to the fact that he still had battles on his hands, and not just with dope. His drinking was of huge concern. He entered a phase when he would check himself into a clinic to dry out but would not stay for long, and was no sooner on the outside than he slipped back all too easily into his bad ways. He confessed: 'I knew I had to do something and I *wanted* to confront my addictions. So, for a period of a month I went every night to a course in Boston of a psychological nature. There, I was effectively humiliated by being asked publicly to recall the times I made an asshole of myself in front of friends and couldn't stand up long enough to carry through a show.' This embarrassing ordeal had no great lasting effect on the grip his addictions had on him, however.

After Aerosmith performed a New Year's Eve gig at Boston's Orpheum Theatre, they settled down to work on songs for their first album with Geffen Records. Although some nights on tour had been a strain and everything still felt dangerously brittle, once Steven and Joe got together to write songs for this come-back album it was obvious to them both that they *did* still have that chemistry. The creative spark between them ignited and they were prolific, producing a song per day. In something like four weeks, Steven felt that they were ready to go into the studio.

In a complete departure from their past, their eighth studio album was to be recorded at Fantasy Studios in Berkeley, California, under the aegis of producer Ted Templeman. When Aerosmith turned up, Steven had the tough task of whittling the song collection down to the nine best numbers. He was anxious that everything should be ready for working with Ted, and it showed.

Ted Templeman was an experienced and much sought after record producer who had publicly expressed an interest in working with the reformed Aerosmith, just when the band had been tossing about names of possible producers to approach. Ted was especially attuned to the raw energy that forms the core of Aerosmith's sound, the rough diamond edginess that, in his opinion, had often been wrongly smoothed down on vinyl. This kind of talk was music to Steven's ears for it chimed with his own feelings. Ostensibly then, Ted Templeman and Aerosmith made a good match, although the band was a bundle of nerves when showing up at Fantasy Studios.

Recognising this, Templeman let the guys believe for the first couple of days that they were simply running through the selected numbers for his benefit. Secretly, he had the tapes running throughout. 'It was his way of getting a live ambience into the sound,' recalled Steven, 'to get us jiving without pressure. We relaxed and let rip.' One of the nine songs was a reworked version of Joe Perry's solo number, 'Let the Music Do the Talking'. Challenged on whether this was appropriate when the band was looking to make a fresh start, Perry pointed out that he had written the song some time before splitting from the band in 1979, and so essentially it had been penned with Aerosmith in mind. Even when he recorded it for his first solo album, it had niggled at him how it would sound with Steven Tyler's vocals. When they toured the previous summer, they had road-tested it as an Aerosmith song and liked it. The lyrics had been slightly altered and the arrangement modified so it felt like a natural for inclusion in the album.

As time went on, however, the band reverted alarmingly to type. They had been given a second chance – a new record deal with a new label. They were working on fresh songs with a new producer and in an unfamiliar studio, and they had people behind them who were, against the odds, prepared to believe in their investment. Yet, at the end of each day, when the guys went back to their respective hotel rooms, the drink and drugs would kick in again.

On a happier note, on 21 September 1985, after Joe and Elyssa Perry's divorce was finalised, Joe and Billie Montgomery married in Maui, Hawaii. Rather than have a lavish ceremony that no one could afford, it was a private, low-key affair and very romantic in beautiful surroundings.

In November, *Done With Mirrors* was released. The ambiguous title tickled Tyler but despite a strong promotional push from Geffen Records, the album petered out at number thirty-six on the US chart, well short of all expectation. The album did not include a lyric sheet, which Steven approved of; his resistance to, as he has put it, ramming the words of songs down people's throats was very real. Just as Rolling Stones' music had formed the soundtrack of his own youth, so he hoped that fans would relate Aerosmith songs to whatever was going on in their lives.

To boost *Done With Mirrors*, Aerosmith set out on a US tour that would take them into 1986. The music industry was changing fast and rock shows had by now largely become a dramatic visual stage spectacle. Aerosmith wanted to move with the times, but Steven still felt it vital that they basically delivered a hard rock gig. Steven started this tour very much in rebirth mode. He declared: 'I feel like it's ten years ago, again. I feel like the band never was and here we are starting out at the beginning.' Privately, though, he had mixed emotions, wondering if he would find the necessary verve to sustain a tour. 'If I'm gonna be good, it can't be bogus,' he once said. 'It's gotta be me gettin' off on stage. When you're on the road for a year, you can go: "Fuck, another show!" But after two minutes of being on stage it's like ... *all right!*'

Tyler threw himself around the stage, delivering his overtly sexual act – suggestively straddling his scarf-festooned microphone stand, lasciviously panting in ecstasy while shoving his sweat-beaded face, bared chest and abdomen in the faces of the fans filling the front rows. A new generation of music lovers was out there, and it interested Tyler that a lot of the teenagers coming to these shows were familiar with the band's seventies' song catalogue. Critics continued to query if Aerosmith could still hope to be relevant, but Tyler was adamant that there was something unique about his band that made it durable. That new bands coming through were citing Aerosmith as their inspiration also helped to keep their name in vogue.

By the tour's end, however, there was certainly no elation in the band. Steven was in reflective mood as he reviewed their situation with a degree of detachment. Some of their shows had been mediocre and their supposed comeback album, *Done With*

*Mirrors*, had barely cracked the US Top 40 – no grounds for joy. Regarding the album, when asked if they had been unduly influenced by the need to live up to other people's expectations, Steven replied: 'When we climbed out of the hole, got back together and did that album, we had tried to do that for a while and it was really uncomfortable.' But Brad Whitford was prepared to be more blunt. He stated: 'We were stupid enough to believe that we could spit on to a piece of vinyl and it would sell.' Joe Perry opined: 'When we did *Done With Mirrors* everybody was goin': "Aerosmith's back. This is gonna be great. Their new record is gonna be fantastic!" and it wasn't fantastic but that was probably about the best thing that could have happened to us, artistically.'

There had been talk of Aerosmith taking their *Done With Mirrors* tour to Europe and the Far East, but no one was in any physical condition remotely to contemplate undertaking an arduous round-the-world trek. Brad Whitford and Joey Kramer were both struggling with serious drink problems. Tom Hamilton was attached to cocaine and, like Joe Perry, Steven was strung out on a variety of his favourite stimulants. Steven had tested his body and brain for far too long. Pushed almost beyond the limit now, surely something would soon snap.

# CHAPTER 9

# Where Angels
# Fear To Tread

**T**HE TURNING point for Tyler and Aerosmith was not too far
down the road, but before that, in spring 1986, an
unlooked-for opportunity came their way. Producer Rick
Rubin had contacted the band's manager, Tim Collins, to ask if
Steven and Joe would perform with Run D.M.C. on a rap rendition of 'Walk This Way'. Run D.M.C. comprised Joseph 'Run'
Simmons, Darryl 'D' McDaniels and Jason Mizell, also known as
DJ 'Jam Master Jay', all of whom grew up in Hollis, Queens, New
York. Formed in 1982 and considered to be pioneers of rap, their
two hip hop albums had failed to breach the Top 50. Working on
a third offering, they thought that it might be interesting to mesh
rap with a rock number. 'Hip hop wasn't a new thing,' said Rick
Rubin. 'It'd been around for about ten years – it started in the
clubs in the Bronx.' Run D.M.C. was more than amenable to the
producer's idea of getting together with the pair from Aerosmith
to rework 'Walk This Way'. Said Joseph Simmons: 'We used to
rap over the original record before we got into makin' records
ourselves.'

Steven found this proposal baffling at first – it certainly took
a bit of thought – but he and Joe went for it and all concerned
met up in early March at a recording studio in Manhattan. Joe

confessed that he had no idea who was who in the rap trio, just as he knew that they could not tell him and Steven apart. The atmosphere was perfectly friendly and curiosity about each other was palpable, but when they set to work, the cracks flew wide open.

Because of their substance abuse, Steven and Joe had difficulty in staying awake. Tyler later said of this shambolic first attempt: 'We just *couldn't* fuckin' do it! I was at the bottom of my barrel. I was on methadone and snorting Xanax. Rick Rubin looked at us and thought: "What the fuck is *this*? They can't even *dribble* straight!"' They persevered, though, and it was finished in five hours. To support the number they filmed a video featuring Steven, Joe and the rap trio at a theatre in New Jersey before an invited audience ready to scream and jostle excitedly below the footlights.

Aerosmith is now synonymous with creating memorable and provocative music videos, but it was a whole genre they had feared missing out on with the state of the band in the early to mid-1980s. Talking of the development of the likes of MTV, Tom Hamilton recalled: 'I remember watching that first video channel and thinking we're not going to be a part of that and it was a horrible feeling.' In the video for this new version of 'Walk This Way' equal time was given to both Run D.M.C. and Aerosmith's two, but Perry's cool rock guitarist image and Tyler's brash in-your-face delivery stole the limelight. In his trademark ragamuffin stagewear, Steven pranced energetically, rode his mike stand and finally literally flipped head over heels. For a man in his condition, he was remarkably athletic and he conveyed an attractive arrogance when watching the black trio figuratively attempt to break down the wall between them. Symbolism in the video had a certain significance, for it was hoped that this crossover number would improve the fortunes of both very different bands.

Run D.M.C. released *Raising Hell* in May with the reworked 'Walk This Way' as its first spin-off single. It reached number four on Billboard, with the video receiving saturation air time on

MTV, and has gone down as the first hip hop track to break into Billboard's Top 10 singles chart. Said Joe Perry: 'As far as I'm concerned, this was just a little side thing that Steven and I decided to do for some fun.' Years later, the rap-rock version of 'Walk This Way' would rank twenty-seventh in *Rolling Stone* magazine's Top 100 Songs That Changed The World. It gave Run D.M.C. the injection it needed, and played a part in jump-starting Aerosmith's comeback, but by September 1986 it was clear that a crossroads had been reached. Although *Done With Mirrors* was considered a commercial flop, Geffen Records still wanted a second Aerosmith album, but no one was under any illusions. It was do or die time, and to have any chance of capitalising on the boost the new version of 'Walk This Way' gave them, the band had to get clean – starting with sorting out their lyricist, vocalist and frontman.

The timing was right. Steven knew that he was a slave to his addictions. He took cocaine and other drugs but he had recognised throughout that summer that heroin had the deadliest hold on him – he was very alive to the danger that heroin could be killing him, bit by bit. It already ravaged his health and robbed him of his creativity. The mental fog caused by drugs had even removed his ability to rhyme when writing lyrics. That was why he had taken steps to try to wean himself off heroin by turning to methadone. This powerful synthetic painkiller, used to treat heroin addiction, helped to an extent but Tyler knew that he was struggling. He was living with his girlfriend, Teresa Barrick, in an apartment in Cambridge, Massachusetts, when life-changing events kicked off.

One night Steven received a message that Tim Collins had convened an urgent meeting at his office for the following day, at the ungodly hour of 6.00 a.m. To make this meeting Steven had to miss receiving his daily dose of methadone, so when he arrived at the office on time he was emotionally and physically shaky. On stepping through the door he realised that he had been summoned under false pretences and that it was, in effect, an intervention.

Six men were present, each primed and ready to confront Steven – Joe Perry, Tom Hamilton, Joey Kramer, Brad Whitford, Tim Collins and one stranger who turned out to be a psychiatrist, Dr Lou Cox. Their collective aim was to pressurise Steven into undertaking a strict rehabilitation programme. To that end, caught cold, Steven was made to listen for hours while the band told him in unsparing detail just how dreadful his behaviour had been because of drugs and alcohol, and how badly it had been affecting each of them. Tyler's knee-jerk reaction was that this was rich. Talk about the pot calling the kettle black! *Every* member of Aerosmith was struggling with addiction problems; not surprisingly Steven took exception to this bruising attack. When he was permitted to respond, at first he ferociously argued back and hurled a few well-aimed metaphorical brickbats at his bandmates. It was highly emotional, and deep down Steven would forever hold on to a tiny kernel of resentment about the way this whole painful business had been handled. In the end, by late morning, his control collapsed. He broke down in tears and agreed to accept professional help to conquer his addictions. Already drained and strung out, Steven learned to his alarm that the deal meant him going into rehab immediately. A room at a clinic was booked for him; a bag was even packed for his admission. It must have been extremely frightening for him to relinquish control of his freedom so suddenly – albeit for the best of ends.

At the clinic Steven checked into that day, there was a strong element of religion underpinning the whole treatment regime. He was expected to make God and prayer a key part of his life. At this facility, he was grilled to a head-spinning degree about his feelings on what seemed to be every aspect of his life from childhood to date; all, it seemed, with a view to attaching assorted labels to him. Some tags he acknowledged as valid, others bemused him, but there was one corner that he was not prepared to be painted into – the need for sex addiction therapy.

The rehabilitation process and coping with all the withdrawal symptoms was really tough. Physically, his pain threshold had sunk so low that he later likened his excruciating suffering to that endured by a third-degree-burn patient. He has a naturally fast metabolism but the medication he was given rendered him catatonic. Losing all interest in his personal appearance, he became for a while a sadly bedraggled wreck. With his long hair hanging lankly about his face, a shawl around his coat-hanger-thin shoulders and shuffling around in loose moccasins, he was painfully aware that as he aimlessly slunk around corridors people were staring at him, whispering, recognising the once outrageous rock star in their desperate midst. It hammered home to Steven just what a leveller drug addiction is. There were people from all walks of life seeking help in this facility – from pilots to postmen. Said Steven: 'There was even a priest who used to shoot up when he heard confession!'

Mentally, Steven was all over the place and he had to draw on untapped reserves to help him survive this gruelling and disturbing experience. There were some saviours. He got back in touch with other aspects of the world. He began to read a lot and Joe Perry's support was of great importance to him. Perry empathised with Tyler going through this harrowing ordeal, and he extended the kind of compassion Steven needed right then. This was one crucial time that proved the strength of the friendship bond between them. As the guitarist's visits also gave Steven the promise of a new future for Aerosmith, he worked hard to develop a sense of purpose and to recover a sense of self-worth. 'Every day, you face a different fight against craving or withdrawal but every day it gets a little better,' he later stressed.

After forty-five days of rehab, Steven was classed clean of drugs. He went from this clinic to attending Alcoholics Anonymous meetings in order to tackle his drink problems. Teresa watched these developments closely, and her support and understanding throughout also played a vital role in the front-man's fight back from the brink. Once back in the real world, Steven's biggest danger was relapsing. To keep up the pressure on him, Joe threatened his friend in no uncertain terms that if he were to fall by the wayside then he (Perry) would take a walk from

Aerosmith again. Tyler, though, was all too aware of how precarious his condition was. He knew that just one glass of beer could result in him heading down town in search of a needle or a mirror.

For all that, he was able to enjoy the obvious upside of being clean of drugs. The world was brighter, had more definition and meaning. His energy levels and mental alertness were coming back up, and for the first time in a long while he was able to appreciate music properly. In the years ahead, the sober Steven Tyler never became evangelical about recovering from addiction; he would not preach to others going the same way he had.

In November 1986, Joe Perry was next to go into rehab to come off of heroin. He, too, went through a gruelling journey of discovery and later said: 'It's amazing how people can be so unaware that they're fucking other people over and hurting people but that's how it was with us.' Joe emerged from rehab clean, and over the next two years Brad Whitford, Joey Kramer and Tom Hamilton each found his own method of tackling his individual addictions. Said Brad: 'We crawled out from under our problems and got in touch with ourselves.'

Drug-free, sober and feeling like a new man, Steven was looking forward to the future when part of his past came into focus. For the past nine years, Bebe Buell's daughter Liv had grown up believing that Todd Rundgren was her father. By the end of the 1970s, the girl's domestic situation had changed. Bebe had become romantically involved with another man, but Liv still lived with her mother and attended school in Portland, Maine. For a period in the early 1980s, Bebe had attempted to launch a career as a rock star, fronting a couple of bands. That had not panned out but she had lost none of her verve, at least around her young daughter. Liv later recalled: 'My mom was so amazing. She had all these beautiful clothes and in the bathroom all her jewellery was pinned to the wall. It was more than a little girl could ever dream of!' Whenever her mother went out, Liv enjoyed dressing up in Bebe's glamorous clothes and experimenting with professional make-up.

In December 1986, Bebe took Liv along to see Todd Rundgren perform a gig in a Boston club. Backstage afterwards, Todd's dressing room door opened and Steven walked in. He had come to visit the musician, but his eyes shot at once to the dark-haired little girl beside Bebe. When Steven had learned in 1976 that, after their brief liaison, Bebe was pregnant, he had not known what to believe, particularly since she and Rundgren had instantly resumed their relationship. Over the ensuing years, Todd was widely understood to be Liv's father. That night, however, Steven was jolted. 'When Liv was very young, I wasn't sure whether I was her father,' he admitted, 'but by the time she was nine I could see my features in her.'

Bebe has always maintained that her reason for allowing Liv to be under the misapprehension that Todd Rundgren was her father was to shield her, because Steven had been so mired in drugs and drink. That December night, it was a patently very different Steven Tyler who strode confidently into the dressing room, looking and sounding better than he had done for years. Bebe introduced Liv to Steven simply as an acquaintance, but for the intuitive youngster it was not quite so straightforward. Liv has revealed: 'I connected with Steven immediately. It was almost like I fell in love with him.' This innocent love she channelled into idolising Steven Tyler, the rock star. That evening, Steven spent a little time in Todd's overcrowded dressing room talking generally with Liv, helping her to knock out a tune on a keyboard. Watching this tableau, Bebe was overwhelmed with emotion, and torn over what she should do, but it was obviously not the right moment to say anything.

In 1977, it had pleased Mick Jagger when speculation had run around that he might be the father of *Playboy* centrefold Bebe Buell's daughter. Jagger's pride might have taken a dent if he knew that in 1986, noting a strong resemblance between Steven Tyler and the Rolling Stone, Liv guilelessly asked her mother if Jagger was Steven's father!

Setting aside the question marks that that backstage visit had thrown up, Steven faced the new year determined to further his drive to get well, and he began to work out in a gym. This physical exercise was also good psychologically, since it provided a trouble-free way of expending any pent-up aggression, and it became a way of finding clarity and purpose.

January 1987 saw Boston blanketed with snow as Aerosmith regrouped to begin rehearsals and to knuckle down to writing material for their next album. Invigoratingly, it became like the old days when Aerosmith was just starting out, with Steven fired up by Joe's inspirational guitar licks. With a clear head, Tyler's creative juices got going and output was rewarding in both quality and quantity. Visiting these sessions weeks later, John Kalodner was encouraged by what he found, but believed that an extra element was needed to sharpen the material even further, and he told Steven that he wanted to bring in outside songwriters to work with the band.

Kalodner first drafted in Desmond Child. The thirty-three-year-old, Florida-born Child had just a year before been recruited to work with Jon Bon Jovi and Richie Sambora on Bon Jovi's third album, also a do-or-die career point. Desmond had driven to the Sambora family home in Woodbridge, New Jersey, where in the basement he had injected fresh blood into the songs Jon and Richie were coming up with. That three-way symbiosis had produced two hits: 'You Give Love a Bad Name', and the blue-collar anthem, 'Livin' On a Prayer'. Bon Jovi's album *Slippery When Wet*, released in August 1986, shot to number one and eventually racked up sales exceeding 20 million worldwide. By bringing Desmond Child's talent to Steven and Joe, John Kalodner hoped that it would likewise help to create the defining moment in Aerosmith's career.

It has been suggested that Tyler was resistant to the idea of outside lyricists coming in; at first, by his own admission, he was not one hundred per cent happy with some of Desmond Child's suggestions, but perhaps the star was showing a touch of territoriality. This was also something strange to deal with when he was already in a raw state, so inevitably he found it a shade intimidating. However, Steven later maintained that he was amenable to the A & R man's determination to make him work with professional lyricists and he quickly adapted to the situation, enabling him and Child to complement one another.

The single three-way collaboration between Tyler, Perry and Child to emerge was 'Dude (Looks Like a Lady)'. Steven had almost nailed this raucous hard rock number – he just stumbled over coming up with the first line. As he had done when working with Jon Bon Jovi and Richie Sambora, Desmond first talked with and listened to Steven to get a feel of where he was coming from, then clicked straight in – providing Tyler with an opener for this song that came vividly to life. That kind of clever clarity impressed Steven immensely, and the lingering resistance he harboured to letting a professional songwriter into his creative world evaporated. He and Child spent hours bouncing lyrics off one another, creating a hit song and cementing the camaraderie between them in the process. In short order, Steven and Desmond created 'Angel', and Child wrote 'Heart's Done Time' with Joe Perry,

After Desmond Child, John Kalodner enlisted the services of songwriters Jim Vallance and Holly Knight, which added 'Magic Touch', 'Simoriah' and 'Rag Doll' to the haul. One aspect of 'Rag Doll' would rankle with Tyler. He had originally titled the number 'Rag Time' but Holly Knight was invited to change that lyric. 'Time' became 'Doll' and Steven was unhappy that someone should get a songwriting credit for changing just a single word. Steven wrote 'Girl Keeps Coming Apart' and 'Permanent Vacation' with Joe Perry and Brad Whitford respectively, while a number titled 'St John' was Tyler's only solo effort.

Between March and June 1987, Aerosmith recorded this new material at Little Mountain Sound Studios in Vancouver, Canada, under the eye of producer Bruce Fairbairn, whose most recent success was the Bon Jovi hit album *Slippery When Wet*. Fairbairn's way of working was different from the producers the band were used to, and it all helped to maintain a crucial discipline that kept this new Aerosmith on the right track. Gone were the days of drug hazes and people falling asleep on the job, although Tom Hamilton was still smoking marijuana. The bass player took a good deal of stick from his bandmates over this, while Tyler contented himself with pinning Tom with some pretty piercing looks. Eventually Tom quit the weed, which meant that all five were finally totally clean.

That summer, Steven and the others filmed the video to accompany 'Dude (Looks Like a Lady)'. It was largely Aerosmith in high-energy performance but incorporated brief cutaway shots showing Geffen A & R man John Kalodner dressed up as a bride and Steven in drag, wearing a pink sequinned dress and looking like a pantomime dame.

*Permanent Vacation* was released in August 1987, and exuded confidence, strength and vibrancy through its new musical layers. *Rolling Stone Encyclopedia of Rock* later recorded: 'Aerosmith forfeited none of their bad boy image and their live shows are among the best of their career. Even critics liked them better the second time around.' *Permanent Vacation* provided the band with their first UK chart success when it ranked number thirty-seven in September. In America it peaked at number eleven, remained on Billboard's chart for seventy weeks and went multi-platinum.

Mid-month, Aerosmith performed 'Walk This Way' with Run D.M.C. at the MTV Music Awards held at Universal Amphitheatre in Universal City, California, but Tyler was fixed on the October release of 'Dude (Looks Like a Lady)'. Aided by heavy rotation airplay of its video on MTV, this single climbed to number fourteen in the US and made it to number forty-five in the UK singles chart.

Success tasted all the sweeter the second time around, and Steven concentrated on positive thinking, but he had not forgotten the past pannings Aerosmith had taken from critics. Proud of their resilience, he said: 'It is almost like the world was asphalt and we were these fuckin' weeds. No matter what they put over us, we grew right through it.' When asked to pinpoint the best revenge he had ever enjoyed, Tyler unhesitatingly stated that it was his band's comeback. Interestingly, for a man who had gone through hell to claw his way back, Steven had moments when he felt spooked by the thought of the huge success that was now clearly going to be Aerosmith's. Towards the end of the 1980s, he maintained that it would frighten him to become as big a star as Jon Bon Jovi, whose band followed up *Slippery When Wet* with *New Jersey*, another triumph. What Tyler had come through had left him with inner scars, for he feared that in climbing so high any fall would be all the more devastating. That said, his renewed health and the success of *Permanent Vacation* gave Steven a new strain of confidence and he was once more passionate about his band.

With his professional life straightening out, in late 1987, aspects of his private life had to be attended to. For Cyrinda and Mia, things had been far from easy. When Steven had visited his daughter, each time the youngster wanted him to stay longer, becoming distressed when he had to leave. To Cyrinda, the lake-front house in New Hampshire was no longer idyllic. It had fallen badly into disrepair and she could not afford to have tradesmen carry out extensive renovation work; at the time Steven had been in no position to help, either. Over time she had relied on help from her circle of friends – local bikers who could turn their hands to plumbing, joinery and decorating. These people were platonic acquaintances and Cyrinda had valued their friendship. She was deeply dismayed when, during the divorce proccedings, some of these friendships were alleged to be something more.

In November 1987, just short of Mia's ninth birthday, Steven and Cyrinda's divorce became final. Cyrinda retained custody of their daughter but she was extremely unhappy with the alimony arrangements – she later publicly revealed the amount to have been a little over $252 per week. She also later stated her feeling of having been badly advised when it came to some aspects of the divorce settlement. From Cyrinda's point of view, the problem was that during the period when these matters were thrashed out, Steven was on the skids, in the grip of drug and drink addiction. Aerosmith was washed up and at that point no one could have predicted a Lazarus-style revival. Cyrinda had hoped to secure a stake in songwriting royalties for Mia but was advised that that would not be forthcoming. Even during the divorce proceedings, although Aerosmith's new album and single had charted, that did not equate with pots of cash instantly pouring into Steven's bank balance.

With a Boston Music Award for Outstanding Rock Band of the Year under their belt, Steven and Joe went on a press tour of Europe. It was Tyler's first visit to the UK in a decade; he talked frankly to the music media about his drug-free, rejuvenated band – preparing the way for Aerosmith going back on the road. The *Permanent Vacation* tour, commencing in autumn 1987 in Binghamton, New York, stretched over the next twelve months and took in more than 150 shows in forty-two US states and overseas. Throughout the tour, Tyler worked himself to the bone to reclaim Aerosmith's crown as a dynamic live act, and it proved to be one of the happiest tours of the band's career. They got themselves a double-decker bus and brought along their loved ones. Steven has particularly fond memories of night journeys across Europe between gigs, when he would gaze through the windscreen at the stars in the early hours, as the countryside flashed by. For an outdoors man at heart, it had a liberating feel. Of gigging around America, Tyler said: 'I'm having so much fun, getting up in the afternoon, flying to a show, rockin' the asses off twenty thousand maniacs, flying home at midnight and sitting up till 3.00 a.m. thinking how beautiful life is.'

As newly recovered drug and alcohol addicts, though, stringent steps had had to be taken to prevent them from falling off the wagon. In advance of Aerosmith arriving in each town and city, their hotel room mini-bars had to be stripped of anything alcoholic. Among those around the band, including any support act, there was a complete ban on drug taking, and if anyone wanted to drink alcohol they had to do it well away from Aerosmith. With a brief break for Christmas, the tour picked up again in mid-January, taking in the southern and western states, and beyond.

On 26 March 1988, Tyler turned forty. That spring, *Permanent Vacation* spawned its next hit single, 'Angel', the sentimental ballad written by Steven with Desmond Child. It lodged in the UK chart at number sixty-nine but soared in the States to number three on Billboard. During the tour, Steven drew immense satisfaction from hearing the audience sing the lyrics of this song along with him. It was moments like these that drove home to him just how wasteful those years had been when he had been too stoned on stage even to stay upright.

Not everyone was in such a mellow mood, and it was now that Steven's ex-wife chose to challenge the financial settlement agreed in their divorce. Aerosmith's comeback was clearly going to be sustained, and Cyrinda still felt deeply aggrieved. Her life with Mia continued to be anything but the comfortable existence that she felt it ought to be. Money remained tight and she found it hard sometimes even to keep warm. Once, when Steven paid a visit to the house in New Hampshire he asked where his boat had gone and Cyrinda had snapped: 'I burned it so that your daughter wouldn't freeze to death, you bastard!' Cyrinda's hopes that legal wrangling would improve her status did not materialise – at least, not to the level that she had hoped for – but changes did occur. Part of the 1987 divorce settlement held Steven responsible for paying for parochial schooling for Mia. When Cyrinda upsticked from the rundown lakeside house in 1988 and relocated to New York, Mia was enrolled at Marymount School. She and her mother at the same time moved into a nearby apartment on Madison Avenue, where they would stay for the next few years. Cyrinda had managed to improve their situation but was sometimes wearied by the fact that everything had to be achieved via lawyers.

Not put off by the demise of his first marriage, during a break in touring, Steven wed for a second time when, on 28 May 1988, he and Teresa Barrick tied the knot during a ceremony held in Oklahoma. At the end of June, Teresa became pregnant and was expecting their child the following spring. Also in June, 'Rag Doll', the third single from *Permanent Vacation*, was released and peaked in America at number seventeen, but was not issued in Britain. Then in July the tour resumed. This time out on the road, Steven was more than ever alive to potential danger, as their support band for the major venues was the turbulent and volatile Guns N' Roses. Signed to Geffen Records two years earlier, Guns N' Roses had supported Iron Maiden and Motley Crue. Their 1987 debut album, *Appetite for Destruction*, was aptly titled, for some of the band's members already had problems with chemical abuse and alcohol addiction. Steven said of Guns N' Roses' frontman, Axl Rose: 'He's just the kind of "trash the dressing room" egomaniac that I used to be, but when you're young, when you're making a lot of money and you're bent out of shape – you trash dressing rooms!'

According to Guns N' Roses' lead guitarist, Slash, even landing the support gig had provoked some over-the-top antics. The band had been asked to meet Tim Collins at a hotel to discuss the possibility of backing Aerosmith on the road; during the course of the evening, while Collins was occupied with something else, the guys in Guns ran up a huge room service bill, then trashed the room. Said Slash to *Rolling Stone*: 'But they must have liked us a lot because they put us on the bill anyway.'

The scope, then, for problems for the rehabilitated Aerosmith was huge. To get around this a system was worked out whereby Guns N' Roses agreed to confine any substance and alcohol abuse to their dressing room. They would play their support gig slot and leave the venue, taking all trace of temptation with them before Aerosmith arrived to headline. On the whole, this revolving door arrangement worked, but on one occasion Steven walked into a dressing room to find Slash still there. By the evidence lying around, the twenty-three-year-old had consumed a fair amount of Jack Daniel's. Tyler started to say something but stopped himself. Tyler maintained in 1988: 'I'm always there if they want to talk about it. I can tell them exactly how screwed up I was and what I did with it but I don't wanna get into the preachin' trip.'

In late August, on the evening Aerosmith was to play at the

Great Woods outdoor arena in Massachusetts, events took a major turn for Steven, personally. Before the gig, Bebe Buell and eleven-year-old Liv visited him in his dressing room. His daughter Mia was already there, and the two dark-haired girls, barely eighteen months apart in age, eyed one another for the first time. Liv recalled: 'We were like identical twins.' When the performance began, Liv sat next to her mother in the audience but her eyes were riveted on Steven. She had idolised him as a rock star but all of a sudden Liv turned and asked her mother straight out if Steven Tyler was really her father and not Todd Rundgren as she had been led to believe. Faced with such a direct question, Bebe could not withold the truth any longer and under cover of the music blasting off the stage, emotionally she came clean to Liv.

Some time soon after, Bebe had to let Steven know that Liv now knew the truth, after which he and Liv had to talk. When Steven confirmed to Liv that he was her real father he found it immensely moving, especially when the girl was patently delighted about it. To regularise matters, a blood test was carried out, paternity was proved and Steven made the appropriate financial arrangements.

It is a treasure to Steven that Liv does not harbour any resentment against him for not having been in her life for eleven years. Liv's inherent maturity was not long in showing. Looking back on her teens, she candidly pointed out: 'I never had much to rebel against because my parents were always so cool. I mean, what was I to do? Smoke a joint? Go to rock concerts? That's all they ever did' – and far more besides! In time, Liv took the Tyler name. She told US Magazine: 'Wanting to be more a part of my real father was only natural and I liked the name. It's a great name.'

Liv's true paternity was not made public knowledge for a further three years. Mia, meantime, would overhear comments about how alike she and Liv were. So Cyrinda sat Mia down one day and explained that as her father had had relationships before they had married, he could have other children to other women.

Mia was thrilled to learn that she had a sister, and the girls went on to become close.

In September, Aerosmith performed for a second year at the MTV Video Music Awards, again held at the Universal Amphitheatre in Universal City, California. For the first time, Aerosmith had been nominated for two awards – Best Group Video and Best Stage Performance in a Video, both for 'Dude (Looks Like a Lady)'. When the *Permanent Vacation* tour came to a close, Aerosmith had played on bills with Deep Purple, Dokken, White Lion and Guns N' Roses, and Tyler's deepest delight was how the fans had been outstandingly loyal and receptive to them.

It had taken a great deal of guts, determination and a sheer passion for life and music, but by the end of 1988, from the depths of drug-ridden despair, Aerosmith had roared back to life. Steven still wrestled with the fear that one slip could bring him crashing down again, this time from an even higher perch. 'It's a bitch to stay straight,' he candidly confessed. Taking his sobriety one day at a time, he promised himself each morning that he would not take dope or drink that day – knowing that he could not vouch for his willpower tomorrow. On tour, he had taken extra precautions to isolate himself from temptation to the point where he had left no one in any doubt that if he caught anyone doing drugs or taking alcohol in his dressing room, there would be all hell to pay.

Primarily, Tyler had found new beauty in his personal and professional lives. The rehabilitation clinic in which he had ditched his addictions had used religion as the bedrock of their therapy, and Steven did believe that other forces were at work. 'There's got to have been a plan for this band,' he maintained, 'either by a higher power, or an angel of mercy because for all the shit I did, *someone* threw me a rope.'

# CHAPTER 10

# Going Up, Mr Tyler?

TOWARDS THE end of 1988 several weeks were devoted to developing ideas for the follow-up to *Permanent Vacation*. Revelling in the creative benefits of his hard-won sobriety, Tyler was typically tongue-in-cheek: 'I've been like a squirrel storing things up and I can't stop fiddling with my nuts!' He maintained that they wanted to keep the material simple and guitar-oriented, but the song collection that evolved over the coming months wove an interesting and intricate tapestry.

Steven collaborated with Jim Vallance on two numbers, 'Young Lust' and a belter called 'The Other Side', both of which came quickly to fruition. Desmond Child's services were called upon to assist Tyler and Perry pull together 'What It Takes', a song that proved immensely popular with the fans live; seven other songs came from collaborations within the band, for they had closed ranks this time. From the band's perspective, exploring collective creativity was always the best, and at this time it could only help to foster their new cohesion. Still, Perry's raucous riffs marrying with Tyler's intrinsic understanding of melody could, even after all these years, leave the others in awe.

A Tyler/Perry number to come straight off the bat was 'Monkey on My Back', reflecting Steven's experience with drug and alcohol addiction, but the two standout tracks were swiftly identified as the diametrically different songs, 'Love in an Elevator' and 'Janie's Got a Gun'. Tyler once confessed: 'I put so much sex in my lyrics because it is always on my mind.' Certainly, the source for 'Love in an Elevator' has become a near fabled tale in rock.

According to Tyler, one evening in a swish hotel elevator, two nubile beauties ambushed him, keen to check out his credentials as a groin-grinding rock god. Not in the least averse to this 'attack', Tyler ended up down on his knees attending to one lady, who was in a startling state of undress. Completely engrossed with making out, the steamy pair forgot where they were until reaching the ground floor lobby, where the door slid smoothly open. Hotel staff and customers queuing to use the lift could not believe their eyes. Said Steven: 'It was very exciting. The door was open for all of six seconds, then closed, but it felt like a millennium!' Steven effortlessly came up with the lyrics to tell this story and they twinned perfectly with a riff Joe had become attached to. The chemistry was right and both Tyler and Perry knew that it would be a stimulating live number – something which always motivates them. Perry later stated: '"Love in an Elevator" really sums up the excitement I feel is all over the *Pump* album.'

In complete contrast, 'Janie's Got a Gun' dealt with a taboo topic. In the basement of his house, Steven had installed a sophisticated keyboard next to the treadmill he used to keep fit. Exercising often energised him lyrically. In 'Janie's' case he had the song title and the melody but no specific direction. He had read a newspaper article about gun crime, and was working out down in his basement with the question of why a girl would get hold of a gun percolating through his head. As lyrics came to him thick and fast, drenched in sweat with his heart pumping, he leapt off the treadmill and began to pen a song about a fictitious girl who is raped by her father and subsequently seeks revenge by gunning him down. As a father of girls, Steven found the idea of sexually abusing one's own daughter a totally alien concept, and he had to reach deep into unknown realms to come up with this song. 'Once I'd tapped into the insanity, the song wrote itself,' he said. Tyler took nine months to perfect this powerfully evocative song, which has since been hailed as one of his finest compositions. It was nearing completion when he presented it to the others in the studio. Not noted for delving into weighty social issues in song, Steven stunned his bandmates this time. Joe Perry stated: '"Janie's Got a Gun" came out of left field. It is rare for us to do a song about anything other than fucking or sucking but this one dealt with child abuse.'

Having rehearsed in January 1989 in a Massachusetts recording studio, the band quit wintry Boston and headed for Little Mountain Sound Studios in Vancouver, Canada, to begin work again with producer Bruce Fairbairn. Tyler was champing at the bit to see how the fruits of all his labour would flourish. Events in his private life were also challenging.

On 6 March, Teresa gave birth to a baby girl they named Chelsea Anna Tallarico. Steven had now had three daughters to three different women in the past twelve years. In his relationship with Teresa, Tyler had not always played it straight. With his trademark candour, he has confessed publicly that he went through a spell of being unfaithful, and gave a stark explanation for cheating on a woman whom he knew had shown him enormous devotion. Referring to all those years he had been drugged to the point of collapse, he expressed a deep frustration that he had missed out on too many girls who had offered themselves to him. When he beat his addiction to drink and drugs, it was a feeling that he acted upon. He declared: 'When I got sober, I started to fuck everything that walked.' Having got married seemed only to increase his attraction, and women made flagrant moves on him. That Teresa hung on in there as this tough spell ran its course is something Tyler was grateful for. He said: 'My wife was with me at the tail end of my addiction when I was living at the Gorham hotel. We shared the madness back then and she shares in my madness now.' At a point in the late 1980s/early 1990s, Steven underwent psychological evaluation in a clinic which sought to help him understand the reasons he had become a drug addict and an alcoholic. This had involved long intensive discussions about his life. Though suspicious of the tendency among therapists to blame everything on a patient's upbringing, at the end of this assessment he said he felt that it had helped.

It was less pleasing by spring that clashes were erupting at Little Mountain Sound Studio. Steven knew the value of having experienced people such as producer Bruce Fairbairn and A & R man John Kalodner involved in this new album, but Aerosmith had changed since making *Permanent Vacation*. That album's success and their strengthening health and sobriety had restored the band's confidence. The five men were harder to handle in the sense that they once more had a strong vision of what they wanted and were capable of doing; it did not come naturally to them to give ground to others whose job it was to keep Aerosmith firmly on track to even headier heights. Steven was passionate about his lyrics and did not want to hear it when the Geffen Records executive tried to persuade him to omit or alter certain words to ensure that the songs were palatable enough to draw the all-important commercial radio airplay. Arguments broke out in the studio as these matters were thrashed out before recording wrapped in June.

In summer 1989, Bon Jovi were one of the world's biggest bands, and were on the road supporting their hit album, *New Jersey*. That August, having headlined the Moscow Music Peace Festival at the Lenin Stadium, they flew to the UK to play some dates, including one at the Milton Keynes Bowl in Buckinghamshire. Five years earlier, on Bon Jovi's first British tour backing Kiss, Jon Bon Jovi had come under attack from critics with one reviewer dubbing him a 'juvenile Steven Tyler'. Although an absurd description, in essence comparisons to Steven had not affronted Jon. He remembered having avidly watched Tyler perform around the New Jersey shore clubs in the 1970s, and he did not argue with the notion that he had subliminally absorbed a smidgen of the flamboyant frontman's stage style. Steven and Jon's paths had crossed a few times over the years and each star respected the other. So, when Steven and Joe Perry went to Britain that summer they attended Bon Jovi's Milton Keynes gig and ended up joining the New Jersey rockers for an encore, blasting their way through a memorable rendition of 'Walk This Way'.

In America, Aerosmith's new single, 'Love in an Elevator', was released. Delivered by Tyler at his usual break-neck pace, the rock song was accompanied by a video that oozed lust from start to finish. It contained stage performance shots with Steven lasciviously thrusting his way through the raucous number, and cutaway shots depicting steamy goings-on in a department store elevator. Dummies wearing bikinis came alive as busty, cavorting models when no one was looking, and Steven played tonsil tennis with a willing shop assistant. The single peaked at number five on Billboard and dropped anchor in the UK at number thirteen. When *Pump* followed in September, the eagerly awaited album attracted Aerosmith's best reviews yet. Its darker, more thought-provoking subject matter found widespread favour, and the new layers in Steven's lyrics earned him high acclaim. In Britain, *Pump* hit number three, while the album stopped at number five in the US but it went multi-platinum, stayed on the charts for over two years and became the fourth bestselling album of 1990.

Aerosmith's stock was rising; sixteen years on from releasing their eponymous album, they were rapidly reaching the realms of elder statesmen in rock. The band provided instruments, stagewear and memorabilia to Boston's Hard Rock Café, which created a wall display dubbed the Aerosmithonian. The Rolling Stones, meanwhile, were on their *Steel Wheels* tour of America, and that October on MTV Mick Jagger had jokingly included Aerosmith among possible opening acts for his band. Talking of Jagger's remarks, Tyler told *Rolling Stone*: 'He was being fa-cetious. I wanted to smack him!' That Tyler was jesting was clear when he got the chance to meet up with Jagger when the Stones' tour hit the east coast, and the two frontmen greeted each other warmly. For Steven, it was surreal. It did not seem so long ago that he was the skinny, hyperactive youth who would hang around outside New York clubs, hoping for a glimpse of the legendary Rolling Stone singer. To be meeting Mick Jagger on equal terms took a bit of getting used to.

Tyler's thoughts quickly switched to Aerosmith's tour plans. What would become a massive worldwide undertaking kicked off in Europe in October 1989. Steven's enthusiasm knew no bounds. He stated: 'The positive response to our music is what keeps it exciting for us and we have come to realise that we're musicians first and foremost and we still love playing together night after night.' In mid-November, Aerosmith played a nine-date UK leg, their first live British concerts since 1977. When they performed at London's Hammersmith Odeon, they were joined on stage by Whitesnake's frontman, David Coverdale, who duetted with Steven on the Beatles number, 'I'm Down'.

Right then, the second single to be released from *Pump* was 'Janie's Got a Gun' accompanied by a dark video depicting the raw emotions redolent in this song. The single did not register in Britain but peaked early in the new year on the US chart at number four. Steven dubbed 'Janie's Got a Gun' as the toughest song he had written. That said, it was very important to him to fire a warning shot across the critics' bows, and he stressed: 'I don't mean to take the piss out of my lyrics on "Janie's Got a Gun", or of how people would like to hear something deep but it really is only rock 'n' roll!' Joe Perry, too, insisted that Aerosmith had not become an 'issues' band – that Steven had not set out to write a message song. That preserve, he felt, was more the domain of Bruce Springsteen and Bob Dylan. 'It was interesting doing the song and getting the reaction we did,' said Joe, going on to vent his opinion on the way the two singles' videos had been received. The groundbreaking video for 'Janie's Got a Gun', directed by David Fincher, was gruesome in places and disturbingly insinuated the incestuous rape contained in the song's lyrics. It also contained an emotionally brutal scene where the character of 'Janie' shoots her abusive father at close quarters. Said Joe: 'It blows my mind. You get oohs and ahs about the half-naked girl in the "Love in an Elevator" video. Then when "Janie" kills her father, blows his brains out over the table, no one raises an eyebrow! Some people's attitude to life sucks.'

Aerosmith returned home before the end of the year to commence the first US leg of this global trot, having taken Skid Row on board as their support act. At the Civic Center in Springfield, Massachusetts, the atmosphere became overheated and missiles went flying – both ways. Though it is far from unknown for bands to be pelted on stage, it is less common for an artist to retaliate. Skid Row's lead singer, Sebastian Bach, was apparently struck on the head by a bottle, and there did seem to be provocation coming from a particular section of the excitable crowd. On impulse, Sebastian Bach tossed a bottle back into the audience and it, in turn, struck someone. The upshot was that Bach pleaded not guilty to assault charges at Hampden County Superior Court in Massachusetts. The tour moved on, and when Aerosmith played three sold-out shows at the Boston Garden, generous fans came with canned food donations – twenty tons worth in all – which was passed on at Christmas to the Boston Food Bank.

Aerosmith won the 1989 Boston Music Award for Outstanding Rock Band of the Year. They also earned two award nominations: the 1989 Grammy Award nomination for Best Rock Performance by a Duo or Group with Vocal for 'Love In An Elevator', and the 1989 MTV Video Music Award nomination for Best Heavy Metal Video for 'Rag Doll'. In mid-February 1990, Aerosmith appeared on NBC TV's top-rated show *Saturday Night Live*, with Steven and the others hamming it up in a wacky skit alongside Mike Myers and Dana Carvey. They also performed two new numbers, 'Monkey On My Back' and 'Janie's Got a Gun'. 'Dude (Looks Like a Lady)' was reissued in Britain, where it reached the Top 20. Then, on 6 March, Aerosmith was inducted into Hollywood's Rock Walk on Sunset Boulevard in Los Angeles. Two days later, *Rolling Stone*'s Critics Award for the Best Heavy Metal Band of 1989 went to Aerosmith – all of which recognition helped Steven to enjoy three sell-out dates at the Great Western

Forum in Inglewood, California. With the award season in full swing, Tyler saw his band mop up, taking five trophies at the Boston Music Awards, including the Outstanding Pop/Rock Album Award for *Pump* and Outstanding Song/Songwriter Award for 'Janie's Got a Gun', and four prizes in Britain when in March 1990 at the *Kerrang* Readers Poll Awards, Aerosmith walked off with the top honours for Best Band, Best Album (*Pump*), Best Tour/Live Gig and Best Male Singer.

In April, 'What It Takes' peaked at number nine on Billboard's singles chart. After a brief respite, Aerosmith's world tour resumed with a second US leg. By late spring, with Chelsea just past her first birthday, Steven's wife Teresa learned that she was pregnant again. That summer, Steven's eleven-year-old daughter Mia, living with Cyrinda in New York, enrolled at Manhattan's Professional Children's School. Twelve-year-old Liv, also in New York, attended York Prep.

Plying his trade on the road, Tyler concentrated on further developing his stagecraft as Aerosmith ricocheted around America and Canada, playing at the end of June at the Skydome in Toronto on a heavy metal bill that included the Black Crowes, Metallica and Warrant. The final single from *Pump*, 'The Other Side', was released and peaked at number twenty-two in America, taking longer in Britain to stall just inside the top fifty. At the end of July, this second leg of the *Pump* tour closed with a gig at the Capital Center in Landover, Maryland, when the band's short break allowed Steven to return to the pregnant Teresa and their baby daughter.

Soon, however, Steven had to hit the live circuit again, playing gigs in the UK and Europe. Most notably, he was looking forward to taking part in mid-August 1990 in the Monsters of Rock Festival held at Castle Donington in Leicestershire. The village lies north of East Midlands airport, and in a huge field nearby 72,500 rock fans gathered to enjoy Whitesnake, Poison, the London Quireboys, Thunder and Aerosmith. It had been thirteen years since Aerosmith last played at an outdoor British rock festival, in Reading, and they were second to Whitesnake on this

Donington bill. 'From where we are at the moment in Europe, I don't think that we are big enough to headline that event,' confessed Joe Perry at the time. 'We will be next year but at the moment [in Britain] we're doing big halls.' Tyler was confident that Aerosmith would connect with the new wave of heavy metal UK fans. He said: 'I don't feel an age gap with music fans but then again, we don't create one. You have to be in touch with what younger fans are going through in their lives and I think we are. Anyone can write mature songs. It's harder to write songs about what you really are and we're all kids at heart!'

To Tyler's delight, during their performance at Donington, Aerosmith was joined on stage by one of their all-time heroes, Jimmy Page, who accompanied them on a rendition of the 1965 Yardbirds classic, 'Train Kept A-Rollin'. Led Zeppelin's famed lead guitarist again jammed with Aerosmith on stage when, two nights later, they played at the Marquee Club in London before a few hundred people. Festival appearances also featured in Europe as the weeks rolled on – at the Swiss music festival in Winterthur, and the Super Rock '90 Festival in Mannheim, Germany, again alongside Whitesnake and Poison, among other bands.

Aerosmith had returned to America when, on 7 September, at the seventh MTV Video Music Awards, they won two trophies – Best Metal/Hard Rock Video and Viewers Choice Award, both for 'Janie's Got a Gun'. With just time to headline at the opening night of the Las Vegas Hard Rock Café, Steven and his band-mates took the *Pump* tour next to the Far East and Australia. From the stage each night, Steven loved to see the blend of ages coming to enjoy his band. Older fans tended to be content to sit further back, to listen and absorb, while the younger rock fanatics still crushed at the front, reaching up at his legs just out of their grasp, and Steven thrived on being able to reward fans by injecting even more zest into his performance. Joe Perry also vouched for the benefits of the new health-conscious regime they were all loyally sticking to. He stated bluntly: 'I'm not spending the whole day of a show looking for drug dealers.' That autumn,

Aerosmith appeared on the MTV Unplugged series, performing at New York's Ed Sullivan Theatre. Then in October, having played 163 gigs to over three million fans spread across fifteen countries, Aerosmith's mammoth *Pump* tour came to an end in Australia. They were one of the top three highest grossing US live acts of 1990, raking in in excess of $25 million in concert ticket sales alone. Aptly, 'What It Takes' in late December won the Top Album Rock Track category in Billboard's Year in Music Awards.

The year 1991 kicked off with the birth on 31 January of Steven's first son, whom he and Teresa named Taj Monroe Tallarico. Steven was present at the birth, and cut the umbilical cord. Now the father of four, clean and sober, the forty-two-year-old star must have wondered – having had a rollercoaster life himself during which he had diced with death at times – just how each of his children would turn out. His own ethos, he has often stated, was: 'I would rather grow up wrong, than be right in someone else's eyes.' As his offspring grew up, though, it would naturally be hard sometimes for Steven *not* to try to give them the benefit of his experiences, and an appreciation of how taking wrong turns can seriously screw up your world.

There were no shadows in the first quarter of the new year – only happiness and yet more success for the band. Aerosmith picked up two American Music Awards for Favourite Pop/Rock Band, Duo or Group and Favourite Heavy Metal/Hard Rock Artist. They were named Best Band in *Rolling Stone*'s Readers Picks Awards and on 20 February the band won its first Grammy Award when 'Janie's Got a Gun' took the trophy for Best Rock Performance by a Duo or Group with Vocal.

Although Steven had two infants at home to keep him on his toes, he kept in touch with his elder daughters, Liv and Mia. The girls had the kind of up-and-down friendship many sisters do. Two very different personalities and independent spirits were bound to make for a lively interaction, with the young girls sometimes competing for their father's attention. Looking on, Cyrinda sometimes felt that Liv, at least on the surface, had more confidence than Mia and enjoyed good-naturedly ribbing her half-sister that she looked more like Steven than she did. Mia had only ever known Steven as Dad, and it felt strange to hear Liv speak of him in that way. It was no more than sisterly rivalry, which levelled out in time.

In July, when Liv turned fourteen, it became public knowledge that Steven Tyler was her natural father. With Aerosmith one of America's biggest rock bands, it was also going to help having taken the Tyler name, for in about a year's time Liv would make a bid to break into the modelling world, with her mother acting as her manager.

Steven and the band had been working on new material at Little Mountain Sound Studio in Vancouver alongside producer Bruce Fairbairn. Although still signed to Geffen Records, in late summer Aerosmith closed a $30 million deal with Sony which would come into effect in 1995. When this was announced to the press in September, it was revealed that a generous royalty rate had also been agreed. This multi-million-dollar record deal established them even more firmly amid rock music's top strata. Sony now owned Aerosmith's original record label, Columbia Records.

In an industry driven by youth, rock journalists were quick to point out that by the time this highly lucrative deal came into effect Steven Tyler would be forty-seven. Such talk only sharpened Tyler's ambition to prove to these sceptics that he and his band still had a great deal more to offer. Aerosmith had just got the wind back beneath their wings for the 1990s, and Steven was determined to stay at the top. That was publicly. Privately, Steven did not let his feet leave the ground. A $30 million deal sounded a fantastic sum of money but, in reality, Sony did not actually hand over that sum on signature; $30 million was worked out as being *potentially* what the record deal was worth.

At the annual MTV Video Music Awards 'The Other Side' picked off the Best Metal/Hard Rock Video Award, and 'Janie's Got a Gun' continued to claw in trophies to add to Aerosmith's growing collection. Their celebrated association with the adopted hometown was further recognised on 14 November, when the band was inducted into the Boston Garden Hall of Fame. Just a week later, Aerosmith lapped up the accolade of a guest appearance in *The Simpsons*, performing 'Walk This Way' at Moe's Tavern in the episode titled 'Flaming Moe's'. On 3 December 1991, Aerosmith took part in MTV's tenth anniversary celebrations, having previously been filmed performing their power ballad, 'Dream On', accompanied by a full orchestra conducted by Michael Kamen.

Over the years, Columbia Records had periodically released Aerosmith compilation albums: *Aerosmith's Greatest Hits*; *Classics Live*; *Classics Live II* and *Gems*. Before the end of the year, Columbia brought out a fifty-two track three CD set titled *Pandora's Box*. Exquisitely packaged, this collection was a mix of early Aerosmith numbers, live performances and some previously unreleased tracks from the band's first decade together; it reached number forty-five in the US album chart.

The multi-million-selling album, *Permanent Vacation*, had been franked by the phenomenal success of *Pump*, and Aerosmith's recent world tour cemented the band's remarkable resurrection. From having stared into the abyss, all five had fought major battles on several fronts to become an award-laden rock band on its best ever footing, and no one was in the mood to take a breather.

Steven was impatient to push on. The work that was under way on new material was stimulating but still fluid, and he enjoyed discovering where his creativity was going to take him next. He could not view an album as a single entity. Each idea, every song, had its own individual importance and could not be corrupted to form a pattern. On the other hand, seeing how a song collection could stitch together to create a cohesive album was rewarding in itself.

Having successfully scaled the heights again, Aerosmith was a source of fascination to the music media and an inspiration to a new generation of rock stars, some of whom already looked ripe to fall by the wayside. Steven was often asked if he would give the young turks the benefit of his experience. It was a strange situation. Although he knew that he was immensely fortunate to have survived his descent into addiction hell, and was constantly aware of having to keep the tightest grip on his recovery, in a certain sense he could not hand on heart totally regret the path he had taken in life, because it had all been an intrinsic part of his nature. Not a man to navel-gaze, he still knows that he can be hypersensitive and that his emotions often spill over in different ways – through his highly demonstrative manner, his volatile temper and in the way he pours his feelings nakedly into his lyrics. Having fought his way back into the rock game, he had every intention of grabbing the ball and running full tilt with it.

# CHAPTER 11

# When Size Really Does Matter

'IF WE hang ourselves, it's going to be on the tree of creativity,' declared Steven. He was certainly suffering for his art during the long and arduous process of finding the follow-up to *Pump*. Managing to nail songs was frustratingly elusive, and when Aerosmith went into A & M Studios in Los Angeles to start recording with producer Bruce Fairbairn in December 1991, problems only worsened. In many ways it might have been expected that the more firmly Aerosmith had their feet back on the ground, the more they would want to wrest total control of the reins. This caused power struggles and tense arguments between the band, its management and the record company. Unable to bottle things up, Steven singled himself out by making his feelings on the issue more clear than the others. He, in turn, came in for vocal criticism from some band members, who felt that the songs he was coming up with were unacceptably sexist. Tyler's risqué style of lyrics has always been one of Aerosmith's hallmarks, but this time they were felt to be too near the knuckle. Tyler did not agree; he made no bones about his enjoyment of sex, nor of his opinion that no matter how people like to deny it, sex makes the world go round. As if to emphasise his stance, he bluntly claimed that he would only cease singing and writing about sex the day he wakes up in the morning, as he put it, 'without a hard-on'.

He had been dubbed immature and a sex addict, and although he did not appreciate either tag, he let such barbs glance off him. Come March 1992, however, he reacted strongly when John Kalodner told Aerosmith that he disliked the material so much that the album would have to be rewritten. Kalodner knew that the band had genuinely worked hard all winter but he had serious difficulty stomaching those lyrics that were devoid of Tyler's usual tongue-in-cheek humour. He felt strongly enough about this issue that he was prepared to dissociate himself from the material. Steven was infuriated, feeling that manager Tim Collins could have been more openly supportive of the band over the issue. Although things got unpleasant and heated, everyone involved only wanted the best for Aerosmith – they just differed on how that could be achieved. Kalodner suspected that the band was not always comfortable with the degree to which he had a say in what happened on their albums, but the experienced A & R man would not budge. He wanted new songs written, and to draft in outside professional lyricists again. Disliking anything that remotely smacked of an ultimatum, initially Steven was livid but inwardly uncertainty set in. One night he would listen to the material and like it, the next night he would be left wondering if some songs worked after all. Despite the fact that some in the band had nursed doubts about certain numbers, actually being sent back to the drawing board by Geffen Records stunned them all. Brad Whitford felt this setback was bound to be sounding alarm bells at Sony, who had recently inked a $30 million deal with Aerosmith. When the material to hand was subjected to intense scrutiny, about five songs survived and Tyler had to just let go of the others.

Away from the cauldron of the recording studio, Steven continued to work on his physical health and fitness. He was kept busy carrying out interviews and would subject himself to marathon photo shoots. Socially, if ever he fell into the company of those getting high on drugs he found the strength to turn around quietly and walk out – to take himself away from temptation. He knew that he needed to be alert and in top form for when he and the others headed to Vancouver to concentrate on creating material that everyone, this time around, could believe in.

Steven and Joe Perry lived about five miles apart, and as summer 1992 progressed they shuttled back and forth between their houses, bent on crystallising their ideas. They were set to work with songwriters Jack Blades, Tommy Shaw, Taylor Rhodes and Mark Hudson, and were also reunited with Desmond Child and Jim Vallance. Said Steven: 'It opens up another door. I thought in the beginning: writing with somebody else? There goes our sound – but that is not what it's all about. You don't go in there to write, say, a Jack Blades song.' John Kalodner had feared that, in the present testy climate, the band might not easily accept external contributions, but productivity proved rewarding. No one looked for any great bonding or social involvement. Collaborators came to Steven and Joe, spent a day or so working on numbers and then they went their separate ways.

To Tyler, the secret was to write more than double the number of songs needed to comprise an album. Usually, he only had a couple of numbers that never made it; top of his selection criteria was to consider how a song would stand up when played live. A song had to be able to energise a crowd and himself, singing it at gig after gig. The upshot of all this industry was a richly diverse musical mosaic.

Steven and Joe teamed up with Jack Blades and Tommy Shaw to come up with a pacy number called 'Shut Up and Dance', which to Tyler smacked of rock and roll, Brits style – distinct, he feels, from Americans' understanding of this genre. He particularly liked the ballsy attitude in the song, and of performing the number he declared: 'It's such a rush, stronger than any drug that I ever took.' Joe stated: 'We wrote "Shut Up and Dance" because we're entertainers. We're supposed to take you away for an hour and a half, or for five minutes.' 'Eat the Rich', co-written with Jim Vallance, was also a slick rock and roll song. 'Gotta Love

It', created by Steven, Joe and Mark Hudson, was a rhythm and blues number that had the power to send Tyler on a drug-free trip, as did the similarly influenced 'Fever', the only Tyler/Perry collaboration in this collection.

'Get a Grip' was another collaboration between Tyler, Perry and Jim Vallance, as was an instrumental called 'Boogie Man'. Lenny Kravitz guested on 'Line Up' and Eagles drummer Don Henley provided distinctive backing vocals to 'Amazing', an emotive rock ballad that Steven had written with an old friend, Richie Supa. It had had its dangers co-writing a song with someone from his days of excessive drug taking and of spiralling out of control. Steven had been very conscious till then of needing to isolate himself from reminders of those times; it was a measure of how much stronger he felt he had become that he could not only work with his old friend but also come up with arguably his most autobiographical song yet.

One of the most unusual results came from creating the song 'Flesh', on which Steven worked with Joe and Desmond Child. This song has been dubbed a weird S & M trip. Steven had not written anything like it with Child before. This departure in style for a lyricist more prone to helping rock stars write commercial power ballads stemmed from when Joe had come up with a guitar riff which evoked an unnerving darkness and reeked of sleazy adult themes. By Perry's own admission the song seemed to delve down strange alleys which Steven and Desmond were lured to explore. Tyler was as surprised as Child at the way it worked out.

'Crazy', Desmond Child's other collaboration with the Aerosmith pair, was a belter of a bluesy ballad, more in keeping with expectations. Said Joe: 'That title probably summed up our career. "Crazy" has a cool rhythm and blues feel to it. I get a real kick out of playing this one live.' 'Crazy' featured Steven's signature harmonica playing, which also punctuated to great effect the other power ballad in the pack, 'Cryin', written by Tyler and Perry with songwriter Taylor Rhodes. Steven cheekily quipped that 'Cryin' was 'the only song I ever got away with that's about a blow job!' In a more serious vein, Joe explained: 'Taylor writes songs from a different angle to us, which gives "Cryin'" a fresh perspective.' Aerosmith had frequently been accused of projecting a Neanderthal mentality in their songs. Said Perry: 'The Stone Temple Pilots said that we were sexist. So we thought: "Fuck it. We'll show 'em!"' The lead guitarist's solo composition was a number called 'Walk on Down', on which Joe sang lead vocal.

Although 'Crazy' and 'Cryin' were almost guaranteed to be hit songs, the number which rose like cream to the top was 'Livin' on the Edge', on which Steven and Joe worked with Mark Hudson. Steven had wanted to steer the boat into unusual waters, and 'Livin' on the Edge' joined 'Janie's Got a Gun' as one of the band's rare forays into social issues. The song was inspired by the fact that America was a tinderbox of civil unrest, which ignited in late April 1992 with three days and nights of race riots in Los Angeles. Four white policemen had just been acquitted of criminal wrongdoing in the case of black motorist Rodney King, whose beating by the officers the year before had been captured on videotape. Tyler knew that they had something special with this song. With an attention-grabbing opener, during which Steven's vocals were deeper register than almost ever heard from him, the number erupts into a thumping hard rock song that takes twists and turns and cleverly changes tempo throughout.

Beginning in October 1992, recording stretched into January, by the end of which Aerosmith had their album in the can. They titled it *Get a Grip*, and along with joy and relief, there was nervous tension. It had been four years since *Pump*'s release and in that time it had become public knowledge that the band's first work on the new album had been rejected by Geffen Records, that they had been sent back into the trenches to collaborate with outside songwriters. So a question mark hung over their heads with music journalists, who were quick to query whether Aerosmith could still cut it – particularly since, in the intervening years, the music scene had changed.

The Aids issue had been shoved to the fore by Freddie Mercury's death in November 1991. The hedonistic, reckless rock world, which had thus far preferred to ignore 'the Aids thing', had suddenly been forced to confront its glitzy but thoughtless way of life. As it fell back on its heels a while, through the centre had emerged a new, low-key, scruffy, alternative rock movement dubbed grunge. A blend of pop metal and a resurrected 1990s version of punk rock, its first exponents were Seattle bands, notably Nirvana, fronted by Kurt Cobain. The high critical acclaim afforded to Nirvana's late 1991 hit album, *Nevermind*, and its spin-off single, 'Smells Like Teen Spirit', had lit the way for the likes of Soundgarden and Pearl Jam. Aerosmith was coming out with its new album at the height of the grunge rock wave, and would have to produce something really special to appeal to critics who only had ears for music from the current grunge trend.

Steven was acutely conscious of the stark contrast between the deliberately downbeat, scarcely moving stage style of grunge bands and the colourful high-octane rock entertainment that Aerosmith personified. He knew that he could not stand still on stage if his life depended upon it – it is in his blood to throw his body around in performance – and Joe Perry was alive to the danger that in 'coming back', a band like theirs ran a huge risk in changing times of looking like a caricature of itself. Steven, though, refused to stand aside and see these grunge bands as the latest spokesmen for a generation.

In April 1993, 'Livin' on the Edge' was the first single to be released from *Get a Grip*. It peaked in America at number eighteen, one place higher than its best performance on the UK singles chart. The song's amazing video had been filmed at Culver City Studios near Los Angeles, and to match the number's unusual start the first shot of Steven is breathtakingly dramatic. With the right side of his face and body painted black, he stands naked, holding his genitals as a bilious green inner demon lunges out of his 'dark' side. There were scenes of roller-skating schoolgirls vandalising cars with hockey sticks, of pupils being scanned for weapons, and to keep the adrenalin pumping there was one particularly clever special effects scene involving Joe Perry. Playing lead guitar while standing on a snowy rail track as a freight train bears down on him from behind, he nonchalantly steps aside at the last second, still playing guitar. For other sequences, Steven had endured being spun back and forth, round and round and upside down while strapped spread-eagled on to a giant gyroscope. There was an oddly evil artistry which suited Tyler when, sheathed in a gauzy black costume, his heavy long black hair hanging about his face, he aims a cigarette holder elegantly into his mouth, his expressive eyes heavily surrounded by black make-up with tiny glittery mirrors stuck to his skin. It is a fantastically weird video, spliced with a visually and musically dynamic stage performance by the band, and Steven was charged with a frenetic energy throughout. He electrified the screen in whatever guise he appeared. Said Tom Hamilton: 'There was something that just came together on that video that, to me, made it so cool!'

Governor William Weld declared 13 April as 'Aerosmith Day' in the state of Massachusetts. Three weeks later, *Get a Grip* was released and became Aerosmith's first album to debut at number one in America's Billboard album chart. It also became the band's bestselling studio album worldwide, notching up sales in excess of twenty million copies. *Get a Grip* took the number two slot in the UK chart; rewardingly, Steven felt that this work encapsulated the best of everything he was creatively capable of giving at that time.

At the beginning of June 1993, Aerosmith kicked off a sixteen-month mammoth world tour at the Expocentre in Topeka, Kansas. They gigged around north America throughout the height of summer, when Steven's stamina and the band's stage mastery drew constant praise. Ira Robbins for *Newsday* wrote: 'Whatever it is that fuels Aerosmith's unforgettable fire after all these years, it must be plentifully stocked backstage. The band's live sets are only building more momentum as their new lifestyles fire them into a natural oblivion on stage.' There were those who were aching to take a swipe at Steven, and some young journalists confronted him with queries as to how a forty-five-year-old man could possibly imagine that he could still get away with singing songs like 'Young Lust'. Tyler succinctly pointed out that that song was not about him lecherously ogling underage girls. He also pointed out that he may be in his mid-forties but he did not look, feel or act it. Steven's daughter Mia was asked by one interviewer what it felt like seeing her middle-aged father clutching his genitals during his stage act. Her spontaneous response, revealing her natural discomfort with this public aspect of her father's life, did not immediately go down well with Steven.

'Eat the Rich' petered out at number thirty-four in Britain and did not chart in America, but recognition continued to mount in a variety of ways. Towards the end of August, Aerosmith received the inaugural star in Boston's Tower Records Walk of Fame – a large brass star bearing the band name was embedded into the shop's stair landing. On 2 September, at the MTV Video Music Awards, Aerosmith won the Viewers Choice Award for 'Livin' on the Edge', which they performed during the show. A month later, 'Cryin'' was released, peaking at number twelve at home and making the UK Top 20.

The video for this power ballad, depicting how a teenage girl exacts a unique form of revenge on her unfaithful boyfriend, again captured the music-loving public's imagination. Some scenes had been shot earlier in the year at the Central Congregational Church in Fall River, Massachusetts, when Steven's emotive delivery breathed extra dynamics into the number. Two young actors were drafted in to portray the main characters in the song's story. They were Stephen Dorff, who starred that year as the doomed original Beatle, Stuart Sutcliffe, in the feature film *Backbeat*, and a sixteen-year-old actress from San Francisco named Alicia Silverstone. The 'Cryin'' video became one of the most requested videos on MTV of 1993 and brought Alicia a degree of local fame. She later reflected: 'All of a sudden it was this huge thing. It was like: "There's the Aerosmith chick!" I was going through puberty.' Alicia would feature in two more Aerosmith videos for songs from *Get a Grip*, which strengthened her fame among MTV viewers.

Aerosmith once again appeared on *Saturday Night Live* before heading to Europe for a series of gigs, performing for the first time in some countries. Soaking up the undiluted adulation he received night after night, Steven curiously sought some anonymity, too, and on a free evening in Amsterdam he and Joe Perry took an acoustic guitar and went out busking on the street. Passers-by threw money into the open guitar case, oblivious of who was entertaining them. It tickled Tyler no end, and when he and Joe called it a night, they tipped their takings into a legitimate busker's case further along the road.

On 26 October 1993, Aerosmith performed live on MTV Europe for the first time. During this leg of their world tour Tyler realised that it was taking a little bit of time to warm up their audiences. Even though 'Cryin'' and 'Livin'' on the Edge' were instant favourites, they had to rejig their set to suit what European fans were familiar with from their back catalogue. Audiences undoubtedly have moods, and Steven was candid that while some shows ignited, others were less successful. Aerosmith hit Britain, playing at London's Wembley Arena in December. Back home, at the Billboard Music Awards, the band was voted the Number One Rock Artist.

By the time they arrived back in the States, 'Amazing' had dropped anchor at number twenty-four. Some in the music industry had been sceptical that Aerosmith could ever exceed the success achieved by *Pump*. *Get a Grip* proved those people wrong. Yet the band never seemed to feature in those endless Top 100 lists, which at times irked Steven. In Europe, he had happily busked unnoticed, but he never normally liked to be overlooked, as Joey Kramer has vouched. Out in public, Tyler loved talking with anybody and everybody, was never precious or pretentious, and thoroughly enjoyed being mobbed. What amused the drummer was that on the very rare occasions that the frontman was prowling the streets and no one realised he was in their midst, Tyler would do something outrageous to ensure he grabbed their attention.

After twenty years in the business Tyler still found the enthusiasm to wake up each day eager to see what else lay around the corner. He was very happy in his marriage to Teresa and as a father to their two children, Chelsea and Taj. Apart from the obvious reasons for refraining from adultery, now that the spectre of Aids loomed large he, like several other rock stars, viewed casual sex while touring as just too dangerous a caper. He knew that he had a wife who deeply adored him, knew too that he was still on a learning curve to becoming a selfless husband; while he had begun by appreciating her unswerving devotion when he had been down and out, he now admitted to loving Teresa more than ever.

After playing sold-out shows at the Boston Garden on New Year's Eve and New Year's Day, in January 1994 Tyler was thrilled for Aerosmith to be undertaking its first tour of South America. During this exotic leg of the *Get a Grip* world tour the band performed at the Hollywood Rock Festival in Rio de Janeiro in Brazil. Their own gigs also took them to Argentina and Mexico. It was an eventful trip, which threw up a few surprises for the experienced frontman. More than a decade earlier, on their first jaunt through Mexico, Queen had been bombarded on stage with boots, bottles, batteries and other hazardous missiles. Coming off stage thoroughly dejected, assuming that the audience had hated them, Queen were greeted by a local official gleefully explaining that, on the contrary, that ordeal was a traditional show of appreciation. In these humid climes, times had not changed and Steven was subjected at some gigs to fans in the front row spitting on him whenever he came near the lip of the stage. The promoter's assurance afterwards that it was well meant did little to excuse this disgusting behaviour.

Aerosmith opened their next north American leg of the tour on 1 February in Florida at the Orlando Arena; that same month they played an exhilarating gig to a sold-out, delirious crowd at New York's Madison Square Garden. Along the way, at the American Music Awards held at the Shrine Auditorium in Los Angeles, they picked up two trophies – Favourite Pop/Rock

Band, Duo or Group and Favourite Heavy Metal/Hard Rock Artist. In March, at the Grammy Awards at Radio City Music Hall in New York, Aerosmith performed 'Livin' on the Edge' and collected their second Grammy for Best Rock Performance by a Duo or Group with Vocal for this increasingly lauded number.

As the rock world had gathered to reward its brightest stars and to backslap each other, another casualty was lining up to make a tragically premature exit. Nirvana's troubled frontman, Kurt Cobain, had been in and out of rehab in 1993 and had over-dosed in a New York hotel suite. While in Italy in early March 1994, the twenty-seven-year-old singer downed a cocktail of prescription drugs, anaesthetic and champagne, and slipped into a coma. He was rushed to hospital, where his stomach was pumped, then transferred to the Rome American Hospital to recover. A week later, he was discharged. Towards the end of that month, back on US soil, Cobain checked himself once more into rehab, this time in California, only to check himself out three days later. On 5 April, he shot himself with a Remington 20-gauge shotgun, in a room above the garage at his home in Seattle, Washington. His body was not discovered for three days. His suicide note quoted the Neil Young lyrics, 'It's better to burn out than to fade away.' Steven felt heart-sore for the young man. He stated: 'When Kurt Cobain did videos, look into his eyes – he could not even face the camera. He was in pain. I'm angry about Kurt. This guy didn't have to die.' The same could have been said about Brian Jones, Jimi Hendrix and Jim Morrison, all of whom, curiously enough, were also just twenty-seven years old when their lives were snuffed out.

In late April, Tyler set sadness aside to enrapture Japanese fans when Aerosmith's world tour took the band to the Far East. They opened at the Yokohama Arena in Yokohama and wrapped up this leg in mid-May at the Budokan in Tokyo. Thoughts now turned to the European and UK dates that were next on the agenda. On 4 June, Aerosmith fulfilled Perry's prophecy and this time headlined at the annual Monsters of Rock Festival at Donington Park in Leicestershire. Said Joe: 'It really means a lot to us to play at Donington. It's one of the few festivals – one of the last ones – that's like a tradition. It's like a fabled gig.' The support bill included Sepultura, dubbed 'Sao Paulo's angriest young men'. Aerosmith had played with them on a bill in Rio de Janeiro but had not actually caught their act. That night, at Donington, before ripping into a hard rock set of their best-loved hits, Tyler had that split second of disorientation when, walking out on stage before tens of thousands of people, he could hardly grasp that anyone was there. Particularly at night, with the bright stage lights in his eyes, it can feel momentarily as if he is completely alone. That night Aerosmith turned in a stupendous performance and Steven was described next day in *The Times*' report of the gig as 'a glamorous stick insect'. A spectacular pyrotechnic finale capped the night, sending the fans home happy. The fifth single released from *Get a Grip*, the rocker 'Shut Up and Dance', was released in July in Britain where it peaked at number twenty-four.

Towards the end of that month the power ballad 'Crazy', the final single from *Get a Grip*, was released. Reaching one place higher than 'Shut Up and Dance' in the British charts, it lodged at number seventeen in America. Its video featured the third appearance of Alicia Silverstone (she had also featured in the video for 'Amazing') and marked the career screen debut of Steven's eldest daughter, Liv.

At 5'10" tall, the beautiful, dark-haired girl had successfully eased her way into the modelling scene at fifteen; in addition to appearing on the covers of teen magazines she had starred in commercials for make-up and for shampoo. The 'Crazy' video makers maintained that she landed the part because of how she had looked and come across on screen in an advert for Pantene shampoo, and that they had not known of her connection to the world-famous Steven Tyler.

The theme of the video, which became one of the most requested on MTV of 1994, was two schoolgirls playing truant, taking off in an open-topped car and basically turning any man they met into putty in their hands, but it was more noted for two specific aspects. One was the suggestion of teenage lesbian romance between the characters portrayed by Liv Tyler and Alicia Silverstone. According to Steven, the original version of the video graphically depicted lesbianism, but on consideration it was decided to tame that element down before its release. Said Liv: 'I understand why people might have a problem with it but I have no problem with it, Steven has no problem with it and if other people have a problem with it, that's their problem.' Then there were the scenes where the girls decide to enter an amateur pole-dancing competition for the $500 prize money. This scene was Liv's spotlight moment. Dressed in silver trousers and bra she very visibly became her father's daughter on stage; spitting out a piece of chewing gum, with a leggy high kick she whirled off seamlessly into a slinky, sinuous stage act, plunging her fingers into her long hair and oozing scintillating sexuality.

Years later the 'Crazy' video ranked number twenty-three in VH1's Top 100 Music Videos of All Time. In March 1995, 'Crazy' won Aerosmith their third Grammy Award for Best Rock Performance by a Duo or Group with Vocal. When Liv was filming the pole-dancing scenes someone had called out to her to give the camera 'a little more ass' – a risky request with her protective father around.

Steven and Liv continued to enjoy a special father/daughter relationship. Affectionately, Liv has maintained: 'I can smell my dad from a mile away. He has this ambery smell that just melts into him.' Liv would visit with her father and whenever they could not sleep, they would sit up all night discussing face creams and the like. Liv must be about the only girl who could – or would want to – purloin a pair of her snake-hipped father's jeans!

Having modelled for less than one year, Liv turned her sights on acting, and stepped determinedly into that tough industry. She later confessed: 'I had never been to an acting class in my life.' Yet in 1994, at seventeen years old, Liv was cast in the psychological thriller *Silent Fall*, written by Akiva Goldsman, directed by Bruce Beresford and starring Richard Dreyfuss and

Linda Hamilton. In the early days of Liv's acting career, film
critics nicknamed her Liv Taylor because with her dark hair and
blue eyes she apparently reminded them of the legendary
Hollywood star Elizabeth Taylor. Liv commented bluntly: 'It's
cool to be compared to her but, honestly, who gives a damn?'
Steven was immensely proud to see his eldest child set out on
this career path.

On his own front, Aerosmith played more dates that summer,
took a brief break, then hit the road again. Twenty-five years
earlier, as a twenty-one-year-old bombed out of his skull, along
with hundreds of thousands of rock fans, Tyler had attended the
fabled Woodstock festival in Bethel. In 1994, Aerosmith headlined Woodstock II, held between 12 and 14 August at Winston
Farm in Saugerties, New York. Over thirty acts took part in this
festival, including Joe Cocker, Nine Inch Nails, Green Day, the
Spin Doctors and Red Hot Chili Peppers. Having shunned the
original 1969 event, Bob Dylan performed on the third day of
this musical extravaganza. Tyler led his band through knockout
renditions of 'Dude (Looks Like a Lady)', 'Walk This Way', 'Love
In an Elevator', 'Janie's Got a Gun' and 'Livin' on the Edge',
among others, radiating an intensity that made his wired audience forget their mud-caked condition. For the hundreds of
thousands of people, the amazing finale was crowned by an
impressive fireworks display.

Aerosmith hung around New York to attend the MTV Video
Music Awards held this year at the Radio City Music Hall on 8
September. Nominated in nine categories, the band won three
trophies, all for 'Cryin' – Best Group Video, Viewers Choice
Award and the coveted Best Video of the Year. Tyler made their
acceptance speeches and later displayed to photographers the
lipstick imprint on his left cheek of the kiss he had received from
Madonna.

Neither Tyler nor any of his bandmates normally displayed
any political affiliations, but days after the MTV awards show, the
band hosted a fundraising event for the veteran Democrat
Senator Edward Kennedy at Brad Whitford's Massachusetts

home. Setting off on the final leg of their world tour then, the band trekked around several US states, pitching up in Texas, Arizona and California among other places.

November saw the release of the compilation album *Big Ones*. Chock-a-block with some of Aerosmith's best-loved hits, it also included two new songs – 'Blind Man', written by Steven and Joe with Taylor Rhodes, which had been recorded at New York's Power Station Studio, and 'Walk on Water', recorded on the Isle of Capri after the European leg of their tour. Said Joe: 'We wrote "Walk on Water" with Jack Blades and Tommy Shaw. We wanted to include a couple of new tracks on the record because it has worked so well for other artists recently.' *Big Ones* peaked at number six in America, one place higher than its best in Britain. It quickly went double platinum and fulfilled Aerosmith's contract with Geffen Records. Columbia Records simultaneously released the box set *Box of Fire*, comprising a CD of every Aerosmith album released by that label, as well as a CD of rare cuts.

That same month, at the inaugural MTV European Music Awards staged at the Pariser Platz in Berlin, Germany, Aerosmith made off with the Best Rock Band and Best Rock Act awards. Close to Christmas, the *Get a Grip* world tour finally came to an end. Although Steven was exhausted, he was up for the opening on 19 December of Mama Kin's Music Hall, a club on Lansdowne Street in Boston, which was co-owned by the band and the Lyons Group. Aerosmith performed before an audience of just under three hundred; it was picked up for live broadcast by two locally based radio stations. Boston continued its love affair with the band when, at the city's annual music awards, they won the Outstanding Rock Band of the Year award for the seventh consecutive year. They also collected the Right to Rock trophy, and Tyler took the prize for Best Male Vocalist.

By the end of 1994, Tyler was entitled to feel satisfied and was unwilling to be drawn on the secret of Aerosmith's success. It is difficult to think of any other hard rock outfit whose recording career had commenced in the early 1970s and was still at the top of its game, still with all its original members. Although Steven Tyler is the central focus, Aerosmith remains a democracy with every member integral to its success – five men with differing personalities that somehow gel. In the mid-nineties, Tyler's bond with Perry was stronger than ever. The pair were consistently photographed together in rock magazines, sometimes choosing to highlight hilariously the contrasts in their personalities. Joe is the epitome of cool and style, Steven an unpredictable vagabond prince. To accusations that Perry can often come across as sour-faced, the lead guitarist once retorted: 'Next to Steven, *anybody* looks moody!' During their recent world tour, Steven did whatever he could to avoid the shows becoming stale. He never wanted to feel that he was doing anything by rote. He had long ago honed his stage act to a T, but he did not lack ambition. He was not content simply to soak in thunderous applause, or to raise stadium girders with howling cheers and whistles. He claimed that one of his next goals in performance was for the audience to achieve 'multiple orgasms'!

# CHAPTER 12

# A Cat With Nine Lives

I N JANUARY 1995, Steven Tyler and Joe Perry inducted Led Zeppelin into the Rock and Roll Hall of Fame during a ceremony held at New York's Waldorf Astoria Hotel, later jamming on stage with Robert Plant, Jimmy Page and the late John Bonham's son, Jason, on drums. After this, Steven went on holiday with Teresa and their children. In spring his thoughts turned to songs for Aerosmith's first album under their new contract with Sony. Progress was steady, and once summer arrived Steven rewarded himself with a hunting holiday, reverting to a boyhood passion.

At the back of Steven's mind were concerns about the band's manager, Tim Collins, whose behaviour had become puzzling. The days when Aerosmith had needed an external hand on the tiller were gone. Like the others, Steven was clean of drugs, sober, focused and in command, so it was perplexing when their manager would tell them that he felt they were in danger of breaking up. It is said that Collins seemed to be in favour of the band undertaking further therapy, but Steven and the others could not see the need for it.

Sidelining this anomaly, as the year progressed Steven concentrated on coming up with fresh material. In addition to

working with Joe, to help inspire him he collaborated with lyricists Marti Frederiksen, Taylor Rhodes and Glen Ballard,
producing 'Something's Gotta Give', 'Full Circle' and 'Taste of
India'. Because it had been a while since the band had played
live, they road-tested the new material and re-oiled the wheels in
early November, performing as the G-Spots at the Middle East
club in Cambridge, Massachusetts. In the new year they flew to
Miami to bite the bullet and create their next album with Glen
Ballard as producer. Steven toiled at a hotel in the city's sophisticated South Beach district. He was joined by his friend,
songwriter Richie Supa, and two other former collaborators,
Mark Hudson and Desmond Child. As they knocked ideas
around, one song quickly emerged, called 'Kiss Your Past
Goodbye'.

As the jewel in Miami's crown, South Beach is a hot spot for
film and music stars, and boasts a vibrant nightlife scene amid
the bars and clubs along Ocean Drive. Sometimes, to unwind
after intensive songwriting sessions, the band gravitated to this
bustling environment, where Tyler was often hit on by buxom
young beauties eager to drape themselves around a guy whose
stock-in-trade was oozing flagrant sexuality. With a grin that
almost split his mobile face in half, he would happily pose for
photos. That was as far as he went, but rumours soon circulated
that he was living it up with women. Talk also surfaced that he
was doing drugs again, which was also untrue, but since trying
to deny these rumours would give them more oxygen, he chose
to ignore them and keep focused on the song collection that had
built up enough for the band to start work at Miami's Criteria
Studios.

In several ways, however, the situation was not good. Joey
Kramer's father had recently died; thrown into emotional
turmoil, the drummer needed time away from work. The unease
over manager Tim Collins was deepening. Aerosmith had not
recorded before with Glen Ballard, and so band and producer
were unfamiliar with each other's ways, and by now Steven had
been sitting with songs for so long that there was a real danger

of him losing impetus with the material. All this was against the irritating backdrop of ugly rumours continuing to circulate.

To help keep a sense of perspective, Tyler touched base often with his family. Liv had left school by now, while seventeen-year-old Mia had recently moved with her mother from New York's Madison Avenue to an apartment on East 68th Street. Come spring 1996, Teresa, Chelsea and Taj joined Steven in Miami. The presence of his wife in town helped to douse the rumours, but the working atmosphere remained strained. A stand-in drummer was found to hold up the absent Joey Kramer's end, but there was not always the sense that they were working as a cohesive unit. Despite this, unique songs were evolving from Tyler's chaotic creativity. Along with Richie Supa and Glen Ballard, Steven had come up with a number called 'Pink'; with Joe Perry and Desmond Child he had created 'Hole in My Soul' and 'Ain't That a Bitch'.

The satisfaction of knowing that a sound song collection was taking shape could not cancel out the fact that matters were coming to a head with Tim Collins. Years later, it was revealed just how difficult Aerosmith felt the situation had become. According to the band members, the manager would tell them to their faces that they were no longer in recovery; presumably Tim Collins believed the rumours flying around Miami. The way Tom Hamilton and Joey Kramer remember it, the manager also told them that Steven was considering their respective positions in the band, which was not the case. And to further muddy the waters, with the boot on the other foot, Steven's frazzled bandmates were apparently strongly urged by Tim Collins to write a letter to their frontman complaining about his behaviour. Joe Perry has described the letter as confrontational. All five in Aerosmith acknowledged that Tim Collins had been of enormous assistance to them at a given time, but they felt that the manager was now seeking to have too much control over their lives. They have since said that at times they felt manipulated and under an oppressive degree of scrutiny. For whatever reason, Tim Collins seems to have believed that Steven was spiralling out of control, but Joe Perry was adamant: 'I know what Steven looks like when he's fucked up. Even though there were times I might have been thinking, he's acting strangely today, I knew that he was not getting high.'

Troublesome and worrying as all this was, Collins finally crossed the line with Tyler when he telephoned Teresa and told her that Steven was being unfaithful to her with girls he encountered on South Beach. Teresa has recounted publicly how shocked she was to receive this telephone call at home. Tyler went ballistic. His temper snapped and he was so angry he quit Miami, along with the rest of the band. Two months later, at the end of July, Tim Collins was fired.

The ex-manager immediately went to the press, and at least two major US publications ran the story that Steven Tyler was suspected of using heroin and needed detox again. Once more, Steven was livid. This kind of coverage he could do well without and, considering that he was innocent of these charges, he also felt deeply aggrieved. In a calmer frame of mind, he did later try to figure out specifically how Tim Collins could have believed that he had begun to take heroin again. He eventually pinpointed one day in Criteria Studios in Miami when he and Joe had been arguing heatedly over a point – not an unusual occurrence. Nor was it strange that Steven had been ranting, as was his wont when passionately fired up about something. Steven believed that someone at the studio, new to his volatile ways, had rung round a few people claiming that he was acting like someone who was high on dope.

In any event, incensed by these newspaper and magazine stories, Tyler categorically denied having relapsed. He declared how proud he was to have stayed sober for ten years. 'I don't drink or do drugs because I don't want to and I like the me I am now,' he stated. 'I like being able to write songs and to be able to be with my kids.' Steven gave a lengthy interview to *Rolling Stone* in which he reiterated that he had not fallen off the wagon at any time in the past decade. Steven was, of course, conscious that Sony would not have much cared for this hugely negative publicity, and he was also acutely aware that such accusations rebounded on more than himself. He was particularly raw that it impacted on his youngest daughter, Chelsea. He revealed: 'She had a sleepover and one of the girls' mothers would not let her sleep over because: "Daddy was back on drugs." When your seven-year-old daughter says that to you . . .' To press queries as to whether he considered himself to be a drug addict, he replied that someone in recovery is *always* a drug addict, you just do not do drugs. It all made for a very difficult and distressing time when Tyler admitted that he found it incredibly hard-going trying to keep everything together and to remain creative. It became so bad while recording their new album that it could have threatened Aerosmith's existence. Recently reflecting on what he termed the 'nasty press' coverage at this time, Tom Hamilton said: 'It was really hard on the band emotionally. We probably came pretty close to saying: "Fuck it!"'

Time would be a healer regarding some aspects. As far as Tim Collins was concerned and the unfortunate manner in which their working relationship unravelled, Steven is still able to separate his anger over the endgame from his genuine gratitude to the manager for the vital role he had played in helping Aerosmith to get sober and back in the saddle as a successful, working band. That said, it was unquestionably true for Steven that after Tim Collins was fired, certain Aerosmith attitudes had the opportunity to resurface and for those and other reasons, he felt rejuvenated.

More changes occurred in summer 1996. Kevin Shirley replaced Glen Ballard as producer for the new album, and A & R man John Kalodner was back on the scene. Having spent some time in California after Miami, Aerosmith returned to Boston when, on 12 August, they issued a press statement that Wendy Laister, who had been working alongside Tim Collins, would be on their management team. Soon after that, they went into a New York recording studio to recut their album. Tyler knew it was of paramount importance that they shaped up to meet everyone's expectations, but he also maintained: 'I think bands get in trouble when they start over-thinking things – dare we do that, or we'll get a bad name, sort of thing. So we just did what we did.'

Even so, considering the accusations that had recently ricocheted around, it was a bold move when Steven, in partnership with Joe Perry, Mark Hudson and Steve Dudas, came up with 'The Farm', a number containing lyrics about a drug addict with a hypodermic needle sticking out of his arm. But not only was Tyler determined not to be restricted in his craft by false rumours or the pressure that stemmed from that, he was writing about something he knew all about, and was not glorifying drug addiction. Likewise, references to New York in the song were rooted in a fear he privately battled with, for there had been a period whenever he arrived in this city that his first action had been to go in search of a drug dealer.

Of the hard rock song 'Nine Lives', by Tyler, Perry and Marti Frederiksen, Joe said: 'We went to see AC/DC and that was the inspiration for that song. We came straight back and wrote "Nine Lives" and we'll keep doing that. We absorb stuff. We're not a band that says: "This is how it's got to be."' Another rock number, 'Falling in Love (Is Hard on the Knees)', saw Steven revert to his penchant for raunchy lyrics. Written in conjunction with Joe Perry and Glen Ballard, the title was inspired by a slogan Steven once saw on a car bumper sticker. Once again challenged on his taste for the near-the-knuckle lyrics of this particular number, he announced unrepentantly that it was like being 'in search of the perfect blow job'. In October, Aerosmith was named the Act of the Decade at the 1996 Boston Music Awards. A month later, recording ended on the new album, appropriately titled, considering Aerosmith's history, *Nine Lives*.

Part of Steven's past life reared its head around the start of the new year when his ex-wife, Cyrinda Foxe Tyler, published *Dream On, Livin' on the Edge with Steven Tyler and Aerosmith*. In this tell-all memoir, Cyrinda pulled no punches when recounting her version of her years with the frontman. In graphic detail, she laid bare some of the most intimate aspects of their relationship. Not long after the book was released, Cyrinda indicated that in the paperback edition she intended to include some nude photographs of Steven. At that point, Steven stepped in to object to this plan. Apparently, these revealing snaps were to have been passed to Steven when their divorce had been agreed in 1987. Steven initiated legal proceedings in order to prevent publication of these privately taken nude photographs, a lawsuit that dragged on for two years.

In February 1997, putting this personal issue behind him, Steven joined his bandmates to shoot the video for 'Falling in Love (Is Hard on the Knees)' in Los Angeles under the aegis of Michael Bay, who had directed the recently released action thriller, *The Rock*. This video was short of the sassy teenage temptresses previously depicted by the likes of Alicia Silverstone and Liv. Buttonholed as to why Liv did not appear in this video, Tyler joked that his daughter's professional fee now for such appearances would have outstripped the video's entire budget. 'Falling in Love (Is Hard on the Knees)', Aerosmith's first single release of the year, reached number thirty-five in the American chart and number twenty-two in the UK.

Sticking to his stance of never getting on a soapbox to lecture about the perils of drug taking, Tyler felt strongly that there was still an unhelpful resistance among anti-drug campaigners to admitting that drugs like ecstasy did, in the beginning, make a person feel great and that therein lay the seductive danger of hard drugs, leading in turn to devastating addiction. This message was promoted by the hit British movie *Trainspotting*, starring Ewan McGregor, Robert Carlyle, Ewen Bremner and Jonny Lee Miller. Steven admitted that he had almost turned off *Trainspotting* midway through, because the sordid life that the fictional heroin addicts led and the dire situations they got into on screen reminded him uncomfortably of real life desperate people he had come into contact with during the depths of his addiction, and the squalid, deadly places he had been forced to go to in order to score a fix. In March 1997, Steven featured in a US TV programme called *Heroin: High School High* that dealt with teenage heroin addiction. There always seemed to be something that, for good or ill, would make Tyler glance back over his shoulder at his past. In the band that spring there was also a general acknowledgement that in a strange sense they had had to melt down in order to have come back as strong as they had.

With its sleazy riffs and lascivious lyrics, on its release *Nine Lives* entered Billboard's album chart at the top. It made number four in Britain, where the *New Music Express* said: '*Nine Lives* is traditional Aerosmith, rasping sub-Stones, third generation removed white blues.' Within a couple of weeks, however, there was controversy over the album cover. The artwork for the album sleeve depicted a man with a cat's head, dancing on top of a collection of snakes. Aerosmith had been under the impression that this was an original design. They were stunned when it emerged that this was not the case and that this image had inadvertently deeply offended the Hindu community. Joe Perry revealed: 'Once the album was on the market, the Hindus saw it and they really freaked out. We were getting emails, lawyers' letters, and there were bomb threats on the Sony building. After that, we went: "That's it! We're changing the cover art," and we stopped the presses.'

In May, 'Hole in My Soul' failed to breach the US Top 50, but made the Top 30 in Britain, where Aerosmith launched their *Nine Lives* world tour with a gig at the Telewest Arena in Newcastle upon Tyne, breaking the house record. After another British date at the Manchester Nynex Arena, Aerosmith headed east to gig around Europe, taking in Germany, Finland, the Czech Republic, Austria, Italy, the Netherlands and Belgium, before returning to Britain for four further dates – one in Birmingham, and their only Scottish gig at the SECC in Glasgow, before pitching up at London's Wembley Arena for a two-night stint, ending on 5 June. Accompanying Aerosmith on this leg were Shed Seven and Kula Shaker. Ever on the lookout for interesting support acts, Steven had enjoyed a live radio broadcast Kula Shaker had given, but all had not gone smoothly on tour as one evening Kula Shaker left the stage after performing just one song, hugely frustrated at the poor quality of their sound.

Unfortunately, on that particular night there had been no time for the support act to have a sound check because Aerosmith's own sound check had taken an age. Joe Perry explained: 'Usually, after fifteen shows we don't sound check unless we want to work on a new song. We'd only rehearsed, though, for a couple of days before the tour.' Teresa had joined Steven in London for the Wembley Arena dates. Backstage that second night, the post-gig gathering included the band members' families, a bevy of the usual beauties and a smattering of stars. Jon Bon Jovi was engrossed talking with one of Aerosmith's business managers and, as a lover of the sixties music scene, Steven was also thrilled that among the band's guests was The Pretty Things' frontman, Phil May.

While the band continued to gig through Europe, at home the *Boston Globe* reported that the proceeds from the sale of Aerosmith T-shirts at the chain of Hard Rock Café restaurants, amounting to more than half a million dollars, would be going to a children's hospital. Back on US soil, Steven was keyed up to play a warm-up gig at the Entertainment Center, Old Orchard Beach in Maine, before leading his band into the north American/Canadian leg in early July. Kicking off at the Corel Center in Kanata, Ontario, he wowed audiences through performances in Montreal and Toronto before giving his all for twenty-five gigs spread across fourteen US states, wrapping up at the Deer Creek Music Center in Noblesville, Indiana, on 31 August.

A second US leg would start in North Carolina in late September, but before that, at the annual MTV Video Music Awards held at Radio City Music Hall in New York, Tyler was delighted that Aerosmith won the Best Rock Video award for 1997 for 'Falling in Love (Is Hard on the Knees)'. That month, Aerosmith also picked up two nominations in the MTV Europe Music Awards – in the Best Live Act and the Best Rock Act categories.

Tyler's attention right through to near the end of October, however, stayed squarely on eliciting the very best response he could from his home-grown fans as the band took in another ten American states before dropping anchor temporarily after an appearance during the Universal Concerts held in Vancouver, British Columbia, Canada. Night after night on this gruelling schedule, with his adrenalin pumping, Steven knew that he was electrifying the performances for loyal fans who had come in their droves from far and wide to see them. Perhaps he could not pick out individual faces in the gloom beyond the stage foot-lights, but the rapturous reception Aerosmith was given everywhere spoke for the Blue Army's continued devotion.

In a more modest situation, it gave Steven immense pleasure when, in early November 1997, Aerosmith performed a benefit concert for the Nordoff Robbins charity. They played for autistic children, and Steven was thrilled when at one point, as he sang them a song that he had been taught as a kid, the children joined in and sang and danced along with him. Aerosmith received the Silver Clef Award at the 10th Nordoff Robbins dinner at the Roseland Ballroom in New York.

Not long after a third north American tour got under way at the Coliseum in Jacksonville, Florida, Aerosmith performed 'Pink' at the Billboard Music Awards at the MGM Grand Garden Arena in Las Vegas, which was broadcast live on US network tele-vision on 8 December. The *Nine Lives* world tour took a break after a New Year's Day gig at the Fleet Center in Boston.

Taking time to relax with his family did not mean that Steven sat about in his moccasins, doing nothing. He had taken up roller-blading and skiing, and he indulged his long-time liking for mucking about on the water by piloting jet boats. For a star who tunes in so passionately to his stage persona, it takes him remarkably little time coming off the adrenalin-driven high of live performance to slip behind the curtain into family life. For just about a week that inbuilt buzz of 'showtime' grabs at him at a certain point in the evening. Once that leaks away, he is happy helping out about the house, being with his wife and children. He does take off on his own – sometimes he puts on the rollerblades, skates off and can be gone for hours. Towards the end of 1997, he was in quite reflective mood, telling his wife that if he died tomorrow then he would die happy. He had not become jaded with success and was grateful to be tasting it a second time around. It still gave him immense delight to hear thousands of fans sing his own lyrics back to him at gigs, and among his fan mail he received letters from drug addicts telling him that *he* had inspired them to at least try to put the needle away, to seek help with their addictions. An emotional man anyway, letters like these touched Tyler very much.

In January 1998, Steven sheathed his skinny frame in his flamboyant stagewear once more when the US leg of the *Nine Lives* world tour resumed in Maryland. By the time it ended the following month in Michigan, Aerosmith had picked up two Grammy Award nominations, for 'Falling in Love (Is Hard on the Knees)' and for *Nine Lives*. The third single from *Nine Lives*, 'Pink', was released, charting at number thirty-eight in Britain, while managing to peak eleven places higher in America. With Steven's harmonica opening, 'Pink' was an unusual song – in places not immediately comprehensible – and its accompanying video was fantastically bizarre. It featured various people including John Kalodner and the band members individually morphed into a wide range of freakish incarnations – Joe Perry, for instance, at one point ambles towards the camera as half man (playing electric guitar) and half horse. Steven's many wild and weird guises included appearances as a child with bunny ears, a dancing skeleton in a top hat, a bronzed bodybuilder flexing his pecs and wearing only a posing pouch, and a shapeless young girl. Steven and Joe briefly showed up as one man with two heads – Tyler's head and Perry's head sitting on one wide pair of shoulders. Each bewildering character sauntering or rushing towards the camera was more outlandish than the last. Finally, Steven's quizzical face fills the screen. He goes cross-eyed, then signs off with a flash of his infectious grin before ducking swiftly down out of shot. While fans struggled to know what to make of 'Pink's' video, Steven came down with viral laryngitis, paying the price for having given his all in concert for much of the past ten months.

He had recovered by the time Aerosmith flew to the Far East for their seven-date tour of Japan. Kicking off on 1 March at the Dome in Nagoya, visiting Osaka and Fukuoka before two gigs at the Tokyo Dome, the tour concluded with two nights at the Yokohama Arena. They left Japan mid-month for America, where eleven days later, on 26 March, Steven privately celebrated his milestone fiftieth birthday.

Showing no sign of slowing down, Steven relished embarking on what would be their fourth US leg when the Aerosmith roadshow got back into gear in mid-April at the Delta Center in Salt Lake City, Utah. After playing dates in Colorado and Washington, the band arrived in Alaska for two gigs at the Sullivan Arena in Anchorage. On 27 April, the day of the first concert there, news was released that Aerosmith songs would anchor the official soundtrack album to accompany an upcoming feature film called *Armageddon*. Two nights later, the world tour literally came to a crashing stop.

The performance had gone well. Then during the encore, while swinging his microphone stand around, in a second's mistiming Steven hit himself with the heavy metal base and he fell awkwardly on to one knee. It was not just an embarrassing tumble on stage. As soon as Steven stood up it was obvious to him that damage had been done. It turned out that he had torn his anterior cruciate ligament and surrounding cartilage. He needed an operation, and so the band was forced to postpone the remaining fourteen US and Canadian dates. They hoped to be able to reschedule these dates for later in the year, but an entire European tour which had been planned to kick off on 26 June at the Petrovsky Stadium in St Petersburg, Russia, and end on 1 August at London's Wembley Arena, had to be cancelled altogether. A proposed South American tour also had to be elbowed.

Once the swelling in his injured knee went down, in early May 1998 Steven underwent surgery. The straightforward procedure went well, and his doctors advised him to stay off the road for at least three to four months. He recovered at his home in the Boston area and in an effort to keep Aerosmith's name in vogue, along with his bandmates he began to look at material for a possible live album release. What most invigorated Tyler, however, was Aerosmith's involvement in the soundtrack for *Armageddon*, the Hollywood science-fiction blockbuster about attempts to stop meteors from hitting and destroying the Earth. Directed by Michael Bay, it starred Bruce Willis, Billy Bob Thornton, Ben Affleck and Steven's daughter, Liv, who played Grace Stamper, Willis's screen daughter.

In the past three years, Liv's acting career had taken off with appearances in *Heavy, Stealing Beauty, That Thing You Do!* and *Inventing the Abbots*. It had been a period of considerable change for Liv. She said: 'I cried on my eighteenth birthday. I thought that seventeen was such a nice age. You're young enough to get away with things but you're old enough, too.' In 1997, at twenty years old, as part of asserting her independence, she had stopped living at home with her mother; that same year, *People* magazine had named Liv Tyler as one of the 50 Most Beautiful People in the World. Her role in the multi-million-dollar movie *Armageddon* was an opportunity to truly exploit her dark-haired, blue-eyed beauty, and to prove her magnetism on the big screen.

Aerosmith contributed four songs to the official soundtrack album: two new numbers – a lush power ballad called 'I Don't Want To Miss a Thing', written by lyricist Diane Warren, and a rock song, 'What Kind of Love Are You On?' – plus their classic number, 'Sweet Emotion', and a cover of the Beatles' song, 'Come Together'. Of Aerosmith's involvement in this project Steven said: 'We got to see what they had of the movie so far and it was so exciting, so fantastic with all this stuff going on, especially where they put "Sweet Emotion" in the film. I immediately fell in love with it. Then I saw the love scene with Ben Affleck and my daughter and at the end [of the film] when she starts crying and yells "Daddy", the tears started running down my face.'

The video to accompany 'I Don't Want To Miss a Thing' was shot in the Minneapolis Armory in spring 1998 when Steven, post-operation, was still having considerable difficulty with walking. In long, black flowing clothes, Steven adopted a dramatic look and his emotive delivery of the power ballad is, for many fans, one of his best ever. The video of Aerosmith performing the number was spliced with scenes taken from the movie and with a touching twist at the end, when Liv as Grace Stamper in mission control cries and reaches out to an image on a huge TV screen, it is an image of her real father's face that she tenderly touches.

Steven had been keeping track of his eldest daughter's career with pride, attending her film openings when he could and visiting the cinema to see her movies, often more than once. With Liv's profile rising, in November 1994 she and her father had appeared together on the cover of *Rolling Stone*, Liv giving her father a peck on the cheek, only to draw criticism from some who claimed that it had somehow looked incestuous. It was an absurd reaction that Steven seriously struggled to comprehend. Asked if he saw Liv as sexy, he resoundingly barked: 'No! Others do.'

As a protective father, a reformed drug addict and a raucous rock star who is never shy of speaking his mind, Steven Tyler is a daunting figure for any young guy hoping to strike up a relationship with one of his daughters. Right then, Liv was dating actor Joaquin Phoenix, whom she had met on the set of the film *Inventing The Abbots*, but Phoenix had managed not to feel intimidated by the formidable, sometimes unpredictable, frontman.

On 27 May 1998, MTV premiered Aerosmith's 'I Don't Want To Miss a Thing' as more details of the film's soundtrack emerged. In addition to Aerosmith's four numbers, the album featured songs from Jon Bon Jovi, Bob Seger, Journey and ZZ Top among others, while composer Trevor Rabin contributed 'Theme from Armageddon'.

Steven made his first live appearance since having surgery on 29 June, when Aerosmith performed a forty-five-minute set at the private premiere party for *Armageddon*, held at the Kennedy Space Center in Cape Canaveral, Florida. He still had to wear a leg brace to support his knee, and before the five hundred invited VIP guests, the band performed the live debut of 'I Don't Want To Miss a Thing'.

*Armageddon* publicly premiered on 1 July 1998 and went on to attract four Academy Award nominations, including a nomination for Best Original Song for 'I Don't Want To Miss a Thing', which debuted that summer in the American singles chart at number one; it was Aerosmith's first ever number one single in their twenty-five years as recording artists. The song remained in pole position on Billboard for four weeks. It also topped the charts in nine other countries including Australia, Germany and Italy. In Britain, the impressive rock power ballad made number four. 'I Don't Want To Miss a Thing' was nominated for a 1998 Grammy Award in the category of Best Rock Performance by a Duo or Group with Vocal, as was 'Pink'. At the Grammy Awards ceremony, held in the new year, 'Pink' took the trophy.

Despite the derailment to the tour caused by his knee injury, Steven was in buoyant mood about Aerosmith's past, present and future. He voiced his frank amazement and gratitude that the band was still hanging on in there, still coming up with the goods. Perfectly aware that it was very easy for their lurid reputation for drug abuse and excess to deflect attention from their musical ability, Tyler stressed to journalists: 'It wasn't anything we shot up or put up our noses that gave us the edge.' It was, he maintained, the various talents each of his bandmates brought to Aerosmith. Keeping the unit intact, he felt, was both their hardest and their greatest achievement.

In his by now acknowledged capacity as an elder statesmen of rock, Tyler was quizzed on what he thought about the violence that was becoming synonymous with certain elements in music. Steven stated: 'You start dancing with your shadow too much and it's obvious. You can either walk around smacking each other or loving each other. The dark energy dies. So, what do you choose?'

Tyler's energy reserves never flagged. To keep his frame stick-thin, Steven started every day with a robust session on a Stairmaster in the gym. His potent attraction to his female fans had in no way been diluted by having turned fifty, although Tyler took a pragmatic view of it all. 'It's just a fantasy that goes hand in hand with rock,' he maintained. 'If they really knew us, it wouldn't be the same – just ask our wives – but I like to keep that little bit of a fantasy.' He also knew how to teasingly suggest his availability. The impudent star confessed to looking at other women and ever so slightly on occasion briefly caressing the odd busty babe backstage but he found no difficulty in leaving things at that.

He had not lost the buzz of turning on the radio and hearing Aerosmith songs belt out over the airwaves. Come the late 1990s, however, radio was changing and older artists were being dropped in their droves from playlists around the country. When Tyler discovered that this was happening to Aerosmith's music at radio stations across Los Angeles he got on the phone personally to find out why. One radio producer told him that that particular station would not be playing Aerosmith because they were classed as a rock act. Steven promptly challenged the guy by reeling off a long list of the band's romantic ballads. Whether or not this mission made a blind bit of difference to those in charge of the station's playlists, Tyler felt better for having at least tried to tackle the issue.

In a less militant mood, Steven took stock of his life and although content enough, he did not believe in resting on his laurels. In summer 1998, he had ambitions of breaking into the realms of acting. With differing degrees of success other rock stars, including Roger Daltrey, David Bowie and Jon Bon Jovi had made it on to the silver screen. Unsurprisingly, Steven envisaged himself cast in a flamboyant passionate role in a high-octane action adventure movie. Since he was planning getting back on the road with Aerosmith and writing more songs for future albums, it was hard to see quite how he would have the time to attempt to break into acting, but he admitted: 'Life's gotta be complicated for me.'

# CHAPTER 13

# The Keeper Of
# The Flame

**FEELING RECOVERED** from his knee operation and buoyed up by the success of 'I Don't Want To Miss a Thing', in summer 1998 Tyler was ready to resume Aerosmith's *Nine Lives* world tour. Plans were announced for a major US leg kicking off in August at the Walnut Creek Amphitheater in Raleigh, North Carolina. During its expected run through to the end of the year, the band hoped to knit in the dates that had to be postponed when Steven picked up his injury. But fate intervened again in July, when drummer Joey Kramer sustained second-degree burns on both legs, his left arm and hand. He had been sitting in his sports car at a petrol filling station in Scituate, Massachusetts, with the engine still running, when a leak in the petrol tank hose caused fuel to set the car ablaze. Joey was very lucky to scramble alive out of the burning vehicle, and was rushed to hospital for treatment for his horrific injuries. Aerosmith postponed their tour plans, and over the next six weeks Kramer made remarkable progress. He later praised: 'Without the care and time taken by the entire staff of the burn unit at the Massachusetts General Hospital, I don't think my rehabilitation would have been so speedy.'

The seventh leg of Aerosmith's world tour finally got under

way on 9 September at the Montage Mountain Amphitheater in Scranton, Pennsylvania. As the band then headed to New Jersey they learned that they had added two more trophies to their collection; at the MTV Video Music Awards they picked off the prizes for Best Rock Video for 'Pink', and Best Video from a Film for 'I Don't Want To Miss a Thing'. By now, the *Armageddon* soundtrack had gone triple platinum. Hurling himself into performances from Clarkston to Cincinnati, Chicago to Columbus, on 24 September in St Louis, Missouri, for their gig the next night at the Riverport Amphitheater, Tyler took time out to throw the first pitch at the St Louis Cardinals baseball game against the Montreal Expos at the city's Busch Stadium.

Hitting state after state, Steven went all out to prove his fitness and enthusiasm. In early October, when Aerosmith took to the stage at the GTE Virginia Beach Amphitheater, his breathtakingly explosive passion enthralled a 25,000 capacity crowd during the ninety-minute show. His energy levels were extraordinary and he wielded his microphone stand with almost careless abandon as he gyrated around the stage. Rock journalists left that evening to scribble that Tyler was now possibly rock's greatest frontman. He does draw an intriguing blend of emotions from his devoted fans, for in addition to responding to the pulsating sexuality he flagrantly exudes, he also elicits an enduringly deep affection.

Come autumn 1998, Steven's public statement mirrored his private feelings, as he confessed that after twenty-five years in the business he and his bandmates had at last lost their sense of insecurity. Steven saw new dimensions to his world and he relished the fact that Aerosmith was in tremendous shape; each night the band played out of its skin in the quest of rewarding the loyal supporters who had stayed true to them through thick and thin. Steven also openly valued the fact that his friendship with Joe Perry had deepened yet further. This relationship still formed the axis on which the band's fortunes turned. It was stimulating, too, that Aerosmith was more than holding its own in such fast-moving times; they were learning how to take advantage of the worldwide web, which was beginning to make a serious impact on the way rock music reaches its audience. On 17 October, their gig at the P.N.C. Bank Arts Center in Holmdel, New Jersey, simultaneously went out as a webcast; over 120,000 people downloaded the performance, making it the largest single artist webcast, at that point in time.

Days later, Aerosmith released a twenty-three-track double live album called *A Little South of Sanity*. Comprising tracks recorded during the band's 1993–1994 world tour and during some gigs on their *Nine Lives* tour, it peaked at number twelve on Billboard and reached the Top 40 in the UK album chart. Steven did not over-enthuse about this compilation. He appeared to view it as an album he would likely find most interesting when he listened to it in his old age. He continued to be fascinated with the breakneck pace of technology, firmly contemplating a time when gigs could be recorded live and CDs made available virtually as fans are streaming out of the auditoriums. This North American leg ended in late October in Toledo, Ohio, but behind the cheeky grins and quick quips to the media, Steven was quietly concerned. Twenty-four gigs in, his operated-on knee was threatening to give him some problems. He preferred not to think about the prospect of needing more surgery, and after donating $10,000 to the Massachusetts General Hospital, where Joey Kramer had been treated for burns earlier in the year, he launched Aerosmith back on the road.

With the tour now renamed the *Little South of Sanity* tour, the next batch of dates commenced in early November at the Bradley Center in Milwaukee, Wisconsin; in the ensuing weeks they performed in fourteen states. Veterans of the road, Aerosmith have notched up their share of hairy experiences and touring mishaps. Joe Perry highlighted one particular hiccup as his favourite rock 'n' roll moment. 'We were at some puddle-jump airport and our jet ran off the runway. It was probably two in the morning after a gig and we all had to get out of the plane and shoulder it back on to the runway to take off. We were all covered with mud.'

At the MTV Europe Music Awards held at the Fila Forum in Milan, Aerosmith won the Best Rock Act award, which the band accepted via video link to Italy and, for the second year running, they took in the new year with a gig at the Fleet Center in Boston. Sticking around home territory for a gig on 2 January 1999 at Worcester's Centrum Arena, just two more dates in Pennsylvania and Tennessee wrapped up their wanderings in time to collect the accolade of Favourite Pop/Rock Band Duo or Group at the American Music Awards.

Away from the spotlight, Steven's concern had deepened. This recent round of dates had proved punishing on the knee that had been weakened last spring, and the prospect of further surgery now made him outwardly nervous. He revealed how distressing it had been to undergo knee surgery, for he had had no guarantees that post-op he would be able to do everything he had taken for granted before – from lifting and carrying his children to careering around the stage. He felt that having successfully come through surgery once, it shortened the odds of him equally well surviving a second date on the operating table. While he hoped that a rest from touring would, in itself, be enough to relieve the worrying pressure on his leg, he tried to relax at home with his family. Spending time with friends, he accompanied Joe to Los Angeles' Whisky A Go-Go club to cheer on the guitarist's eighteen-year-old son (by his first wife, Elyssa); Adrian Perry was performing there with a band called Dexter.

Not everyone was in the mood to play happy families, however. Tyler's troubles with Cyrinda Foxe's wish to publish nude photos of him in the paperback edition of her memoir, *Dream On: Livin' on the Edge with Steven Tyler and Aerosmith*, came up again when Steven won the latest round in their court battle. Steven's stance remained that his ex-wife did not have the right to publish these snaps for commercial gain, without his consent. In March 1999, a New York State Supreme Court granted a temporary restraining order preventing Cyrinda from publishing these revealing images until their ownership could be legally established. This was not the end of the matter. Following this temporary restraining order, the case was remanded to a lower court for further adjudication.

That same month, changes occurred in the management, publicity and legal departments handling Aerosmith; the band ultimately signed with a Los Angeles-based management firm and hired a new legal team. It had become almost a given that Aerosmith would mop up at the annual Boston Music Awards, and in April they lifted four trophies: for Act of the Year; Best Rock Band; Best Video for 'I Don't Want To Miss a Thing'; and Best Male Vocalist. As this embarrassment of riches further cemented Aerosmith's ties to Boston, Tyler wanted to give something back to the city that had taken him so firmly to its heart; he donated money to help build an Oprah Winfrey 'Angel House' for a needy family in Boston. Steven also donated the rights to the song 'Fallen Angels' to the chat show star's organisation, Angel Network.

After the three-month lay-off, Aerosmith had by now resumed their tour in Columbus, Ohio. It was a bitterly cold spring, with the foul weather ensuring that winter illnesses continued to cut down people across the whole country. Already feeling poorly, when the band took to the stage on 1 May at the Fiddler's Green Amphitheater in Greenwood Village, Colorado, Steven came down with the flu, and despite his condition worsening over the coming six days he stubbornly fronted Aerosmith when the band played at the famous Hollywood Bowl. Situated on North Highland Avenue in the Hollywood Hills, with its distinctive concrete band-shell stage, the Hollywood Bowl has a romanticism all of its own among performers. Joe Perry confessed: 'We knew that we were putting Steven's voice at risk but there was no way we were going to blow out the Hollywood Bowl!' That night, resplendent in eye-catching silk, Steven pouted, pirouetted and thrust his way through the set, gamely disguising his weak condition from the fans, but ending the night with laryngitis that was severe enough to force some cancellations to allow him to get his voice back and to recover from the flu. When the tour resumed, as Aerosmith prepared to play at the Delta Center in Salt Lake City, Utah, on 17 May, they were saddened to hear that record producer Bruce Fairbairn, with whom they had worked on their multi-platinum albums, *Permanent Vacation, Pump* and *Get a Grip*, had that day been found dead in his Vancouver home. Just under a week later, Aerosmith wrapped up their North American stint at Tinley Park in Illinois.

A year on from *Armageddon*'s release, Aerosmith was still garnering awards for 'I Don't Want To Miss a Thing', and in June the power ballad won Best Song from a Movie at the 1999 MTV Movie Awards. The number has also become one of the most requested songs ever played on British radio. One bum note that summer concerned Woodstock '99. Intended to mark thirty years since the original music festival, this event was slated to take place in Rome, New York, between 23 and 25 July. Back in April, Aerosmith had been confirmed as one of the few acts that had played at Woodstock '94, and would again be taking part this time around. However, due to unforeseen scheduling conflicts and other obligations, it was not now going to be possible, and Aerosmith had to back out. The band issued a statement setting out its decision not to take part in Woodstock '99, in which they said that they 'regretted the inconvenience and sent a heartfelt apology to fans who had purchased tickets to see them perform as part of the weekend festival'.

Meantime, back in vocal form, Steven set out to strut his stuff for the final leg of a world tour that had kicked off over two years earlier. Opening on 10 June at the Globen in Stockholm, Sweden, it was a trek around Europe playing at outdoor arenas. Having racked up appearances in Germany, Austria and Switzerland, Aerosmith hit Britain for a single gig at London's Wembley Stadium before heading to Belgium. On 11 July, they took part in the Monza Rock Festival, appearing the following evening at the Neapolis Festival in Naples before quitting Italy for one gig in Spain, then winding everything up on 17 July with a performance at the Super Rock event held at the National Stadium in Lisbon, Portugal. Over the course of this mammoth undertaking,

Aerosmith's opening acts and guest performers had included Spacehog, the Black Crowes, Lenny Kravitz, Bryan Adams and Stereophonics.

Back home with his family for the remainder of that summer, Steven was well rested by the time he was invited to sing 'The Star-Spangled Banner' in mid-September prior to the New England Patriots and the Indianapolis Colts football game held at the Foxboro Stadium in Foxboro, Massachusetts. More changes came into effect in the business and accounting areas of the band's working world while publicly their star continued to rise. On 8 December, at the Billboard Music Awards, Aerosmith was honoured with a Lifetime Achievement Award.

For many artists, the new millennium was a chance to stage a spectacular showcase gig. Aerosmith chose to greet the dawn of a new century by playing a mini-tour of Japan, dubbed the Roar of the Dragon. Commencing on 29 December at the Dome in Osaka, they played six shows. The stage setting for each gig had a striking theme incorporating dragons and other representations of East Asian culture. Their second gig at the Osaka Dome was on New Year's Eve, spilling over into 1 January 2000. The band's American fans had hankered to see them perform on home soil at this unique moment in time. However, they were able to enjoy a small segment of this show when ABC television's *New Year's Eve Millennium Celebration* special programme streamed Aerosmith's performance of 'I Don't Want To Miss a Thing' live from Osaka. On 2 January, they performed at the Nagoya Dome. A single stop in Fukuoka followed, then there were two consecutive nights at the Tokyo Dome, bringing the tour to a close on 7 January. It had been a huge success, and their Japanese hosts and fans had made the band feel most welcome.

For many, this historic dawn ushered in a burgeoning optimism; people felt inspired to hit new heights – in Tyler's case, literally. During his off-duty periods he had become addicted to extreme sports such as hang-gliding. Wearing a parachute and hang gliding several thousand feet above the ground gave Steven the kind of heady rush that illegal substances once used to. He also enjoyed waterskiing and careering around on a mountain bike. Watching his family of four grow up and spread their wings thrilled him, too. Nine-year-old Taj and eleven-year-old Chelsea were happy, healthy youngsters, each developing their own distinctive personality, while Steven's two older daughters continued to carve their individual career paths.

Throughout 1999, Liv had appeared in three movies, *Plunkett & Macleane, Cookie's Fortune* and *Onegin*. She would soon be seen in *Dr T and the Women* but her biggest screen role was just around the corner. Liv felt frustrated whenever film magazine and newspaper features labelled her as Liv Tyler, 'daughter of Aerosmith rock legend Steven Tyler'. It was no reflection on her pride in, or her love for, her father, but she had begun to feel suffocated by the tag to the extent of thinking she should have kept the surname of Rundgren. Liv landed roles on her own merit as an actress but undoubtedly the Tyler name attracted attention – the lifeblood of any performer.

Twenty-one-year-old Mia was working on a career as a plus-size fashion model (plus size in America being a ladies size 10–12). At 5' 7" tall, with long dark hair, she had developed into a strikingly beautiful young woman, who was often refreshingly candid in interviews. Said Mia: 'I was always chubby as a kid. We're a family of big eaters and if you look at my older sister Liv, you'll see that she's not super-skinny either. She is totally happy that she has a womanly shape.' Pointing out that that is a rarity in a country and an industry that favours waiflike figures, Mia was frank that while she had grown up comfortable that she was not sylphlike, it could have been made easier. 'I know that it would have been better if I had seen role models who had figures like mine. Beauty comes in all different packages,' she maintained. 'My dad has a fast metabolism when he is touring and running around on stage but my family never pressurised me to be skinny. We're very tolerant and supportive of each other.' Mia would go on to become a catwalk queen, taking part in a provocative plus-size lingerie fashion show in New York, among other things. At a time when the danger of anorexia was fast gaining publicity, both Mia and Liv helped promote a healthier body image for women.

Regarding Aerosmith, Steven was having to fend off any notions that with the band entering its fourth decade in music, it was really time to shuffle quietly away into muted retirement and leave the stage for the young, mainly media-manufactured pop stars coming along. The Rolling Stones, who had started their career a clear decade before Aerosmith, were still touring the world, and Tyler boldly pronounced that so long as he was able to draw breath, he would continue to perform live. To prove that there was life in the fifty-two-year-old yet, Steven now let it out that work had begun on Aerosmith's thirteenth studio album.

As had been the case for the past thirty years, Steven and Joe Perry sparked creatively off one another, but Perry also revealed: 'Lately, we've found it more exciting to work with other people. Steven and I have sat there in an empty room with a blank tape, me with a guitar in hand and he at the keyboards, a lot of times. I'm not saying we won't sit down and write songs again alone, but for now it's fun to bring in other people.' The outsiders included former collaborators Mark Hudson, Marti Frederiksen and Steve Dudas. Over time, songs emerged including 'Just Push Play', 'Beyond Beautiful', 'Under My Skin', 'Light Inside', 'Sunshine' and 'Jaded'. Written by Tyler and Marti Frederiksen, 'Jaded' particularly excited the frontman. He declared: 'It felt phenomenal when I hit on that melody. I didn't tell the band for two months. I loved the way the song wrapped around itself and within a couple of weeks it went from "Jaded" to "J.J.J.Jaded" with the rhythm and everything. It helped a lot that I was a drummer first.'

The songs were written at the Boneyard, a recording studio Joe Perry had had built in the basement of his house at the ranch he owns near Boston. The demos they made of these songs sounded so good that Steven believed they were as professional as anything then playing on radio. They played music round the clock, creating such a great feeling that it spurred them to record the album in this studio and to produce it themselves, with assistance from Mark Hudson and Marti Frederiksen. Tyler quipped that so many record producers had said that Aerosmith was a pain in the ass to work with, that they had wanted to find out if it was true. Seriously, Steven relished the band taking this aspect of their work into their own hands. They had learned a lot over the years from working with experienced producers and were itching to spread their own wings.

The entire band believed strongly that they now had no need of a coach. Said Tom Hamilton of this new work: 'We did it all close to home and as one long, continuous, very organic process, as opposed to in the past when there would be a four-week blast of writing then there'd be some appearance we'd have to make that would completely break up the momentum.' When it came to shooting a video to accompany 'Jaded', however, the band was happy to work with director Francis Lawrence. Aerosmith already had a trophy cabinet crammed with awards for their innovative and outlandish videos, but the video for 'Jaded' still stirred the normally supremely laid-back Joe Perry.

Aerosmith had thrashed out their ideas with the director and between them they had come up with a storyboard depicting the tale of a young woman who is losing touch with reality. The set design was elaborate and extravagant, even for a band accustomed to excess. Said Perry: 'It was the first time I'd ever walked on to a set and got goose bumps. When I saw that first shot, the big staircase, all those performers and the giraffe, I felt like I was in a Fellini movie. It was incredible!'

The invigorating experience of making this new album, the fresh freedoms enjoyed by having recorded and produced it themselves, did not mean that there were no spats between Tyler and his 'twin'. They still got embroiled in heated arguments, but they were productive ructions and always about the music. Anyone visiting the Perry family home and overhearing the rumpus going on down in the basement had to file it under 'Keep Out! Volatile Men At Work'.

Mainly, though, they had a ball at Perry's ranch. Joe owned a sizeable collection of off-road vehicles, of which the band made full use. At times they were as headstrong as a bunch of unruly teenagers. Joe recalled one occasion when they could have come a nasty cropper. 'We were riding around on dirt bikes and somebody forgot that I have a swimming pool. They came up over the hill and slammed the brakes on really hard and we got to see just how many times a dirt bike can go end over end. Fortunately, there were no broken bones.'

In mid-September, Steven poked his head above the parapet long enough to clock up that Aerosmith was among sixteen artists being tipped for possible induction into the Rock and Roll Hall of Fame in 2001. Among the others were AC/DC, Black Sabbath, Lou Reed, Michael Jackson, Paul Simon, Queen, Bob Seger and Steely Dan. Several hundred people from across the music business, including artists, record producers, journalists and industry figures, all voted on the nominees, whittling the number down over a period of weeks to those who would be inducted. To be eligible for induction to the Rock and Roll Hall of Fame, an artist or band had to have been in the recording business for at least twenty-five years, but Tyler was not holding his breath. They had been passed over before for this industry honour. On 12 December 2000, however, it was announced that alongside Paul Simon, Queen, Michael Jackson and Steely Dan, Aerosmith would be inducted. By the end of the year, some music commentators were touting Aerosmith as arguably *the* pre-eminent American hard rock band; in VH1's '100 Greatest Artists of Hard Rock' they ranked number eleven. And the accolades kept coming.

In January 2001, at the American Music Awards, Aerosmith received the Award of Achievement, which had at that point only been given to Michael Jackson, Prince and Mariah Carey. Aerosmith performed at the ceremony, debuting their as yet unreleased single 'Jaded', and were rewarded with an enthusiastic standing ovation. Weeks later, on Sunday 28 January, Aerosmith performed at the half-time show during America's NFL Super Bowl XXXV game between the Baltimore Ravens and the New York Giants, held at the Raymond James Stadium in

Tampa, Florida. Nearly seventy-two thousand people packed the arena, and the whole event was also watched live by 750 million television viewers worldwide. Other performers included Nelly, Mary J Blige, N'Sync, Tremors and the Earthquake Horns and Britney Spears. The half-time show culminated with all the performers joining Aerosmith for a rendition of 'Walk This Way'. When later challenged as to how it felt as hard rockers, performing with breezy young pop stars, Joe Perry drolly remarked that if they could get away with appearing on stage with Britney Spears, then the band was surely bullet proof!

In March, Aerosmith's thirteenth studio album, *Just Push Play*, was released. It lodged at number two on Billboard and quickly went platinum. In Britain, the album made number seven; 'Jaded' soon reached the same peak in the US singles chart, stopping six places lower in the UK. A further three singles would spin off *Just Push Play*: 'Fly Away From Home'; 'Sunshine', and the title track, but 'Jaded' was the most successful and in 2001 its video won the Billboard Music Award for 'Best Hard Rock Clip of the Year'.

Without doubt, the landmark event of 2001 was being inducted into the Rock and Roll Hall of Fame on 19 March at a ceremony held during a black tie dinner at New York's Waldorf Astoria Hotel. In anticipation of receiving this recognition, Steven remarked: 'Not bad for a bunch of guys that got kicked out of clubs for playing their own songs.' Aerosmith was the only band to be inducted into the Rock and Roll Hall of Fame at the same time as having a hit song ('Jaded') played on radio across the nation.

Aerosmith was inducted by Kid Rock, who said during his introduction: 'Aerosmith are to rock and roll what Fonzie was to *Happy Days*.' While the audience politely tried to work out the significance of this remark, Kid Rock carried on with his speech and ended by inviting Aerosmith up on stage as 'the greatest rock and roll band in American history'. After receiving their coveted statuettes, Aerosmith launched into blistering renditions of 'Sweet Emotion', 'Train Kept A-Rollin' and 'Jaded'.

If some recipients of this honour preferred to play things cool backstage after the induction, Steven was far from blasé. Openly thrilled, he declared: 'To know that you've got a place next to Elvis Presley? This is totally overwhelming!'

# CHAPTER 14

# A Road Paved
# With Passion

**H**AVING LATELY performed at the NFL Super Bowl and at the Rock and Roll Hall of Fame, on 27 May 2001 Steven completed a hat-trick of appearances at grandiose events when he sang America's national anthem at the pre-race ceremony of the 85th Indianapolis 500. This legendary car race, held at the Indianapolis Motor Speedway, sees dozens of drivers compete for the million dollar first prize over a two and a half mile circuit, before a crowd of over a quarter of a million. Vehicles had displayed band names before but this was the first year that an Indy 500 race car sported the image of a rock band. The Aerosmith vehicle was painted pink and silver, carried Aerosmith's winged logo and an image of the scantily clad female robot that featured on the cover of the newly released album *Just Push Play*. In deference to Tyler's nickname, the car was called The Screaming Demon and displayed on its conical nose a caricature of a yelling Tyler, plus Steven's autograph. After Steven performed the national anthem, veteran Indy racing driver Jeff Ward slid behind the wheel of this customised car and joined battle with the other competitors.

Quitting Indianapolis, Tyler hightailed it back to his bandmates, who were excitedly anticipating the imminent launch of the *Just Push Play* tour. Regardless of how many times he had gigged around the globe, Steven was not jaded. 'You gotta keep it fresh, coming up with new stage designs and places to go. You always want to outdo what you did last time,' he said. Asked how Aerosmith could do that this time, Steven riposted: 'We could have bombs and blow-up dolls, but it's better to keep my sex life out of this!' In keeping with *Just Push Play*'s cover design, the stage set for this tour had a futuristic theme in silver and white. There would be two impressively sweeping staircases and a huge video wall, which Joe Perry had faint reservations about. 'The biggest thing on this tour, literally and figuratively, will be the video screen in back. We've never brought a screen with us before, so we hope it will add to the live performance, not take away from it,' he said.

With Fuel as the warm-up act, Aerosmith launched the world tour on 6 June at the Meadows Music Center in Hartford, Connecticut. They delivered a playlist that alternated between hard-rocking numbers and soaring ballads in a show designed to appeal to all ages, rounding off with an encore that included the haunting and powerful 'Livin' on the Edge.' One MTV gig report stated: 'The band seemed under-rehearsed at times – Steven Tyler missed his harmonica cue during "Cryin'" – but Tyler went into charismatic hyperactive ringmaster mode and, overall, the band hit a groove and stuck in it.'

Gigging over a handful of states throughout the month, Aerosmith played a single Canadian concert at the Molson Amphitheater in Toronto before reverting to more North American performances; they completed this first leg on 23 July in Englewood, Colorado. After a two-week break, a second US leg got under way, with scintillating performances creating such a lust among fans for more gigs that, on a high, Aerosmith announced several extra dates to be added to their itinerary between October and December. Fired up, the band quit North Carolina for a gig on 11 September 2001 at the Verizon Wireless Amphitheater in Virginia Beach, when everything came to a hideous halt with the terrorist attacks that were launched on the United States.

Sent reeling like the rest of the world, Aerosmith cancelled the Virginia gig and pulled the plug on dates in New Jersey and Maryland. Less than a week after that mind-numbing tragedy, they went back on stage in Atlanta, Georgia. Steven was uneasy about whether it was right to carry on with the tour. The mood in America was understandably like a tinderbox, with unimaginable sorrow and grief for the thousands of people who died in the attacks, mixed with an equally understandable collective volatile rage. When performing in Nashville, Raleigh and West Palm Beach to conclude this stint, the band remained sensitive to the situation. Would people feel guilty about going out and trying to have a good time for a few hours? Or would they welcome being able to get out from under the blanket news of this atrocity and somehow begin to get on with their lives? There was a remarkable sense of defiant resilience resonating at street level.

Although Steven concentrated on walking a fine line at concerts, aiming to maintain a positive vibe, like every other American he was inwardly gutted. He told Alex Beam for the *Boston Globe*: 'You have to stand at ground zero to experience the magnitude of the hot heaping helpings of hate that people have. I visited ground zero at the Pentagon. The giant hole – the devastation! They rocked America's world.'

Ten days on from the terrorist attack, with America a cauldron of seething emotions, a hastily arranged two-hour telethon called 'America: A Tribute To Heroes' was broadcast live from New York, Los Angeles and London (by satellite) on all major US television networks; the kaleidoscope of feelings was reflected by the evident state of mind of many of the performers through their telling choice of song. Belligerence shone out when Tom Petty opted to perform his band's hit, 'I Won't Back Down'. U2 offered more subtle strength in the face of intense adversity with 'Walk On'. Paul Simon turned in a soul-searching rendition of his classic, 'Bridge Over Troubled Water', and Jon Bon Jovi and Richie Sambora performed a hauntingly introspective version of 'Living on a Prayer'.

Ten days into the third leg of the *Just Push Play* tour,

Aerosmith decided almost at the last minute to take part, on 21 October 2001, in the United We Stand: What More Can I Give? benefit concert for the 9/11 victims held at the RFK Stadium in Washington DC. Other performers included Rod Stewart, Bette Midler, America, Carole King, Mariah Carey and Michael Jackson, each artist being restricted to a five-song set. Aerosmith took to the stage in the afternoon. Wearing a long jacket emblazoned with the American flag, Steven led his band through a gripping set which included performances of 'I Don't Want To Miss a Thing' and 'Livin' on the Edge'; in a nation then living on a knife edge the latter took on an evocative new depth.

Straight after coming off stage at the RFK Stadium, Aerosmith flew to Indianapolis to honour their scheduled tour date that same night, at the Conseco Fieldhouse. In a charged state, Steven turned in a riveting show for the equally emotional audience. Inescapably, it was difficult to perpetuate a business-as-usual atmosphere – the reckless spirit of any normal rock concert was wholly inappropriate – but Tyler kept trying to find the right balance. For some time to come, every gig threw up this extra challenge, and nightly it very much depended on the mood of the fans.

With so many people bereaved and suffering, it was not the climate in which to feel sorry for yourself, and so when Steven began to feel tired and unwell, he kept it firmly to himself as long as he could, but eventually a show in Pittsburgh and one in Toronto had to be cancelled. Aerosmith returned to the stage on Halloween for a gig at the Molson Centre in Montreal, Quebec, but Tyler's throat gave him so much trouble that he had to rest his voice. A date in Ohio was scrapped, while gigs in Boston and Rhode Island were postponed. The band planned to resume the tour in early November at the First Union Center in Philadelphia, but that too had to be rescheduled as Steven's problems persisted stubbornly. He was well aware of the dangers of placing too much strain on his vocal cords, but a machine used to create dry ice smoke on stage was not helping him, either. The particular machine Aerosmith had been using at indoor arenas was designed for outdoor use; breathing in its emissions so close to the machine for a couple of hours every night on tour had been inadvisable. Tyler saw a pulmonary specialist and for a while was using inhalers, while the dry ice smoke machine was replaced.

The show got back on track on 10 November at the Rupp Arena in Lexington, Kentucky. Nights at New York's Madison Square Garden and the Continental Arena in East Rutherford, New Jersey, also went without a hitch, but Tyler's sigh of relief was premature. The tour stalled again briefly when their gig at the twelve-thousand-capacity Jefferson Convention Complex Arena in Birmingham, Alabama, on 1 December had to be scrapped at the eleventh hour after a giant scoreboard at the venue fell seventy feet to the ground and was destroyed, just hours before the gig was due to start. Nobody was injured in the incident and it was suspected that the collapse had been due to a snapped cable, but health and safety issues ruled out allowing people into the venue that night. Six more performances brought this eventful leg of the tour to a close in mid-December at the Gund Arena in Cleveland, Ohio. Then Steven was keen to get back to his family.

Back in the summer, for a magazine spread in *Harper's Bazaar*, Tyler had been photographed surrounded by his parents Susan and Victor Tallarico, his sister Lynda, wife Teresa, sister-in-law Lisa and his children, Liv, Mia, Chelsea and Taj. Now, as 2001 began to draw to a close, he needed to catch up with events on the home front.

The complexion of Liv's love life had changed. She and actor Joaquin Phoenix had split up in late 1998 and she had subsequently met and fallen in love with Royston Langdon, then lead singer with the British rock band, Spacehog. In February 2001, Liv and the twenty-eight-year-old frontman became engaged and were living together in a New York apartment. Professionally, Liv had hit the big time for she had been cast as the elven princess, Arwen Undomiel, a leading role in the blockbuster screen version of J.R.R. Tolkien's *The Lord of the Rings* trilogy; other main roles were played by Ian McKellen, Ian Holm, Sean Bean,

Viggo Mortensen and Cate Blanchett. Liv would star in all three films of this fantasy tale, which was shot on location in New Zealand over eighteen months. Of her screen character, Liv said: 'I got to play someone three thousand years old, so that's quite an acting challenge.' As the mythical princess, Liv looked enchanting. Behind the scenes, however, she had her hiccups when the prosthetic ears her character sports melted in the sun. 'I was so upset,' she revealed of this mishap. 'The ears were amazing and I kept them on the dashboard of my car but they're made of gelatine so, of course, by the end of the week one of them had melted into a sticky mess.' The first film in this multi-million-dollar trilogy, *The Lord of the Rings: The Fellowship of the Ring*, had its glitzy world premiere in London at Leicester Square's Odeon Cinema in December 2001, when Liv walked the red carpet alongside co-stars Sean Bean, Christopher Lee and Elijah Wood as a two-thousand-strong crowd of film fans crammed up against the crush barriers.

Steven, then still on tour in the States, was bursting with pride. With her profile sky-high, it was even more inevitable during media interviews that Liv would be quizzed about her parents, particularly her colourful father and the fact that she had grown up for years calling another man Dad. With unwavering candour, Liv talked of the wild and wayward lives her mother and father had led, but she was not prepared to prudishly judge either of them; off the bat, she established that she had been raised always knowing that she was loved by both parents. Of Steven, she declared: 'He has been through rehab and he's clean now but he had some very bad years. The drugs gave him seizures and he could have died. Because of his experience with drugs, I will never go near the stuff.' Of her mother, Bebe Buell, Liv revealed: 'I forgave my mom for deceiving me as to who my real dad was. My mom and I are still close, but my dad and I are true soulmates!'

Offsetting Steven's pleasure in the positive path Liv's life was taking, was his concern for Mia. Her modelling career continued to flourish but in 2001 her mother, Cyrinda Foxe, suffered a stroke that left her partially paralysed, and her ill health would drastically worsen. The downside of being a successful touring rock star is being unable to be there at crucial times for one's family. Steven's wife, Teresa, knew how much that aspect of his fame tortured him. That said, she and Tyler's eldest daughters each knew how committed he was to his craft. Steven once confessed poignantly that when he is on the road during these gargantuan world tours, in the absence of having his loved ones around him, each night at gigs the fans filling the front row become his 'family'. Let loose on tour, Tyler knew that he had to toe the line and look after himself. He still remembered those decadent days when a drug cocktail would await him backstage in his dressing room, but ruefully he accepted that nowadays with grown-up daughters ready to catch him out, the wildest defiance left to him was to hack into a fresh cream cookie when no one was looking!

In early January 2002, Steven limbered up for a fourth, though short, seven-date North American leg of the *Just Push Play* tour. Commencing in Denver, it wrapped mid-month in San Diego. Some things never changed, though. While Tyler remained absolutely focused on every minute detail of each show and its sound, his best mate Joe Perry continued to take a more laid-back approach. When these separate approaches clashed, Steven and Joe would lock horns. Perry has admitted that he can be deliberately contrary, just to annoy his friend. Then, having thought about things, he sometimes has to concede that Tyler is right. No one in the know took any notice of these noisy arguments, for all they did was spark up the dynamic between the men, which in turn spiced up the band.

Out on stage, Tyler continued to hold court as the consummate showman, and such was the enthusiasm Aerosmith met on this leg that when they played at The Joint, a two-thousand-seat venue within the Hard Rock Hotel in Las Vegas, Nevada, on 11 January, they recorded the show for future release as a live album. After a stint in Japan, the *Just Push Play* tour ended in February, with the statistics reading nicely. The tour ranked as the eighth highest grossing of the previous year – the total gross was more than $43.5 million – and over the entire length of the tour Aerosmith had performed to nudging one million fans.

Back on home turf, Steven faced a different kind of crowd when on 1 April, to help kick off the new baseball season, he belted out an inimitable rendition of 'The Star-Spangled Banner' before more than thirty-three thousand sports fans packed into Boston's Fenway Park to watch the Red Sox take on the Toronto Blue Jays. Mid-month, Tyler was truly over the moon when Aerosmith was afforded MTV Icon status – the first rock band to be honoured in this way – the previous year, Janet Jackson had been crowned the inaugural MTV Icon. MTV Entertainment president, Brian Graden, issued the statement: 'Aerosmith is one of those very few bands whose influence pre-dates and spans the entire history of MTV. They have become a fixture at the network and we are thrilled to be able to honour them in this fashion for their continuing contribution to music and music video.'

A tribute show titled *MTV's Icon: Aerosmith* was taped in Los Angeles, during which various acts performed Aerosmith hits. Among those performers were Kid Rock, who had inducted Aerosmith into the Rock and Roll Hall of Fame in 2001, Pink, Papa Roach, Shakira and X-Ecutioners. Janet Jackson offered a testimonial to the band, and others taking part included the actress Alicia Silverstone. Although a few performers had teamed up to produce their version of the classic 'Walk This Way' video, Aerosmith themselves provided the event's finale; this tribute show aired three days later, on 17 April 2002.

That spring, Steven and the band went to Maui, Hawaii, for a working holiday; while relaxing after the *Just Push Play* tour, they wanted to come up with some new material for possible inclusion in an upcoming greatest hits compilation. Tyler spent much of his time on the beach, writing lyrics. One song, 'Girls of Summer' hit the spot with him; he still adored the whole process of creating. He said: 'I just love melody, wherever it takes you. It's in my Italian blood. We pushed up the rhythm guitar on that song. It was almost better as an acoustic song, rather than done with the whole band.'

Aerosmith swapped Maui for Miami when it came to shooting the 'Girls of Summer' video. Working with director David Meyers on South Beach, the band hired more than two hundred female models to take part in a caper that told the tale of young girls out to have fun. Steven said: 'They're hotties and the guys are always trying to hit on them. At the beginning, the main character takes a Polaroid of a guy she spent the night with and shows it to the rest of them. It's a lot of good stuff.'

In July, Aerosmith released the double album, *O, Yeah! The Ultimate Aerosmith Hits*, which charted in America at number four, and number six in Britain. This compilation included the summer anthem, 'Girls of Summer', which was released in the States as a single. It did not chart on Billboard, but picked up a Grammy Award nomination for Best Rock Performance by a Duo or Group with Vocal.

In August, Liv's mother, Bebe Buell, published her tell-all memoir, titled *Rebel Heart: An American Rock 'n' Roll Journey*, in which she relayed tales of her time with her famous lovers, including details of her racy exploits with Steven. Tyler, meanwhile, concentrated on Aerosmith's short North American tour, planned to back the greatest hits album. Dubbed the Girls of Summer tour, it kicked off mid-month in Holmdel, New Jersey. Opening acts for this tour were Kid Rock and Run D.M.C. Crisscrossing states from Pennsylvania to Illinois, after a single incursion into Canada, the band was back on America's east coast to play a gig at the Tweeter Center in Camden, New Jersey, on 7 September when Steven received the tragic news that his ex-wife Cyrinda had just died.

Having survived a stroke the previous year, Cyrinda had since been diagnosed with brain cancer. Although Steven had battled Cyrinda's plans in the past to include nude photographs of him in her memoir, court wrangling and bad feeling were swept aside when he learned of this dreadful diagnosis, and he and his first wife had patched up their differences. Anxious also to do what he

could practically for Cyrinda, Steven had weighed in with financial assistance to help cover her medical expenses, and he
donated an electric guitar for a fundraiser in her name. Cyrinda
had become involved with a musician named Keith Waa, whom
she married on 28 August 2002, a mere ten days before her
death. While undergoing cancer treatment, Cyrinda was staying
at the Gramercy Park Hotel in New York, and she and Keith had
married at her bedside there. Her third husband later said: 'She
was very sick and we wanted to do it before it was too late.'
Cyrinda was just fifty when she passed away. Heartbroken for
twenty-three-year-old Mia losing her mother, Steven paid his
respects at Cyrinda's funeral on 10 September.

The first leg of Aerosmith's tour ended twelve days later in
Noblesville, Indiana, which concluded Run D.M.C.'s stint as a
support act. Less than a fortnight later, the second round of gigs
began in Mayland Heights, Missouri, only for news of yet
another death to reach Tyler's ears. On 30 October, as Aerosmith
was due to perform at the C.W. Mitchell Pavilion at the
Woodlands in Texas, the shocking news broke that Run D.M.C.'s
musician and mixer Jam Master Jay (real name Jason Mizell) had
been fatally shot by an unknown gunman in a recording studio
in the Jamaica section of Queens, New York. Early reports said
that two men had walked into the recording studio's waiting
room where Mizell was and opened fire with a .45 calibre gun.
Jason took a head shot, which killed him instantly. As lurid
rumours circulated about a possible motive for this brutal, cold-
blooded murder, Aerosmith joined others in the music industry
in paying respects to Jason Mizell and contributed to a fund set
up to try and find the shadowy gunman. The second leg of the
Girls of Summer tour segued into its final trek, which wrapped
up on 21 December at the MCI Center in Washington DC, by
which time Aerosmith again ranked in the Top Ten Touring Acts
of America, sandwiched between Neil Diamond and the Eagles.
The runaway top touring artist in the world in 2002, by a huge
margin, was Paul McCartney, who raked in a staggering $126.1
million, according to *Billboard*.

There was an edginess in the music world, however. Already alive to the dangers faced by its stars from stalkers, its fears were further fuelled by the murder of Jam Master Jay. Following John Lennon's point-blank slaying in 1980, some stars had at least considered carrying weapons for their personal protection in America. Even before this recent murder, both Steven and Joe Perry had been granted New York police department permits to carry a gun.

Relegating dark fears to the back of his mind, Tyler ended 2002 happy. Liv's second outing as Arwen Undomiel in *The Lord of the Rings: The Two Towers* hit the US silver screen in December, by which time she had been voted the sixth Sexiest Female Movie Star in a poll run by the *Australian Empire* magazine. Steven made a small screen appearance that same month when he played Santa Claus in an episode of the US children's television show, *Lizzie McGuire*.

On 25 March 2003, Liv and her fiancé Royston Langdon married at a private ceremony held at a villa in Barbados. Reportedly, neither Steven nor Bebe was invited to the Caribbean wedding and were each said to be upset about this. The young couple, however, held a reception a month later in New York, which their family and friends attended.

Tyler, in contrast, was very much of a mind to pay public tribute to his mother and father when he received an Honorary Doctorate from Boston's Berklee College of Music. Founded in 1945, this independent music college is considered to be one of America's top institutions for the study of music outside classical and jazz music. Its buildings are clustered around Boylston Street in Boston's Back Bay area, and Steven had passed the college countless times when living and gigging around this part of the city as a lean and hungry would-be rock star.

Rigged out in graduation gown and tasselled hat, Steven accepted the Honorary Degree at the College's commencement ceremony on 10 May. Delivering his address on stage at the Reggie Lewis Track Center in Boston, Tyler was inimitably irreverent. He told his amused audience: 'All of us in this room may be different shapes, sizes, colours, may have different interpretations of a G-string and come from different places but it's the DNA that tags us as members of the same tribe. In other words, we're all here 'cause we're not all there!'

Speaking of his passion for music and his staunch belief in its sheer power he credited his mother, Susan, for ensuring that music had been woven into the very fabric of his life from a tender age. He praised his father, Victor, for having passed down to him some of his magic as a gifted classical pianist. Recounting a loving home life where his mother had nightly read him fairy stories until he had fallen asleep, and where he had crouched happily beneath his father's Steinway grand piano as Victor had diligently practised, Steven allowed his enraptured audience a very personal glimpse into where the raucous rock star had come from and how his destiny had been shaped. In summing up, he also thanked his wife Teresa and his children for their understanding of his need to get out in the world and express his music.

Thereafter, Steven dropped off the radar, but news started to leak out that Aerosmith was working on an album that would comprise mainly covers of blues numbers by the likes of Muddy Waters, Willie Dixon and Blind Willie McTell. The band had been rehearsing songs at Joe Perry's home studio near Boston, and the album was to be co-produced with Jack Douglas. It was said that they were looking to include some original gritty songs that would resonate with a live energy. Of these efforts, Joe confirmed: 'Some of the songs sound like classic Aerosmith from the 1970s, others sound like old blues songs, but we had a really good time playing them all. We really wanted to get back into the basement and play a live record. This seemed like the obvious way to go.'

Aerosmith emerged from the background that summer to co-headline a US tour with Kiss. Called the *Rocksimus Maximus* Tour, it was launched on 2 August at the Meadows Music Theater in Hartford, Connecticut. A new hard rock band, Saliva, had the task of whetting the audience appetite for each double-header gig before Kiss put on their flashy theatrical show and were followed by Aerosmith's hard rock set. From Connecticut, the bandwagon rolled two days later into Wantagh, New York, to play the Jones Beach Amphitheater, impressing Jon Wiederhorn for MTV to report: 'Even after thirty-three years with Aerosmith, Tyler sounds hungry and lustful. His cigarette rasp soars over the group's ragged rhythms and he still has a fierce, glass-breaking, banshee wail.'

As the tour worked its way around the country Steven, Joe and Brad found time on 4 September to perform at the NFL season kick-off in Washington DC. The second anniversary of the 9/11 terrorist attacks in America was just around the corner, and Aerosmith and Kiss were among those performers who had decided to avoid playing on that emotive date. September 11 had largely become a day for solemn reflection to honour the dead. It was also thought that this anniversary date could attract a threat to any large gathering. The Rocksimus Maximus Tour got back in the groove on 12 September with a performance in West Palm Beach, Florida.

For Steven, personally, the first leg of this tour ended memorably when, seven months on from Liv's wedding, Mia also decided to get married. She had met Papa Roach drummer, Dave Buckner, at the taping of the *MTV's Icon: Aerosmith* tribute show in spring 2002. Now the pair chose to tie the knot very publicly by marrying on stage during Aerosmith's performance on 26 October 2003 at the MGM Grand Garden Arena in Las Vegas. Tyler later recalled how Mia and Dave had turned up for the gig and sprung this plan on him. Said Steven: 'I got my road manager and had him talk to the manager of the MGM Grand and he got me a judge. The judge came down and married them.' According to Tyler, after Aerosmith performed 'Walk This Way', he announced to the twenty-thousand-strong audience: '"Hey, Vegas, I need a favour. My daughter wants to get married tonight. Can I get a witness?" They roared and I brought Mia out and the place went crazy!' The gig carried on after this unscheduled event, with Steven launching, perhaps inauspiciously, into 'Cryin'.

Steven revealed that a little corner inside him had wished that Mia had waited, but so long as she was happy, then he was too. He pointed out: 'All you can really do is look your kids in the eye and ask: "Do you *really* love him? Do you think you're doing the right thing?"' Tyler also conceded that his two eldest daughters in their mid-twenties displayed a great deal more maturity than he had shown at that age, which kind of compromised his chances of passing judgement on them in any way, even had he remotely wanted to.

The second leg of the Aerosmith and Kiss tour, which began in Omaha, Nebraska, in early November, ended just before Christmas in Fresno, California. Throughout, Steven had belted out Aerosmith hits but he had also showcased each night a three-song set of blues numbers that were to feature on the band's next album. This new offering was different, but having tested the water a little, Tyler was keenly awaiting the fans' reaction to it.

# CHAPTER 15

# Shouldering Secrets And Sorrows

**M**ID-JANUARY 2004 it was announced that Aerosmith would once again provide entertainment during America's NFL Super Bowl – this time headlining the pre-game show on 1 February at Reliant Stadium in Houston, Texas, when the New England Patriots took on the Carolina Panthers. Excited by the prospect, Steven waxed lyrical: 'The Super Bowl is rock 'n' roll. It's sexy, it's slammin', it's precision, it's passion and pure energy.'

Tyler was typically spontaneous, too, when it came to naming the band's much anticipated forthcoming album, *Honkin' on Bobo*; a title with no explanation, which both baffled and amused the others. Steven was deadly serious, however, about this new work, which mainly comprised covers of classic blues songs. Their fans had been yearning for some time for the band to return to the harder sound of their 1970s' material, and since Aerosmith's roots are embedded in a love of raw rhythm and blues, it was a challenge that resonated with them. The timing was good, as blues music was enjoying a revival around the world.

The twelve-song collection included the Ruby Fisher and Kenyon Hopkins number 'Shame, Shame, Shame', Fred Mcdowell's 'Back Back Train' and 'You Gotta Move', the Sonny Boy Williamson song 'Eyesight to the Blind', Willie Dixon's 'I'm Ready' and 'Never Loved a Girl', which was a reworked version of Ronny Shannon's song, 'I Never Loved a Man'. The only original song was a slow ballad called 'The Grind', written by Steven, Joe and Marti Frederiksen, which had been in the works for some time.

*Honkin' on Bobo* was recorded in three studios (including Perry's home studio, The Boneyard) and was co-produced with Jack Douglas. Not having worked with Douglas since the late seventies, they found it a surreal experience to look over and see Jack at the helm. Perry once described it like having 'wicked flashbacks – twenty years had passed but not a moment had passed'. It had proved invigorating, though, particularly as they had laid down the tracks as live sessions in a bid to bring an intrinsically charged energy to the songs. For Steven, recording this way showcased just what his band's best strength was. Released at the end of March, *Honkin' on Bobo* peaked at number five in the US album chart and made the UK's Top 30. The album only went gold, and no cut released from it made it on to the Billboard singles chart, but this blues collection added to a rising Aerosmith album sales tally worldwide that was cementing the band's standing as one of America's greatest rock bands.

In support of *Honkin' on Bobo*, and backed by Cheap Trick, Aerosmith went back on the road. They aimed to play smaller arenas than in the past; to complement this, their stage set resembled an intimate blues club. Kicking off on 11 March at the United Spirit Arena in Lubbock, they gigged around Texas before moving to Little Rock, Arkansas. Concentrating on centres in the likes of Tupelo, Tallahassee, Atlanta and Dayton, in mid-April they played two shows in Canada before winding up in Green Bay, Wisconsin. Only one of the twenty-one gigs had to be cancelled, but the second leg did not escape derailment. Commencing in early May at the Hilton Coliseum in Ames,

Iowa, the tour rolled along for a few weeks until illness in the band knocked out shows in New Jersey, Pennsylvania and Virginia Beach. Managing to get through a performance in Star Lake, Pittsburgh, they had to postpone the next gig, scheduled for the P.N.C. Bank Arts Center in Holmdel, New Jersey; it was tagged on at the end of this leg, which got back on track on 22 June at the Jones Beach Theater in Wantagh, New York. Gigs in Mansfield, Hershey and Cuyahoga Falls, Ohio, completed their North American jaunt. There was scant time for Steven to recharge his batteries before undertaking the final segment of the *Honkin' on Bobo* tour, and if anything was likely to remind him of his age it was the news that he would become a grandfather before the end of the year.

On the back of the blockbuster *Lord of the Rings* trilogy, Liv was now not so much labelled as the daughter of Aerosmith's once wild-living frontman, but more as a gifted actress with the film world at her feet. Liv herself declared: 'I don't live a very posh life. There are no drivers waiting or people doing everything for me. I pretty much live like a normal person. It's not good to have a life without responsibilities.' Soon after her wedding to British frontman Royston Langdon she had expressed a desire to have a family. In summer 2004 she revealed that she was pregnant. 'Roy and I are both overjoyed and looking forward to the arrival of our child,' she said. Steven so anticipated this baby's arrival that he had an added spring in his step as Aerosmith took off for a two-week tour of Japan, which got under way at the Sapporo Dome. Between appearances in Osaka and Nagoya, a gig at the Green Arena in Hiroshima had to be cancelled due to Steven picking up an injury. Then, after a tumultuous night at the Tokyo Dome, Aerosmith brought an end to the tour by headlining at the Rock Odyssey Festival, which climaxed on 25 July at the Osaka Dome. Over two evenings, the festival had also featured performances from The Who and Paul Weller.

Back home near Boston, Steven had to rest up. His vocal cords were in a fragile condition and he had suffered badly with his throat behind the scenes on tour. In addition to coping with his own health problems, Tyler continued to do what he could to advise people dealing with addiction. He devoted time to a variety of causes, and not always in the full glare of the media. Steven was involved at this time with the Musicians Assistance Program, which offered help to artists struggling with substance abuse problems. He also lends a hand to those aiding addicts in the street who are battling the same demons. In November, Tyler went to the Women's Hope facility in Boston, which deals with treating substance abuse. There, he helped to serve up a traditional turkey dinner for Thanksgiving Day and afterwards spent time listening to and talking with the residents about addiction. While Steven still does not set himself up as a crusader hell-bent on reforming addicts, he is passionate about giving hope to those who are at rock bottom and desperate to get clean. He is the first to admit to being a prime example of someone who could scarcely have sunk any lower but lived to claw his way back to sobriety. His emphasis to the women at this treatment centre was that it *can* be done. The star's visit had been strictly under the radar, and the struggling addicts appreciated it.

In a broader sense, Steven was in the mood to take stock of the rollercoaster nature of his colourful life to date; having once lost everything, he spoke publicly about the perils of now having too much money. Having left the days of his drug and alcohol addictions long behind him he was, nevertheless, conscious of having to keep a rein on the compulsive element of his nature. One valuable aspect about being wealthy and having his wits was that he could target the best use of his money; right then this translated into purchasing extra acres around his existing property in order to increase his privacy. He keeps a small amount of poultry and other birds, and he enjoys taking long walks around his land accompanied by a couple of pet dogs. He stated: 'Being in the limelight, I can't go out for an hour. I can't really go anywhere any more. So my home is my refuge.'

While on tour, when keeping up with the family news from back home, Steven had heard that Liv had been an expectant

(*Above*) Tyler's drive to entertain draws devotion from Aerosmith's staunchly loyal fans, known collectively as The Blue Army.

(*Left*) Steven performing on the Aerosmith and Kiss World tour, 2003, with his trademark scarves hanging from the microphone stand.

(*Above left*) Tyler's first marriage to model Cyrinda Foxe (*right*) ended in an acrimonious divorce. They are pictured here in 1994, celebrating their daughter Mia's sixteenth birthday.

(*Above right*) Tyler, his daughter Liv (*left*) and Bebe Buell at the *Stealing Beauty* premiere, 1996. Liv was conceived during Steven and Bebe's brief relationship in 1976, but she grew up for years thinking that Todd Rundgren was her father.

(*Above left*) This November 1994 *Rolling Stone* cover shot provoked criticism that it looked incestuous; an absurd reaction that greatly angered Tyler.

(*Above right*) Steven's second wife, Teresa (*left*), and their children Taj (*below left*) and Chelsea (*centre*), with step-sister Mia at the MTV Icon tribute to Aerosmith, 2002.

(*Above left*) Tyler received an honorary doctorate from Boston's Berklee College of Music in 2003. He quipped to his audience, 'All of us have different interpretations of a G-string'.

(*Above right*) Tyler salutes the crowd at Fenway Park, Boston, as the Red Sox baseball team take on the Detroit Tigers in 2008.

A passionate biker, and designer of his own Red Wing motorcycle, Tyler takes a spin in Beverly Hills with girlfriend Erin Brady in 2007.

Giving something back: Tyler, alongside Guns n' Roses guitarist Slash, performs at the fourth annual MusiCares Map Fund Benefit Concert in Los Angeles, May 2008.

(*Above left*) Steven and Erin Brady pictured at the Hard Rock Hotel and Casino, Las Vegas, April 2007.

(*Above right*) On the surface Tyler is irrepressibly cheeky, but it is also his strong will and serious approach to music that make him a superstar.

mother who glowed throughout the pregnancy, and he knew how much his daughter and her husband were looking forward to their first baby's arrival. On 14 December 2004, in the early hours of the morning, at a hospital in Manhattan, New York, Liv gave birth to an eight-pound baby boy whom she and Royston named Milo William Langdon. According to *People* magazine, Liv delightedly told a friend: 'My baby is so handsome. He also has full lips!'

Steven was over the moon to be a grandfather and was thrilled for Liv and Royston, but his delight in this new addition to the family was seriously counter-balanced by the deep, private pain that his marriage to Teresa was in trouble. He had managed remarkably well to mask in public that his domestic situation had been crumbling; as he would later reveal, his marriage was falling apart at an extremely bad time for him in another way. He and Teresa had been married for seventeen years, which in show business circles is an enviably long time, and their children, Chelsea and Taj, were sixteen and thirteen years old respectively.

Steven and Teresa, however, split up, and on 20 February 2005 Aerosmith's publicist, Mitch Schneider, released a press statement on Steven's behalf which said: 'Before the tabloid media makes more of this than it is, I am announcing that my wife, Teresa, and I are currently separated. We are just a family trying to work through a difficult time. A little privacy and sensitivity – for Teresa, my children and myself – would be nice.'

News of this split was widely reported across the media and raised a few eyebrows, for despite Steven's overtly salacious public persona, the Tylers' marriage was thought to have been as solid as a rock. That said, Roger Friedman for *FOX* News appeared to feel that he had the inside track. He stated: 'No reason was given for what seemed like surprising news, but I have known that all was not well in the Tyler household.' Inevitably, speculation surfaced as to who was to blame for the split, but although some commentators expressed views, no one was privy to the truth, and Steven and Teresa preferred to keep a lid on their private business.

Teresa had played a massive part in helping Steven through one of the worst phases of his life and it must have been heart-breaking for them to be parting company. Steven found solace in spending time with his first grandchild, Milo, and his public life went on as before. With his ties to Boston, he had recorded a tape for a city tour called 'Boston: City of Rebels and Dreamers'. He lent lead vocals to Carlos Santana's hit single, 'Just Feel Better', and in April he appeared in a cameo role as himself in the feature film *Be Cool*, a comedy directed by F. Gary Gray starring John Travolta, Uma Thurman, Harvey Keitel and James Woods. In the film, Steven is seen performing a duet of 'Cryin' with a would-be vocalist played by Christina Milian.

On 3 June, Steven collected his second honorary doctorate – this time from the University of Massachusetts in Boston. It was in recognition not only of his music, but also for his support of philanthropic causes from literacy and homelessness, to rehabil-itation for alcoholism and for his support for families of soldiers killed in Iraq. Over two thousand students attended the commencement day ceremony, held on the lawn at the univer-sity's Dorchester campus. In graduation garb and dark glasses, Steven received his scroll from Jack M. Wilson, the president of the University of Massachusetts, and J. Keith Motley, the interim Chancellor.

That summer there were sporadic rumours that Steven was working on a solo album, but it was Joe Perry who released his fourth such effort, titled simply *Joe Perry*. It had been twenty-one years since *Once a Rocker, Always a Rocker*, and on this new album, which had been recorded at his home studio, Joe had handled everything himself (including the vocals) except the drum work, for which he had enlisted the services of his co-producer, Paul Caruso. At the 2006 Grammy Awards, Joe was nominated for Best Rock Instrumental Performance for the track 'Mercy'. Joe Perry releasing solo work was not a sign that there was trouble in the band; indeed, Aerosmith was said to be lining up rehearsal sessions in preparation for an autumn tour.

Steven continued to have his reasons for lying low. He also

needed to spend time with his son and three daughters. He wanted to do all he could to help Chelsea and Taj come to terms with their parents' split. It warmed him to see Liv so happy and settled, but he was concerned for Mia, for her marriage to Papa Roach drummer Dave Buckner had foundered. Hitched so publicly, on stage during an Aerosmith gig in Las Vegas, two years on Mia and Dave had filed for divorce.

Mia's professional profile was developing. She now revealed that her late mother, Cyrinda, had given her a few modelling tips, advising her always to remember to keep her chin up, to wear nude underwear and be sure to work her strong eyes to the best advantage. In 2005, Mia took part in the US reality television series, *Celebrity Fit Club*, when she shed eighteen pounds. It was not Mia's first experience of subjecting herself to this sort of regime. In the early 1990s, she had attended a camp to help over-weight children to slim, and it had been a trying ordeal for her. She lost thirty pounds in six weeks, but had felt so miserable throughout those weeks that when it was over she regained all the weight she had shed and more besides. Although her experi-ence of the *Celebrity Fit Club* series was appreciably better, in general terms she felt that she could never recommend anyone to undertake such regimes.

With her father's and her half-sister's stardom it could be easy to feel overshadowed, but Mia does not. She is independent, with her own reservoir of self-confidence, and she can come away with telling quips about her rascally, unorthodox father, often remarking on the fact that there are two Steven Tylers – the private man, who is Dad, and the larger-than-life rock icon. Said Mia recently: 'He is a family man. Then he puts on his tights and make-up and goes on stage. He's totally cute, like a little boy in an old man's skin. I can see him rocking out when he's eighty, with scarves tied around his walker!'

As the leaves were turning brown around Boston, with Aerosmith rehearsing, news emerged that no studio album was forthcoming. Instead, in October, the band was releasing the live album, *Rockin' the Joint*, comprising tracks culled from a performance during the *Just Push Play* tour three years earlier at The Joint at the Hard Rock Hotel in Las Vegas. *Rockin' the Joint* peaked at number twenty-four on Billboard, while Steven and his bandmates hit the live circuit yet again.

With the Brooklyn-born singer Lenny Kravitz as support act, Aerosmith opened the *Rockin' the Joint* tour at the end of October 2005 with a gig at the Mohegan Sun Arena in Uncasville, Connecticut. About a month into the tour, it was reported that after an Aerosmith gig in Pittsburgh, Steven and Joe Perry were to take a swift detour to New York to perform at a bar mitzvah party.

This private bash, to be held in The Rainbow Room, was thrown by the multi-millionaire David H. Brooks for his daughter, Elizabeth. Brooks apparently had Tyler and Perry ferried from Pittsburgh to New York by chartered jet. At this extravagant celebration, other star performers were reported to include drummer Don Henley and lead guitarist Joe Walsh of the Eagles, the rocker Tom Petty, 50 Cent and Fleetwood Mac singer Stevie Nicks. According to the press, David H. Brooks shelled out a total of $10 million to hire this stellar line-up of entertainment; one report broke down how much each performer was earning for the gig. But the multi-millionaire disputed this, telling the *New York Daily News:* 'All dollar figures are vastly exaggerated. This was a private event and we do not wish to comment on details of the party.'

From late November to mid-December, Aerosmith rolled through seven US states, then Steven packed away his microphone after a show at the Van Andel Arena in Grand Rapids, Michigan. It could not hope to be the same holiday period for Steven without Teresa to come home to, and perhaps it was as well that the ticker tape and streamers had barely been brushed away after the celebrations in New York's Times Square that rang in 2006, when the *Rockin' the Joint* tour resumed on 5 January in Orlando, Florida, again backed by Lenny Kravitz.

A handful of gigs later, having returned to Florida for a show in Tampa, at one point Tyler was joined at the microphone by

Robin Zander, lead vocalist of Cheap Trick; days later came an announcement that Aerosmith planned to extend their tour by adding a third leg, starting in early March, and to be opened by the 1980s band. In the meantime, Lenny Kravitz continued to hold down the warm-up duties.

While Steven dedicated his energies to whipping up a frenzy of excitement, on a personal note, his and Teresa's divorce became official in January 2006. The powerhouse band behind Steven ensured that Aerosmith fans left each venue soaked in delirium, and despite the fact that the band members were each well into their fifties, they still attracted the new teenage generation into the arenas. Aerosmith had specifically set out to reaffirm its standing as a premier hard rock band. Their success in recent years with romantic power ballads had, for some, diluted that, and there was a keener edge than ever to each performance.

The band was also talking about beginning work later in the year on the follow-up to *Honkin' on Bobo*, and they had a clear direction in mind. Tyler told *Rolling Stone*: 'It's going to be just like what White Stripes are doing, like a couple of songs on Sheryl Crow's new album. You'll listen to it and be like: "I've heard that before," but you never did.'

Behind the high-energy stage performances and plans for a new studio album, however, Steven was in trouble. His zest in live performance means that during any gig he literally loses several pounds from his already skeletal frame, and he comes off stage drenched in sweat and almost dehydrated. Getting sufficient rest while on tour is virtually impossible, and because he takes a relentless interest in every aspect of Aerosmith's business and performances he is practically never off duty. Giving each song the full throttle treatment had also been stacking up problems. He managed to conceal them until the second leg of the *Rockin' the Joint* tour ended at Arrowhead Pond in Anaheim, California – but that was about to change.

With Cheap Trick taking over from Lenny Kravitz, just six days later, on 2 March, leg three kicked off at the Seminole Hard

Rock Live venue in Hollywood, Florida. Eighteen gigs were planned to take Aerosmith through to a performance on 9 April at the General Motors Place in Vancouver, British Columbia in Canada, but after the first gig Steven's throat problems forced cancellations to kick in. Eight gigs from Pensacola in Florida, to London, Ontario, were called off to see if the rest would be enough to help him, but his condition showed no sign of improvement and after another examination by doctors it became patently obvious that the remainder of the tour would have to be axed. Steven needed surgery.

A band press release on 22 March 2006 stated: 'Despite Aerosmith's desire to keep the tour going as long as possible, Steven's doctors advised him not to continue performing to give his voice time to recover.' News that Tyler would undergo surgery for 'an undisclosed medical condition' quickly gave rise to rumours that he was battling throat cancer. Publicist Marcee Rondan moved swiftly to scotch these. She told MTV News that rumours claiming that Steven had throat cancer were 'completely untrue'. When pressed, she was not prepared to elaborate on what the problem actually was. It was then said by some that Steven required surgery to correct a popped blood vessel in his throat.

At the time, Steven and his representatives preferred not to detail why he was going under the knife, but eighteen months later the procedure he underwent to repair his right vocal cord featured in the television programme *Incredible Human Machine*, which aired in the US on the National Geographic channel. The leading laryngologist who had operated on Steven was Dr Steven Zeitels, a director at Massachusetts General Hospital, who had dealt with opera stars and other celebrity singers. Dr Zeitels said: 'Singers are the athletes of the performing arts but the stress on the vocal cords eventually creates problems like nodules, polyps and, in Steven Tyler's case, haemorrhaging from a blood vessel that was abnormal from years of singing.'

Steven was on the operating table for less than thirty minutes and Dr Zeitels described him as an exemplary patient. Impressed by the star's determination to understand exactly what had been happening to the blood vessels in his throat, Dr Zeitels said of Steven: 'He's an algorithmic thinker, amazingly bright.' The upshot of the surgery and subsequent post-op vocal therapy was that Steven would not be able to sing for some months to come.

His situation that spring was pretty bleak. He had had surgery twice (for his knee, now his throat), Aerosmith was thrown into an indefinite limbo because of his temporary inability to sing for prolonged periods, and his second marriage had been dissolved. All of these problems were public knowledge. But what only a very select few people knew was that Steven – who had already survived so much in his life – had for a couple of years already been waging a secret battle.

CHAPTER 16

# The Vagabond
# Prince

**N**OT YET ready to publicly divulge the secret he harboured, with remarkable resilience Steven decided in late spring 2006 that he was sufficiently recovered from the throat surgery to join the rest of Aerosmith in knuckling down to work on the follow-up studio album to *Honkin' on Bobo*. Tyler was happy to consider once again collaborating with outside song-writers but, always stimulated by earthy hard rock, his leanings were strongly towards revisiting a sound more redolent of the 1970s. Kicking about with material in the studio, of course, meant testing his vocal cords. As throat surgery can alter a singer's voice, Steven was a shade apprehensive, but a swift glance in his lead guitarist's direction put his mind at rest. Said Joe Perry that summer: 'Steven is sounding better than ever. Even just listening to him talk, his voice has this timbre that I haven't heard for years.'

Proof that Tyler was truly back in harness came in June when Aerosmith announced that they were to hit the road again in just over two months' time. Aerosmith and Motley Crue would co-headline on the so-called Route of All Evil tour. In the old days of drink, drugs and debauchery, these two bad lad bands touring together would have provided an incendiary mix. Even in 2006, it was a pairing that sparked the music media's imagination. Rehearsals got under way for the tour, but Steven's first major public appearance since his throat surgery came when he and Joe Perry performed with the Boston Pops Orchestra at a Fourth of July spectacular concert staged on the city's Charles River Esplanade. During this event, which was broadcast live nationally on *CBS* television, Steven sang 'I Don't Want To Miss a Thing', 'Walk This Way' and 'Dream On' – the audience rewarding the star with cheers and resounding applause when he nailed his famous scream towards the end of this power ballad. Tyler's other appearance that summer was a cameo role in the US television sitcom *Two and a Half Men*. During the episode titled 'Who's Vod Kanockers?' Steven played himself as an obnoxious neighbour from hell.

In late August the focus, health-wise, switched from Steven to bass player Tom Hamilton, when it was announced that he would be unable to take part in most of the upcoming Route of All Evil tour because of having to undergo treatment for throat cancer. Anxious for their bandmate to make a full recovery, Aerosmith enlisted David Hull, a bassist who had played with the Joe Perry Project, to fill Tom's shoes. News then emerged that their plans to release a new studio album in 2007 had had to be pushed back. Perry stated: 'We just could not do it. There wasn't enough time.' Instead, it was decided to release a compilation album. Comprising hits from throughout the band's career, this work also featured two new songs – a hard rock number, 'Devil's Got a New Disguise', and by contrast a mellow country rock song called 'Sedona Sunrise'. As work on this tide-over release began, the tour loomed large, and although Steven had been on song performing live in Boston and in the recording studio, there was concern that the strain of singing night after night in concert for over three months could take its toll.

The Aerosmith and Motley Crue Route of All Evil tour of north America and Canada kicked off on 5 September 2006 with a performance at the Germain Amphitheatre in Columbus, Ohio, and quickly into this trek such fears evaporated. The hard rock spectacle went down a storm with fans and critics alike. *Kerrang* magazine enthusiastically weighed in with its opinion of one of the early shows: 'Aerosmith proved why many deem them America's greatest rock band whether it was born in the 1970s, '80s or '90s. Aerosmith seamlessly create a scrapbook of everything good rock was and, God willing, will always be.'

Less than three weeks later, with everyone on a high, having just played in Camden, New Jersey, Aerosmith had their sights set on a gig at the Tweeter Center in Mansfield, Massachusetts, when Steven dropped the bombshell news that he had been keeping under wraps for so long. Interviewed by Nancy O'Dell on the US television show *Access Hollywood*, he revealed that he had been diagnosed three years earlier with hepatitis C. When the show was aired on 25 September, this news went global.

Hepatitis C is a blood-borne viral infection most commonly spread through unprotected sex or sharing needles. It can damage the liver, potentially leading to chronic conditions such as cirrhosis or liver cancer. Being hard to detect, it is labelled the silent killer, because people can have it and not know. Steven had specifically got himself tested for hepatitis C, and although he was diagnosed with the infection in 2003, he discovered that he had had it for a long time, asymptomatic. Steven revealed: 'The band took a break about three years ago and my doctor said it's eleven months of chemotherapy. So I went on that and it about killed me.' He underwent a year-long ordeal of prescription medication and injections of the powerful anti-viral drug interferon to treat the condition and to strengthen his immune system. The result was that hepatitis C was non-detectable in his bloodstream.

With this tough battle fought in such secrecy now out in the open, Steven could tell television audiences and newspaper readers how extremely difficult it had been for him. He spoke movingly of times at home when he had suffered blackouts because of the treatment and had woken up disoriented, with nosebleeds. He also revealed: 'Your hair falls out, your nails turn yellow, you throw up, you sweat all night.' As he told the *New*

*York Daily News*: 'It really hurt. It was a bad, bad period. I'm in Alcoholics Anonymous and I tried to go three, four, five months with nothing and it, too, about killed me!' What made his ordeal even more poignantly sad is that he had been struggling with this devastating diagnosis and arduous treatment at the same time as his marriage to Teresa had gone on the rocks. He later said of this testing experience: 'It was pretty catastrophic. I got through, one day at a time. Anybody who has been through chemotherapy knows, it sucks.'

When news of Steven's ordeal became public, it was often pointed out that other celebrity sufferers of hepatitis C include *Dallas* star Larry Hagman and *Baywatch* babe Pamela Anderson but, according to the World Health Organisation, there are around six hundred million people around the globe suffering from hepatitis B and C. Now that hepatitis C was non-existent in him, Steven had chosen to reveal his own private battle in order to help raise awareness about this pernicious condition. He wanted to stress that ignorance was not an option – that people potentially at risk would do well to get tested, because hepatitis C is treatable.

Following this revelation, all eyes were fixed on Steven when Aerosmith took to the stage on 26 September in Mansfield, Massachusetts, for the first of two dates there. Perhaps going all out to prove that he had come through the trauma and was back to fighting form, Steven turned on the magic in stunning form. The tour trundled on.

Around this time, Aerosmith released the compilation album titled *Devil's Got a New Disguise – The Very Best of Aerosmith*, which charted on Billboard at number thirty-three. The title track was released as a single, but did not make that US survey. At the end of October, the album was released in Britain and Europe.

After gigging through Kansas, Tennessee, Virginia and North Carolina, and playing to crowds on the west coast of America, Aerosmith headed east through Texas to Florida where on 24 November they played in West Palm Beach at the Sound Advice Amphitheatre. Earlier that day, Tyler was back in helpful mode as, once again, he dished up Thanksgiving dinners, this time to the needy at a restaurant in town. When the band took to the stage in the Joe Louis Arena in Detroit, Michigan, at the beginning of December, Steven was thrilled to officially welcome a recovering Tom Hamilton back to the band. The bassist often jests that he, Brad Whitford and Joey Kramer are somehow viewed as less important Aerosmith members than Joe and Steven but there was no disguising the Blue Army's pleasure at seeing Hamilton back in place.

With a further four gigs around Canada and three US pit stops, the Route of All Evil tour culminated in mid-December 2006 at the ARCO Arena in Sacramento, California. The critical acclaim that greeted the launch of this tour had been sustained throughout, and to Steven's great relief his voice had held out well. He still had to concentrate on building his health and strength, however, after the battering his system had taken during his treatment for hepatitis C, but there was every reason to feel optimistic. Good news also came on 20 December, when Tom Hamilton officially announced to fans that, following a recent scan, he was now pronounced to be cancer free.

For Steven, stepping off tour meant disappearing back into the recording studio to pick up where Aerosmith had left off on work for their next album – but not for long. By late January it was all change again when it was announced that the band planned to embark on a 2007 world tour that would embrace new challenges by pushing into new territories. It sometimes seemed physically impossible for Aerosmith to stand still.

This itch to keep on the move did not prevent Steven from once again taking stock of his personal life. A year on from his second divorce, he was prepared to cite the hectic touring side of his career as having played a significant part in the disintegration of his marriage to Teresa. While it cannot be considered a great life following a husband around from concert to concert saying wow every night and living on the road, in and out of hotel rooms, travelling across America and the world, Steven's stance was that that was what he was – a rock star who loves to be out on stage, entertaining. He has made no secret that he adores what he does – giving live performances particularly – and that it is not a shallow existence to him. Sharing that demanding life, right then, was a new long-legged blonde girlfriend, tour promoter Erin Brady. She and Steven had met and become an item during his recovery from throat surgery the previous year.

Steven considered himself very fortunate that his elderly parents were still alive, and was patently excited that his daughter Chelsea, now eighteen years old, was showing signs of being drawn to his craft. He was thrilled when one day he walked in and found her trying to compose a song. He enjoyed keeping tabs on the development of all four of his offspring and his grandson, Milo.

As a father and grandfather, Steven found himself focusing even more on issues outside music. America's military involvement in Iraq and Afghanistan and the tension with Iran exercised the minds of most Americans, and an organisation called the Peace Alliance supported a campaign in the United States to have a department of peace set up within the government. Over the weekend of 3–5 February 2007, the Peace Alliance held a conference in Washington DC that was attended by nearly one thousand people, including a number of prominent individuals from several walks of life – Steven was one of them. The conference climaxed with a rally held at George Washington University's Lisner Auditorium, at which Steven gave a crowd-stirring performance that punctuated proceedings and left the peace activists optimistic that they had made a mark on America's seat of power, Capitol Hill.

Tyler was on a more familiar platform soon after when Aerosmith flew to London to play a 'secret gig' at the capital's Hard Rock Café on 19 February. It had been eight years since they had last played in London, at Wembley Stadium. This somewhat more intimate 150-strong invite-only crowd was served up a set that blended blues, rock and ballads. Band and audience enjoyed indulging in this celebration of Aerosmith's past glories, but queries regarding the band's future persisted; these were only strengthened when it transpired that their already long-awaited fifteenth studio album would not see the light of day until 2008.

All their energies had to be channelled into preparing for the world tour, which commenced with a sold-out gig on 12 April at the Morumbi Stadium in Sao Paulo, Brazil. Moving on to an appearance at the River Plate Stadium in Buenos Aires, Aerosmith headed from Argentina to Mexico where, three gigs later, they concluded the Latin American leg at the Foro Sol in Mexico City. A single north American concert in late April at Mandalay Bay in Las Vegas then signalled a month's rest before the band took off again.

Steven was more keyed up than usual. Over the span of the six-week second leg, in addition to playing on familiar turf, Aerosmith would be performing live to fans in five countries for the first time; the first of these was the United Arab Emirates. Arriving in the Gulf in late May, however, Tyler had a special appointment to keep. Along with Tom, Brad and Joey, he visited American sailors and marines aboard the aircraft carrier USS *Nimitz* which, commanded by Captain Mike Manazir, was on its first Middle East port visit. For most of the US servicemen and women, this came as a complete surprise and their excitement was palpable. Storekeeper First Class Jacob Rico, an ardent Aerosmith fan anyway, could not believe his eyes when he spotted the frontman in the flesh. Rico later enthused: 'It was cool! Steven Tyler just looked up at me and said: "This is a big ship!" I said: "Yeah! Come on up!"' The four rock stars were cheered and applauded as they were given a guided tour of the ship. Over the vessel's address system, Steven yelled: 'Hi every-body. This is Aerosmith. Hope you guys are playing safe.' Then he spent time on the ceremonial quarterdeck, talking with fans, signing autographs and posing for pictures.

The next evening, 31 May 2007, Steven led Aerosmith out on stage before sixteen thousand fans corralled into the Dubai Autodrome, to be greeted with a rapturous reception. During the two-hour show, Tyler's voice got a rest when in particular songs, after the opening line, the fans took over and sang the hit back to the band. The audience especially appreciated it when for the encore Steven – famous for his dance moves in performance – took time to learn how to throw new shapes from the traditional Arab dancer who accompanied the band on stage.

From the Gulf, Aerosmith travelled to India, touching down just as monsoon conditions were forecast to sweep in. Their single gig in this country took place in early June in Bangalore's impressive Palace Grounds, situated in the heart of the bustling city. Bangalore was no stranger to rock shows, having played host to British hard rock acts including the Rolling Stones, but this again was virgin territory for the American stars. With another nod to an unfamiliar culture, Steven had learned some Hindi words, which he tried out on their massive audience, who managed to stay dry as the predicted downpour never materialised. It did not matter whether the star's attempt at this language was entirely accurate – the fans who had come in their droves from around the subcontinent appreciated the courtesy.

At fifty-nine years old, Steven defied the odds in so many ways; to the excitable crowds he was akin to a disreputable Peter Pan. From the back of packed arenas he appeared to have remained unchanged for the past three decades. Time could almost stand still in this respect for the duration of an Aerosmith gig. Tyler admitted that he had no idea what the secret of the band's longevity was. In the past thirty-seven years he had seen other acts blow themselves out, crash and burn or never get off the starting blocks, and while all the turmoil he and the band had endured would have finished many others off, in a weird way these travails formed part of the glue that essentially bound the band together. Although there was still an element of volatility in the band, each man had become more adept at keeping things in perspective.

One aspect of his busy life Steven would never get used to was missing milestones in his family's lives. While Aerosmith was in the Middle East, Chelsea had graduated from high school. Steven would have preferred to be there and felt bad at having to explain to her that in order to be present at her graduation it would have meant unravelling a multi-million-dollar-earning world tour. When asked about his home life, Steven declared emotionally: 'I am one proud papa and grandpa. It's strange how life works out. One day, you're in a haze, the next you are a family man.'

Steven's ambitions for where his band could yet go remained undiminished. On this tour he maintained: 'Every day brings us something new and we do it, we try it.' But Joe Perry used a broader brush stroke. 'Steven lives and breathes Aerosmith,' he told the UK's *Daily Telegraph*. 'For me, sometimes, it's just a way to make a living. I'm not part of that celebrity thing. I don't need that.'

Tyler had long ago shrugged off comparisons to Mick Jagger, but at times he happily aligned certain aspects of their respective public personas. Citing Jagger, Iggy Pop and himself as singers with not the greatest voices in the world, he pointed out that the vital factor common to all three of them was that they each had attitude!

After India, Aerosmith targeted Scandinavia, commencing in Randers, Denmark, where Tyler's manic on-stage energy gingered up proceedings before the massed crowd in Essex Park. A few rock festival appearances had been sewn into this leg, including appearances in Solvesborg, Sweden, and at the Hessentag Fair in Frankfurt. Quitting Germany in mid-June, after a single gig at the Bercy Arena in Paris, France, the band joined other acts performing at Belgium's Graspop Festival in Dessel. Aerosmith's strong appeal to European fans had been brought home to Steven and, already exhilarated by the tour's runaway success, he was wildly anticipating the next pit stop, for when he and the band boarded the plane from Belgium, the destination was London where they were to headline at the two-day Hyde Park Calling Festival.

On the weekend of 23–24 June 2007, Britain was battered by torrential rain, but nothing could dampen Steven's enthusiasm. Even the normally laconic and laid-back Joe Perry was visibly wired. He declared: 'It is really exciting to think that Hyde Park is going to be filled with eighty thousand maniacs and we get to play for them!'

The two-day Hyde Park Calling festival had been launched the year before, when headliners included Primal Scream and the Who. For this year's event it was expanded to include three stages. On 23 June, Peter Gabriel and Crowded House held court on stage number one. The next night, Aerosmith were to cap the festival. Revved up during the day, Tyler told journalists that he could not wait to get up behind the microphone and 'kick some ass'. He stressed: 'At the end of the day, it's really about having a good time and letting loose. My dad used to tell me: "Musicians and cooks – they are the ones, because everyone has to eat and at the end of the day they want to get up and dance."'

On Sunday evening, as the heavens again opened and drenched the 45,000-strong horde jostling in front of stage number one, acts Jet, the Answer and Chris Cornell played their sets before Aerosmith erupted on stage to power their way through a scintillating one-hour show, belting out one blistering hit after another. One reviewer recalled: 'Strutting around the stage like only he can, Tyler had the audience in the palm of his hand from the opener, "Love in an Elevator".' The climax of the show saw Aerosmith joined on stage during the encore by rapper Darryl McDaniels of Run D.M.C. for a riotous rap-rock rendition of 'Walk This Way', which sent the already delirious audience into orbit. Darryl McDaniels spoke soon after to the media about the experience: 'The thirty years I have been in this business just ran past my eyes. It was awesome because you feed off the crowd.' With immaculate timing, the show ended on the dot of the 10.30 p.m. curfew imposed on the event by London authorities. Tyler told the crowd: 'The cops are turning off the power.'

In the nine months since Steven revealed that he had undergone chemotherapy to conquer hepatitis C, he had received even keener attention, but the star was just as frenetically untamed on stage as ever, still displaying his trademark long flowing locks, and just as hairpin-thin due to constant dieting and working out.

He confessed: 'I do two hundred and fifty press-ups religiously every night before I get into bed.'

Tyler put his natural youthfulness down to his lineage. 'My Italian grandfather on my mother's side had a full head of hair in his old age and my paternal grandfather was a wiry Portuguese sailor,' he said. He did not shrink from questions about his former wild child days, but preferred to move on. He did want, however, to continue to stress that for addicts sunk in the mire the only way to sobriety was to go through the rigours of rehab, and he maintained that it was being clean of drugs that enabled him once more to hit the high notes in songs.

Aerosmith made their mark at Marley Park in Dublin, Ireland, before returning to eastern Europe. They wove gigs in Germany, the Netherlands and Finland around the remainder of their groundbreaking appearances in this corner of the world, which saw them entertain audiences at the Skonto Stadium in Riga, Latvia, the A Le Coq Arena in Tallinn, Estonia, and during performances in Russia at the SKK Arena in St Petersburg and the Moscow Olimpijsky Arena.

Jetting across the Atlantic, they were committed to participating in two Canadian events – the Sarnia Bayfest in Ontario and the Blast at the Beach in Charlottetown, Prince Edward Island – before heading to sunny California, where an appearance at the Mid State Fair in Paso Robles preceded wrapping up this leg on 27 July with a gig at the Konocti Harbour Resort in Kelseyville.

Taking August off to catch their breath, Aerosmith was one of the acts to perform at the star-studded yearly extravaganza, Fashion Rocks. Recorded at Radio City Music Hall in New York on 6 September, it aired nationally as a two-hour special the following night on CBS television.

On 8 September, Aerosmith embarked on the fourth leg of their 2007 world tour, opening at Clarkston in Michigan. With Joan Jett and the Blackhearts as support act, only nine gigs were scheduled; concentrated in an eighteen-day period, the pace was brisk. Six days into this leg, they turned up in Mansfield, Massachusetts, to play the Tweeter Center. The last time they had been there, Steven had just dropped the bombshell news of his secret battle with hepatitis C, which had stunned and worried his fans. Of this night the *Boston Globe*'s Joan Anderman was moved to write next day: 'The stage was sleek and uncluttered, a clean palette for Steven Tyler's star power. Tyler strutted the catwalk, a model rock god, scarves flowing from his hat, his neck and his mike stand, gripping fans by the wrists, dipping his fingers into a woman's drink and rubbing it behind his ear.'

Because Aerosmith had been so much on the road since getting their second wind, they inevitably revisited venues fairly frequently and were concerned that they could become stale to the fans. It seemed unlikely, if for no other reason than the basic psyche in the band. As Joe Perry put it: 'This band has always felt like the underdog. We come from a time when you earned your bones by playing better than the other guy and there is always a "competing with ourselves" kind of thing. We are forever saying: "What did we do last time we were here? We gotta kick some ass this time."' The tour ground to a halt in late September in Illinois.

To add to Steven's contentment with how the tour had gone, he was privately pleased in early October, when Mia, who had suffered the loss of her mother and the demise of her first marriage, found happiness again with a guitarist named Brian Harrah. They had newly become engaged and Mia was thrilled with her father's reaction. She told the media: 'We went over to my dad's hotel to show off the ring. He grabbed Brian and hugged him and was like: "Good job, son!" My dad absolutely loves him.'

On 5 November at the 2007 *Classic Rock* Roll of Honour Awards, held at London's Landmark Hotel, Aerosmith's headlining performance at that summer's Hyde Park Calling Festival won the trophy for Event of the Year. During these awards, Jimmy Page received the Living Legend Award, which Steven presented.

In his spare time, Tyler was able to indulge in one of his strongest passions outside music – motorcycling. Despite a serious motorbike accident years earlier that landed him in hospital, he retained a love of these powerful machines. So much so that in 2007 he had teamed up with an engineer, Mark Dirico, and A.C. Custom Motorcycles based in Manchester, New Hampshire, to launch a new line of custom-built bikes called the Red Wing motorcycle. Steven had designed the sleek motorbike, which its makers claimed had thirty-five per cent more horsepower than a stock Harley Davidson motorcycle. The flashy, glamorous Red Wing had been unveiled at the New Hampshire International Speedway that September. Said Steven: 'You get on one of these bikes and you can ride for days. These bikes are damn cool and just amazing to look at!'

Completely at home with the biker fraternity, Steven travelled to Hollywood, Florida, in early December to attend an annual Bikers Bash shindig held in the Pangaea Lounge, a nightclub inside the Hard Rock Hotel and Casino situated in a Seminole Reservation. A small disturbance in the club's VIP room made the national newspapers when it was reported that Steven's girlfriend Erin Brady got into a dispute with a Seminole Indian woman. One witness told the *New York Post*: 'A woman from the tribe was trying to take a picture of Steven Tyler. Steven's girlfriend was coming back from the restroom. Apparently Erin got in the way of the picture or something and words were exchanged. Next thing everyone knows, the two girls are going at it – scratching, hair pulling, hitting. It lasted about six seconds, then security broke it up.'

After the club's security people calmed matters down, a spokesman for the establishment quipped to journalists: 'There's nothing like a catfight and an ageing rock legend to make an evening entertaining.' Newspaper headlines said that Steven and all involved in the fracas waited at the club to be questioned by officers from the Seminole police department. Steven was questioned as a witness to the spat but no charges were laid and around dawn everyone was free to go.

Those taking an interest in Tyler's love life wondered if there would ever be a Mrs Tyler mark III. Asked directly about his views on wedlock, the twice-divorced Steven mused: 'I guess I'm just not the marrying type. It's been proven time and again. It's not that I am not capable of loving another person. I am. But, spending our lives together? That's where I run into trouble.'

On 26 March 2008, Steven turned sixty. There may have been bleak days in his distant past when he had wondered if he would ever reach this milestone birthday, but when specifically asked once what he envisaged himself being like at that age he had inimitably responded: 'I'm always going to love Jimi Hendrix. "Purple Haze" will still give me a hard-on when I'm hooked up to a life support machine.'

Nothing like infirm, at sixty Steven looked forward to the release of Aerosmith's fifteenth studio album, and talk of a tour quickly surfaced. Impressively, the band's average earnings on tour are one million dollars a show. Having sold around 150 million albums worldwide, Aerosmith ranks as the second bestselling American group – the Eagles hold the top slot – and has inspired a new generation of rock artists to follow in their wake.

Over the course of almost four decades in the business, Steven has branded his unique stamp on rock's firmament. His strong survival instinct has seen him beat addictions for heroin, cocaine and alcohol. Tasting the heady heights of moneyed stardom, he lost it all and descended into squalid penury, only to rise again to become a bone fide living rock icon, battling hepatitis C along the way. Tyler is the best kind of reformed addict – not a sermonising preacher, rather a man who, having sunk to the darkest depths of drug addiction, knows what that hell looks like and so can speak the language that struggling addicts can truly relate to.

Steven has a fascinating personality. With a hilarious sense of humour and utterly irreverent, he can be highly entertaining company, but he is also a smart cookie. Strong-willed, yet he runs full tilt at life and has been reckless near to destruction; this curious blend of traits is what makes him a larger than life star. He has stated that he would not go back and change a thing in his colourful rollercoaster life – not because he believes that he has always done what was right for himself or for others, but rather through an unwillingness to tamper with the tapestry of his life. Although he has mellowed in many ways, there is no sign of his light bulb getting dim, and with his boundless energy he is far from ready to pack away his microphone. Unfazed by the plethora of fresh-faced boy and girl bands swamping today's music scene, Tyler irrepressibly declared: 'I don't buy into this idea that you're not supposed to rock after a certain age. I'm looking to be the lounge act on the space shuttle so that I can sing "Walk This Way" on the ceiling.' It is hard to escape the feeling that if it's possible for any rock star to achieve such an ambitious aim – Steven Tyler will.

# Index